An
**Outdoor
Family
Guide** to

Lake Tahoe

An
Outdoor
Family
Guide to

Lake Tahoe

Second Edition

LISA GOLLIN EVANS

THE
MOUNTAINEERS
BOOKS

Dedicated with love to my mother

Published by
The Mountaineers Books
1001 SW Klickitat Way, Suite 201
Seattle, WA 98134

© 2001 by Lisa Gollin Evans

First edition, 1993. Second edition, 2001

Published simultaneously in Great Britain by Cordee, 3a DeMontfort Street, Leicester, England, LE1 7HD

Manufactured in the United States of America

Project Editor: Julie Van Pelt
Copy Editor: Marni Keogh
Cover and Book Design: Ani Rucki
Layout: Alice Merrill
Mapmaker: Tony Moore

All photos by the author unless otherwise noted.

Cover photograph:
Frontispiece: *Crag Lake*

Library of Congress Cataloging-in-Publication Data
Evans, Lisa Gollin, 1956–
      An outdoor family guide to Lake Tahoe / Lisa Gollin Evans.— 2nd ed.
        p. cm.
      Rev. ed. of: Lake Tahoe, 1993.
      ISBN 0-89886-752-5 (pbk.)
      1. Hiking—Tahoe, Lake, Region (Calif. and Nev.)—Guidebooks. 2. Family recreation—Tahoe, Lake, Region (Calif. and Nev.)—Guidebooks. 3. Tahoe, Lake, Region (Calif. and Nev.)—Guidebooks. I. Evans, Lisa Gollin, 1956- Lake Tahoe. II. Title.
      GV199.42.T16 E93 2001
      917.94'38—dc21
                                                             2001001621

CONTENTS

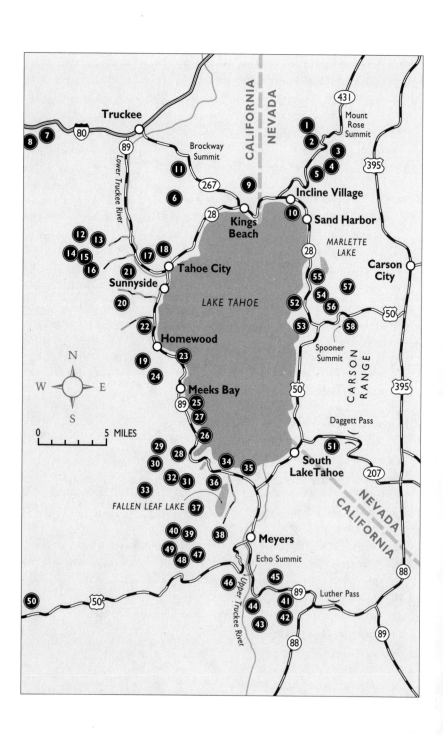

MAP LEGEND

(80)	Interstate Highway	⌣⌣	Bridge
(395) (50)	U.S. Highway	▲	Camping
(28) (260)	State or County Road	〒	Picnic Area
540	Forest Service Road	▣	Point of Interest
═══	Interstate	— ·— ·—	Wilderness/Park Boundary
▬▬▬	Paved Road	⊶⊶⊶⊶	Fence
═══	Unpaved Road	(P)	Parking
+++++++	Railroad	(T)	Trailhead
- - - - - -	Main Trail	⌣	Pass
- - - - - -	Other Trail	▪ ▬ ▬ ▬	State Line
∼∼∼	River/Stream	▲	Peak
∼∼≈	Falls	■	Structure
⬭	Lake	0 1 2 MILES	Scale
⁂⁂⁂	Wetland		

PREFACE

The lake burst upon us—a noble sheet of blue water lifted six thousand three hundred feet above the level of the sea, and walled in by a rim of snow-clad mountain peaks that towered aloft full three thousand feet higher still! . . . As it lay there with the shadows of the mountains brilliantly photographed upon its still surface I thought it must surely be the fairest picture the whole earth affords.
—*Mark Twain,* Roughing It

Many books about Lake Tahoe open with these eloquent lines. In this there is great irony. It is true that Mr. Twain's enthusiasm for Lake Tahoe was so great that he staked a claim in the basin, but his motivation was not scenic beauty. Twain longed for the profits to be made by cutting the land's valuable pine forest. In 1861, however, his unattended campfire scorched a mountainside and destroyed his dream.

This bit of unlikely history says much about the Tahoe Basin. For more than one hundred years, white settlers admired the overwhelming beauty of the basin, even as they moved swiftly to obliterate it. Today the basin is a study in contrasts. When viewed from a mountain peak or from a secluded cove, there is no lovelier place. But Tahoe is also home to unsightly commercial strips, where tourists, breathing in exhaust, crawl bumper-to-bumper in frustration around what could have been the most beautiful lake in the world.

Clearly all is not lost. Beauty, solitude, wildlife, and unspoiled nature still can be found in the Lake Tahoe Basin. The purpose of this book is to reveal this side of Lake Tahoe, for it is a wonderful place to introduce children to the excitement and pleasure of wilderness. Its weather is delightful, its trails are accessible, and its hiking and biking routes are filled with natural enticements for every age. From granite-rimmed lakes that are perfect for swimming to smooth trails exquisite for mountain biking, Tahoe's offerings for families are extraordinary.

We should, however, learn a lesson from the past. Instead of "loving it and losing it," visitors to Lake Tahoe today must protect the area's fragile beauty. By practicing minimum-impact hiking, biking, and camping; by supporting conservation efforts; and, most importantly, by encouraging children to love and respect nature, we can make a positive impact that will long survive our time here.

Take the lead from the erudite but careless Mr. Twain. The loss of his lucrative timber stake did not dim his opinion of Lake Tahoe. About his months of camping on its shores, he wrote, "The air up there in the clouds is very pure and fine, bracing and delicious. And why shouldn't it be? It is the same the angels breathe." If visitors behave a little more like angels and a little less like consumers, developers, and gamblers, Lake Tahoe has a chance to be blue forever.

Acknowledgments

This book could not have been written without the help and support of my family. Because of their enthusiastic participation, my trips to California were easy, joyful, and unforgettable. I therefore would like to express my heartfelt gratitude to my wonderful family: foremost, my husband, Frank; my daughters, Sarah, Grace, and Lilly; my mother, Hannah Gollin; my father, Morton Gollin; my mother-in-law, Anne Evans; and family member extraordinaire, Mary Anne Fomunyoh.

I'd also like to thank the many good friends who gave me help and support during the writing and research of this book, including Patty Yoffee and family, Joy Zimmerman, Hut Landon, Michael Lobue, John and Sue Feder, Dan and Allyn Carl, and Lisa Grossman.

In addition, I'd like to express great appreciation to Don Lane of the U.S. Forest Service, Lake Tahoe Management Unit, who graciously lent his expertise to review the manuscript. His expert fact-checking was invaluable. I also thank Linda Kjer of the Tahoe Rim Trail for her substantial assistance. For my very beautiful and luxurious accommodations, I thank the Resort at Squaw Creek, a fantastic place for families exploring the Tahoe area.

Last, but not least, I'd like to thank the staff of The Mountaineers Books, who have mastered the tough task of being thoroughly proficient and awfully nice at the same time.

INTRODUCTION

We have the ability and capacity to destroy the earth or do exactly the opposite. It will take a commitment to do that, but if you make it, providence intervenes . . . Boldness has magic in it.
  —David Brower, *speaking at the Conference on the Future of Lake Tahoe, July 25, 1992*

This book describes fifty-eight hiking and biking trips in the Lake Tahoe Basin. The trips are divided into four groups—North Shore, West Shore, South Shore, and East Shore—according to their location around the lake. Donner Pass trips are included in the North Shore section. Routes in Granite Chief Wilderness are found in the West Shore section. Desolation Wilderness hikes are in the South Shore chapter. Lastly, the East Shore chapter includes trips in and around Lake Tahoe–Nevada State Park.

How to Use this Book

The hikes and bike routes are classified as easy, moderate, or strenuous, according to their length, starting elevation, elevation gain, and terrain. Generally, easy hikes are 0.5 to 2 miles one way, moderate hikes are 2 to 4 miles one way, and strenuous hikes are more than 4 miles one way. For bike trips, easy trips are up to 3.5 miles one way, moderate trips are 3.5 to 6 miles, and strenuous trips are more than 6 miles. Because these ratings are both general and subjective, consult the detailed descriptions for specific information about trail conditions.

The trail descriptions do not provide estimates of walking or biking time. Hikers and bikers, especially children, travel at variable speeds, making such approximation unreliable. To estimate roughly the time required for a hike, use an average walking rate of 2 miles per hour on level ground for adults carrying packs, plus 1 hour for each 1000 feet of elevation gained. Rough terrain and hiking children obviously increase the time needed. After a few hikes, you can work out estimates for your own family. Generally, strenuous hikes require a full day; moderate hikes, a half day; and easy hikes, 1 to 3 hours.

To help you quickly choose a hike or bike trip that fits your needs, Appendix A contains a trip matrix that concisely lists information such as difficulty, distance, location, and attractions for each route. For more general information about the Tahoe area, including its campgrounds, weather, natural history, and cultural attractions, consult Chapter 1. Information on Lake Tahoe's many beautiful beaches is found in Appendix B. Appendix C contains a recommended reading list for children and adults that includes numerous books on nature and the natural history of the Tahoe Basin. Appendix D contains information on conservation groups serving the Lake Tahoe Basin.

Hiking and Biking with Children

The suggestions listed below apply to all trips. Following these tips will help you and your children make the most of your time on the trails.

Choosing the Right Trip

Hiking or biking a trail that's too difficult for your children is sure to lead to frustration for all. Read trail descriptions carefully to find trips that match your children's abilities. If you are uncertain how far they can walk or bike, choose a trip that has intermediate points of interest so that you can shorten it if necessary. Try also to match a youngster's interests with a trail's attractions, whether fishing, rock climbing, swimming, or wildflowers.

Exploring sagebrush in Tahoe Meadows

Snacks

Let children snack liberally on their favorite treats during a hiking or biking trip. They will be working hard, and snacks high in carbohydrates, such as "gorp," are energy boosters. Offer salty snacks to replace salts lost through perspiration. Good-tasting treats can also be used as a motivating force for reaching the next rest stop. Remember to bring plenty of water or juice, particularly in summer, when humidity is low and temperatures are high. Mild dehydration causes crankiness in children, and more severe cases can cause extreme discomfort.

Motivation

There are numerous ways to motivate children to reach a destination. The promise of a picnic or a treat is enough for some children. For others, encouraging good-natured competition with siblings or peers does the trick. When a child's motivation wears thin, distraction can be the best solution. Songs, trail activities, games, and stories often invigorate sluggish youngsters. One's creative energy, of course, must be high to engage children. For suggested trail activities, see books listed under "Books for Parents" in Appendix C.

Leaders

Allow the children to lead the group. When the novelty wears off, assign the lead role to another, rotating the honor among the youngsters. The trail will fly by!

The Pace

Let the children determine the hiking or biking pace. Your progress will probably be slower than desired, but the trip will be much more enjoyable. Adults will also benefit from slowing down: you may cover only half the distance, but you'll experience twice as much.

A Positive Attitude

Praise children for all their achievements on the trail. Positive reinforcement for beginners is essential and will build a solid base of good feelings about the activity. Refrain from criticism if children disappoint you. Nagging and scolding will not necessarily improve their performance, but it will guarantee unhappiness.

The Right Stuff

Pack items in your backpack to keep children happy on the trail, especially when hiking. Magnifying glasses, binoculars, bug bottles, sketchbooks, or materials for simple projects like bark and stone rubbings provide welcome diversions for youngsters who need a break. For additional suggestions, see books listed under "Game and Activity Books" in Appendix C.

Relax and Enjoy

When hiking and biking with children, the joy is in the process, in the small achievements and discoveries that you can share. To appreciate this, you must relax. With children, you travel slowly enough to take joy in the sweet smell of the woods and the squeals of delight from young, curious, and still-able-to-be-amazed children. You may miss the thrill of a peak or the rush of a downhill run, but the quiet rewards of sharing nature will last a lifetime. With luck, you will find the child within you on the trails and be able to progress contentedly at "child speed."

Wilderness Ethics

During your time at Lake Tahoe, it is essential to use the natural areas in a con-scientious and ethical manner. The environmental health and beauty of the Lake Tahoe Basin is dependent upon the treatment it receives from its users. Dete-rioration and environmental stress from overuse and abuse are evident through-out the basin. Abide by the following rules and teach them by example to your children. In this way, you can help to keep the Lake Tahoe Basin natural and beautiful.

Make a Positive Impact

The oft-repeated slogan "take only pictures, leave only footprints" no longer works for today's overcrowded natural areas. The Rule of Positive Impact asks that visitors consciously try to leave a natural area a better place. For example, by picking up waste, you enhance the beauty of the trail for the next visitor. Give children a small bag that can be stuffed into their pockets for their own litter as well as for stray wrappers left by others. Parents should carry their own litter bags as well.

A second way to create a positive impact is to set a good example by hiking and biking joyfully, attentively, and considerately. Your model will be contagious. Just as a crowd gathers to look at a sight in which others are showing interest, so other visitors may follow your lead if you set a good example.

Respect Other Visitors

Parties with children are likely to travel more slowly than other groups. As a courtesy, parents should be aware of others on the trail who wish to pass and

Kayaking at Sand Harbor State Park, Nevada

should see that their children move aside to let them do so. Also, picnics and rest stops should be conducted off the trail, so as not to block the path.

Leaders should discourage excessive noise. Children can't be expected to march or ride silently, but neither should they make unnecessary noise.

Do Not Feed the Animals

Do not feed the numerous squirrels and birds who beg for handouts throughout the Tahoe Basin. Feeding can be dangerous for both you and the animals. Human handouts are detrimental to wildlife for two main reasons. First, snack foods nutritionally cannot replace an animal's natural diet. If handouts become its primary source of food, the animal may become malnourished and prey to disease and injury. Second, feeding an animal disrupts its natural foraging instincts. As a result, animals that depend on human feeding may not survive the winter.

Feeding animals in the wild can also be harmful for people. Tahoe's small mammals have been found to carry rabies. Rabies aside, a rodent's sharp incisors in your finger is painful. In addition, fleas carrying bubonic plague have been found on Tahoe area rodents. Although rare, instances of human contraction of bubonic plague from flea bites have occurred. Also, deer carry ticks that can transmit Lyme disease.

Let Wildflowers Flourish

From May through September, wild gardens grace the Tahoe Basin. To ensure that all visitors have an opportunity to enjoy the flowers, it is essential that everyone refrain from picking even one blossom. Moreover, wildflowers wilt quickly after being plucked. The fragile bouquets usually droop miserably even before the end of the trail. At high elevations, picking wildflowers poses a particularly critical problem because plants have little time in which to set seed. Removing plants from any part of the basin means removing seeds, thus preventing annuals from reproducing.

Stay on the Trail

To maintain the integrity, beauty, and safety of trails, do not shortcut. Shortcuts are most tempting where a trail switchbacks down a steep slope. Yet when hikers or bikers aim straight down a slope, they damage the vegetation between the switchbacks and contribute to erosion. If shortcutting occurs frequently, a trail may wash away, leaving a scarred and barren hillside. Also, leaving a trail on a precipitous slope is not only dangerous, it may cause you to lose the trail entirely.

Observe the Rules

If you are hiking or biking in Tahoe's national forests, designated wilderness areas, or state parks, there are important rules to observe. Depending on the area's designation, different regulations apply. Below are some of the most important, and most commonly violated, rules. For a more complete set of regulations, check at a visitor center or park entrance station.

- Carry out all refuse. Leave nothing on trails or in campsites. Do not attempt to burn or bury noncombustibles.
- Do not cut, remove, deface, or disturb any tree, shrub, wildflower, or other natural object. Carving on trees is a harmful and unfortunately widespread practice. It scars trees permanently and can even kill them if the carving girdles the tree. Never cut down living trees, or portions thereof, for your own use. Also, never break branches from standing trees, even if they appear dead. The tree may not be dead, and breaking a branch may injure it.
- Do not tease, molest, or feed wild animals.
- Fishing in California and Nevada requires a fishing license for those 16 years of age and older.

Strolling at Sand Harbor State Park, Nevada

Leave Horses Behind

Horseback riding may seem like a romantic way to tour the backcountry, but it takes a heavy toll on Tahoe's natural areas. Choose instead to hike or bike. Horses harm the backcountry in many ways. They spoil Tahoe's meadows by selectively chomping away attractive plant species. Livestock-grazed meadows have distinctly fewer wildflowers and less plant diversity. Horse manure fouls backcountry lakes, streams, and trails. Also, the impact of horse hooves on trails causes rapid erosion. Insensitive riders have caused environmental damage in the past. Today's riders are expected to follow no-trace techniques for livestock use. If you must ride, obey the strict regulations regarding horse travel, including the requirement to carry supplemental feed.

Day Hike in Desolation Wilderness

It is recommended that you visit Desolation Wilderness by day only, unless you are willing to abide strictly by minimum-impact camping standards. Camping harms the land far more than day-hiking. Stressed areas that are devoid of topsoil and vegetation surround many of Desolation Wilderness's lakes. This damage was caused by the great number of backpackers camping in Desolation Wilderness each summer. Much of the environmental stress, including that caused by the disposal of human and cooking wastes and the construction of campsites, can be avoided if visitors hike instead of camp. If you wish to camp in Desolation Wilderness, ask a Forest Service Wilderness ranger where to set up camp in order to minimize your impact.

Light Stoves, Not Fires

Know the local fire restrictions, and never build fires in prohibited areas. Note that campfires are prohibited in all of Desolation Wilderness. Even when fires are allowed, this book recommends against building one. Use a portable cooking stove whenever possible. Fires leave unsightly scars on the land, rob the forests of decomposing matter, and create haze in pristine skies. Also, ashes carried by runoff contaminate lakes and streams. If you feel you can't camp without a fire, make it small, don't use it for cooking, limit its duration, extinguish it carefully, and leave no trace. Lastly, to make a positive impact, dismantle extra fire rings by scattering the rocks and condense overly large fire rings to discourage big fires.

Small Is Beautiful

Enter the backcountry in small groups. The larger the group, the greater the impact on the wilderness. If possible, camp with no more than six others. If you

Camping at D.L. Bliss State Park

seek the company of larger groups, avoid pristine wilderness and choose an area that has already been highly impacted.

Respect the Lakes

The treasure of the Tahoe Sierra is its many subalpine lakes. The lakes are fragile, however, and easily damaged by careless visitors. To protect the lakes, set up camp, eliminate waste, wash dishes, and keep fish entrails at least 200 feet from lakes and streams. If you decide to picnic on a lakeshore, choose a boulder or use areas already trampled or heavily impacted. It is unlikely that such highly impacted areas will recover, and you will avoid spreading the damage. In addition, don't use any soaps in or near lakes and streams, because all soaps pollute, even those that claim to be biodegradable.

Care for the Meadows

Meadows and marshes in the Tahoe Basin play a critical role in filtering nutrients and pollutants out of the runoff and groundwater flowing into Lake Tahoe. Due to unwise development, the Lake Tahoe Basin has already lost 75 percent of its marshes and 50 percent of its meadows. Consequently, Lake Tahoe produces more and more algae. It coats the shoreline rocks and could eventually turn the lake's famous blue color to green. Hikers and bikers should protect meadows and marshes by staying on the trail and by never camping in these sensitive areas.

Deconstructionist Theory

Don't build anything in the wilderness. Don't build cairns, fireplaces, benches, or soft places to sleep. These structures linger long after you've gone and blight the landscape. When camping, "naturalize" your camp before you leave by making the site look as if no one had camped there. Then make a positive impact and pack out any waste left by previous campers.

Doggone It

Dogs do not belong in the wilderness. They frighten and harass wildlife, disturb other hikers and cyclists, and foul water sources. If you must bring your dog, leash it and maintain control at all times. Especially, do not allow it to leave waste within 200 feet of lakes or streams. In addition, protect your pet: uncontrolled dogs may be exposed to rabies through unexpected encounters with wildlife.

Ethics for Mountain Bikers

Mountain bikers are relative newcomers to the Tahoe Basin. Courtesy and minimum-impact biking are critical to their longevity. Abiding by the "Rules of the Trail" of the International Mountain Biking Association (IMBA) is a good first step.

1. Ride on open trails only. Respect trail and road closures (ask if you're not sure) and avoid possible trespass on private land. Granite Chief and Mount Rose Wilderness Areas are closed to cycling. Additional trails may be closed because of sensitive environmental concerns or conflicts with other users. Your riding example will determine what is closed to all cyclists!

2. Leave no trace. Be sensitive to the dirt beneath you. Even on open trails, you should not ride under conditions where you will leave evidence of your passing, such as on certain soils shortly after a rain. Never ride through Tahoe's wet meadows or marshes. Observe the different types of soils and trail conditions. Practice low-impact cycling by staying on the trail and not creating any new ones. Be sure to pack out at least as much as you pack in.

3. Control your bicycle! Inattention for even a second can cause disaster. Excessive speed maims and threatens people; there is no excuse for it! Watch your speed constantly and be alert for sudden changes in the terrain.

4. Always yield the trail. Make known your approach well in advance. A friendly greeting (or bell) is considerate and works well; startling someone may cause loss of trail access. Show your respect when passing others by slowing to a walk or even stopping. Anticipate that

other trail users may be around corners or in blind spots.

5. Never spook animals. All animals are startled by an unannounced approach, a sudden movement, or a loud noise. This can be dangerous for you, others, and the animals. Give animals extra room and time to adjust to you. In passing, use special care and follow the directions of horseback riders (ask if you are uncertain). In general, your best bet is to dismount, walk your bike, and, if possible, pass horses on the low side of the trail, since horses are more frightened by objects above than below them. Running cattle and disturbing wild animals are serious offenses. Leave gates as you found them, or as marked.

6. Plan ahead. Know your equipment, your ability, and the area in which you are riding—and prepare accordingly. Be self-sufficient at all times, keep your machine in good repair, and carry necessary supplies for changes in weather or other conditions. A well-executed trip is a satisfaction to you and not a burden or offense to others. Keep trails open by setting an example of responsible cycling for all mountain bicyclists.

Safety

This section summarizes the basic precautions you should take when you hike or bike in the Tahoe Basin. Be alert to the dangers described below and be prepared

Swimmers at Sand Harbor State Park, Nevada

with the appropriate gear to minimize hazardous situations. The checklist at the end of this section lists the essentials that you need to take on every outing.

There are three caveats to this section. First, it cannot replace a good first-aid book, of which there are many on the market. Second, neither the following information nor a first-aid book can substitute for a firm base of practical knowledge and experience in first aid. One way to sharpen your skills is to enroll in a first-aid course. Finally, safe hiking and biking requires the exercise of caution and common sense. Know the limitations of your group and read the warning signs of trouble, including fatigue, stress, and bad weather.

Hypothermia

Hypothermia is the lowering of the body's core temperature to a degree sufficient to cause illness. The condition is always serious and is sometimes fatal. Signs of mild hypothermia include complaints of cold, shivering, loss of coordination, and apathy. More severe hypothermia causes mental confusion, uncontrollable shivering, slurred speech, and a core temperature low enough to cause permanent damage or death.

Because small bodies lose heat more rapidly than large ones, children are more vulnerable to hypothermia than adults. Early signs of hypothermia in children may be crankiness and fussiness, which can also be caused by ordinary fatigue. A child may not even realize he or she is cold until serious shivering begins.

Hikers, especially children, can become hypothermic when temperatures are well above freezing. Wind chill is a critical, and often overlooked factor in hypothermia.

Parents can guard against dangerous chills by observing the following precautions:

- Carry an adequate supply of warm clothing, including wool sweaters, socks, gloves, and hats, to insulate against heat loss. Gloves, hats, and scarves are particularly effective because they protect hands, heads, and necks—areas that are especially sensitive to heat loss. Carry these items even when the weather looks warm and sunny, especially when at or above tree line. On cool rainy days, avoid cotton clothing; it is not warm when wet and it wicks warmth away from the body.
- Dress in layers and remove unneeded layers to prevent excessive sweating, which lowers body temperature through evaporation. Parents must react quickly to a child's temperature changes, whether occasioned by weather or changes in activity levels.

- Avoid excessive exposure to wind and rain. Always carry rain gear (or at least a spare large plastic garbage bag).
- Carry food high in carbohydrates and sugar that the body can quickly convert to heat.
- Carry warm liquids, such as hot cocoa, when hiking or biking in cold weather.
- Avoid resting against ice, snow, or cold rocks, which draw heat away from the body. Place an insulating barrier, such as a foam pad, between the body and cold surfaces.
- Cover the mouth with a wool scarf to warm air entering the lungs.

If a member of your group shows signs of hypothermia, stop whatever you are doing and take immediate steps to warm the person. Promptness is particularly important when treating hypothermia in children. Add layers of clothing. Replace wet clothes with dry ones. If possible, administer warm liquids or food. If necessary, build a small fire to warm the victim and dry wet clothing. Holding a cold child close to your body while wrapping a parka or blanket around the two of you is particularly effective. Crawling into a sleeping bag with the victim is recommended for cases that do not respond readily to other treatment.

Heat-Related Illness

Hiking or biking at high altitudes, in warm weather, or in the open sun can cause excessive loss of water and salts (electrolytes). Failure to replace water and electrolytes can lead to dehydration, heat exhaustion, or even heat stroke. To prevent heat-related illnesses, consume adequate amounts of water and electrolytes. Avoid salt tablets in favor of liquids and salted snacks, which you should always carry in amounts greater than you are likely to need. Flavored powders containing electrolytes may be added to water to replace those lost through perspiration. Remember that thirst is not a reliable indicator of the need for water. Schedule regular water stops to ensure against dehydration.

Sun Exposure

In the Tahoe Basin, precautions against overexposure to the sun are necessary in any season. During the dry, sunny summers, it is particularly important to avoid excessive exposure, especially on summit hikes. Harmful ultraviolet radiation increases with altitude. Take additional precautions when in or near lakes, as radiation reflects off bodies of water.

To avoid sunburn, take the following precautions:

- Protect exposed skin with sunscreen and be sure to reapply it regularly.

Remember that children, especially babies, burn easily. Be particularly careful when carrying young children in back carriers, for their exposure may be prolonged and can go undetected.

■ Wear brimmed hats, long-sleeved shirts, and sunglasses.

■ Don't be fooled by cool temperatures: you don't have to feel the sun on your skin to get a dangerous burn. Despite the frigid wind on a mountain ridge, a sunburn develops quickly in the thin air.

High Altitudes

The decreased oxygen in the air at high altitudes can result in mountain sickness: symptoms include headaches, fatigue, loss of appetite, muscle weakness and dull pain, shortness of breath, nausea, and rapid heartbeat. If ignored or left untreated, mountain sickness can be fatal. Do not overlook its early, easily treated symptoms.

Mountain sickness strikes unpredictably. It affects both young and old, whether fit or not. Some members of a party may be affected while others are not. Some people may experience no symptoms on one day but quickly develop them on another. In any case, the cardinal rule when the early symptoms of mountain sickness strike is to descend at once to a lower elevation.

To reduce the likelihood of mountain sickness, acclimate your family to high altitudes gradually. At the beginning of your visit, choose trips at lake level, or at least those in the high country that are not strenuous. Because children are often inarticulate about their physical condition, be attuned to crankiness as a sign of altitude discomfort. If suspected, rest and retreat to lower elevations as soon as possible. To aid the family's acclimation, make sure everyone eats lightly, drinks plenty of fluids, gets plenty of rest, and limits physical activity for the first few days. Adults should limit their intake of alcohol at high elevations.

Lightning

Deep blue skies and low humidity are typical throughout the summer and fall in the Tahoe Basin. In the afternoons, however, fine summer weather is frequently interrupted by sudden thunderstorms. If you are hiking during an electrical storm on an open ridge, above tree line, or in an open area with few trees you may be in danger of being hit by lightning. Lightning often strikes the highest object in a landscape, which could well be you or your family in a treeless area.

If you do get caught in a thunderstorm, take the following precautions:

■ Do not seek shelter under natural features, such as lone or tall trees, rock overhangs, or large boulders, that project above their surroundings.

Exploring one of Tahoe's creeks

Such large, exposed objects are more likely to be hit by lightning because of their height.

■ Do not seek shelter in a tent; the metal rods conduct electricity. For the same reason, do not wear a metal-frame backpack during a lightning storm.

■ Do not remain on or next to a horse. Sitting on a horse increases your height; standing next to a horse gives lightning a larger target.

■ Do not lie flat on the ground. To do so is to increase the body area exposed to electrical current in the event of a nearby lightning strike.

■ Do not seek refuge in caves.

■ Assume the safest position—huddle on your knees with your head down. Crouch near medium-size boulders, if available.

■ Keep away from puddles, streams, and other bodies of water, because water conducts electricity.

■ If you are retreating to safety during a storm, stay as low as possible, remove children from back carriers, and walk with your legs wide apart.

■ Safe places during thunderstorms include cars and large buildings—the larger, the better.

Be aware of the fickleness of Tahoe weather. Storms can approach extremely rapidly. If you see a storm, the most prudent course is to retreat at once to a safe area. Don't proceed to a summit if you hear or see signs of an electrical storm.

Snowfields and Ice Fields

Be extremely cautious when traveling over snow or ice. Never venture near the edge of snow or ice slopes or cornices. These areas can be treacherous and unstable. If you are hiking at high altitudes early in the season, check with rangers for snow conditions. At higher elevations in the Tahoe Basin, snow may persist until late July. If you do venture into areas where snow remains, be prepared with the necessary gear, such as crampons, ropes, and ice axes.

Streams and Waterfalls

Streams and rivers can be dangerous. The current of even a small stream can be strong, especially in the spring and especially for children. Take appropriate precautions when crossing streams, and do not allow children to play unsupervised on stream banks. The frigid temperatures of snow and groundwater-fed streams quickly disable even good swimmers.

Waterfalls also present significant hazards. Slick rocks and steep drop-offs near waterfalls warrant a close watch on children.

Drinking Water

Always carry a large quantity of safe drinking water—at least a quart per person. It is not safe to drink from any of the lakes and streams in the Tahoe Basin. The waters may be infested with *Giardia lamblia,* a parasite that wreaks havoc in the human digestive system. *Giardia* infestation is caused when mammals such as muskrats defecate in or near the water, or when water has been contaminated by the careless disposal of human waste. Symptoms of giardiasis in humans include diarrhea, abdominal distention, gas, and cramps. The symptoms appear 7 to 10 days after infection. If you suffer these symptoms, you must obtain treatment from a physician.

To purify water, boil it for 3 to 6 minutes. You can also disinfect the water chemically or by filtration, but these methods have not been proven as effective as heat. All water that might be swallowed must be treated, including water used for cooking, cleaning dishes, and brushing teeth.

To help prevent the spread of giardiasis and other harmful diseases, dig temporary latrines at least 8 inches deep, 8 to 10 inches wide, and 200 feet away from water sources, trails, and campsites. After use, fill the hole with loose soil and tap down lightly. Of course, campers should wash hands thoroughly after using the latrine. Parents should teach children safe toilet practices to protect their health and to keep lakes, streams, and rivers clean.

Ticks

Deer ticks can transmit Lyme disease. The symptoms of Lyme disease in advanced cases are severe and include arthritis, meningitis, neurological problems, and cardiac symptoms. These symptoms can occur anywhere from a few weeks to more than a year after the tick bite. Early signs may include a rash around the infected tick bite and flu-like symptoms. Timely diagnosis and treatment can cure or lessen the severity of the disease. If you or your family experiences these symptoms after a tick bite, immediately contact your physician.

To avoid tick bites, take the following precautions:

- Use an insect repellent containing DEET or permethrin, and spray it on shoes and clothing—especially socks, pant legs and cuffs, and shirt sleeves and cuffs. Avoid direct application of DEET to children's skin, as this potentially harmful chemical can be absorbed through the skin. DEET can also damage rayon, acetate, and spandex, but is safe on nylon, cotton, and wool. When buying DEET, choose a formula containing approximately 35 percent DEET. Tests have shown that this amount provides as much protection as formulas containing higher concentrations.

- Tuck pants into boots, and button cuffs and collars.
- Wear light-colored clothing to help you spot ticks more easily.
- Check frequently for ticks on skin, scalp, and clothing. This may be done on rest breaks during your hike. Ticks often spend many hours on a body before they transmit the virus, so there is no need to panic if you find a tick. Infection can, nevertheless, be transmitted soon after the tick attaches, so it is prudent to check regularly.
- Avoid areas of heavy tick infestation, such as tall grass, in spring and early summer.
- Do not approach or feed deer. They may be hosts to ticks carrying the disease.

If you should discover a tick, remove it using tweezers, pulling it straight out. It is important to remove all head and mouth parts to prevent infection. After removal, wash the area with soap and water. Even though ticks are rare in late summer and fall, you should still check your family regularly.

Bears

California black bears are found throughout the Tahoe Basin. They frequent many of the area's campgrounds, looking for food. You should take the following precautions:

- Do not store food in your tent. Use few odorous foods, and seal all food in clean resealable plastic bags or other airtight containers; seal also trash, soap, sunscreen, toothpaste, used sanitary napkins, and anything else with a strong scent. Campers should hang this cache in a tree at least 10 feet above the ground and at least 5 horizontal feet out from the trunk of the tree. Car campers should carefully wrap their food and store it in the trunk of their vehicle. Ice chests are not bear-proof.
- If you encounter a bear, do not approach it. Bears are not usually aggressive, but they are unpredictable. Be particularly cautious if you see a sow with cubs. Never approach bear cubs; an angry mother bear will seldom be far away.
- If a bear approaches your camp, bang pans, shout, and wave coats in the air. Usually the bear will retreat. If not, immediately abandon the camp.

Lost and Found

Carry current topographic maps for the areas in which you plan to hike or bike. Outdoor supply stores and visitor centers sell a variety of maps, including USGS maps. These are particularly useful because they show terrain features and elevation by means of contour lines. If you have old maps, make sure they are up-to-date. Finally, buy waterproof maps, or carry the maps in a waterproof pouch.

Always carry a reliable compass and know how to use it in conjunction with your topographic maps. If you don't feel confident, check with outing clubs in your area for instruction. Good books providing instruction in compass use are also available (see "Books for Parents" in Appendix C).

Children are particularly vulnerable to getting lost and are less able to care for themselves if they do. When hiking or biking, it is essential that children never stray from your sight. Take the following preventive measures to guard against potentially traumatic or dangerous situations:

- Teach children to stay with the group.
- Give children whistles, with strict instructions to use the whistles only when lost.
- Instruct children to remain in one place if they become lost. That way, they can be found more easily.
- If children must move, teach them how to build "ducks" by placing a smaller stone on top of a larger stone. By leaving a trail of ducks, the child will build a trail for rescuers to follow.

Special Gear for Children

The following special gear can make your outings safer and more enjoyable.

Carriers

Small infants ride in front carriers; those able to support their heads graduate to back carriers. The best carriers on the market are large enough so a child has room to grow. Choose a well-padded carrier that has a storage compartment attached.

When hiking with a young child, it is wise to bring a back carrier, even though the child might feel that he or she has outgrown it. If the child becomes tired, the carrier will be invaluable. Carrying a child in a back carrier is much easier and safer than lugging the child on your back or shoulders. Carriers can also be useful if quick evacuation is required.

Footwear

Lug-soled hiking boots, broken in and well-fitting, are the best choice of footwear for children. These sturdy boots are essential for long hikes on rocky or steep terrain, or when children are carrying backpacks. Sturdy boots are also necessary when biking over rough trails where youngsters may need to walk their bikes or use their feet as stabilizers. The boots' stiff uppers and strong construction will provide support and protect feet from injury. Before the outing, make sure waterproofing is fresh and effective.

Sturdy athletic shoes with good traction are a common alternative. Athletic shoes can be an adequate and comfortable substitute on short outings and relatively easy, smooth trails. Athletic shoes, however, don't provide much support or protection on rough terrain. Also, sneakers are not waterproof and if soaked may result in cold, blistered feet.

Children should wear wool or wool-blend socks. Even when wool socks get wet, they still keep feet warm. When hiking or biking in cool weather, wear two thinner pairs of socks instead of one thick pair. The layers provide more warmth. Always bring an extra pair of socks for each child. Mud puddles and streams are too attractive to be passed up by the youngest in your group. Extra wool socks can also be used as emergency mittens.

Clothing

Because of the changeable Sierra weather (especially in the spring and fall), always carry warm clothes and rain gear. Layers are the best for warmth. Carry extra wool sweaters and rain ponchos or waterproof jackets and rain pants. Before your trip, test all seams for watertight seals, and reseal if necessary. Sweatshirts are not recommended because they are useless when wet. In addition, bring hats and gloves for everyone on high country trips and when hiking or biking in the spring and fall.

Helmets

Both children and adults should wear protective helmets while biking. Whether you're on a busy bike path or a rugged trail, the risks of head injury from a collision or fall warrant protective headgear. Proper fit and positioning is critical to the helmet's effectiveness. Consult a knowledgeable bike shop if you are uncertain about helmet size and fit.

Emergency Gear

First-Aid Kit

It is essential that you carry a first-aid kit on every outing. Once you've assembled one, tucking it in your backpack or bike bag will quickly become routine. Commercially packaged kits are available in convenient sizes, and some are quite good. If you wish to purchase one, check its contents against the following list and supplement when necessary. In addition, ask your family doctor to suggest medications that are specific to your family's needs. To make your own first-aid kit inexpensively, simply purchase the items listed below and place them in a nylon stuff bag, zippered container, or aluminum box. If size and weight are not problems, the box is recommended because it keeps supplies organized, allowing you to tell at a glance when items need to be replenished. Your first-aid kit should include the following:

- Adhesive bandage strips (bring an abundant supply; their psychological value to children cannot be underestimated)
- Butterfly bandages for minor lacerations
- Sterile gauze pads (4 inches by 4 inches) for larger wounds
- Adhesive tape to attach dressings
- Antibiotic ointment to treat wounds and cuts
- Moleskin for blisters
- Triangle bandages for slings
- Athletic tape for multiple uses
- Children's pain reliever

Rocks at Sand Harbor State Park, Nevada

- Adult pain reliever
- Betadine swabs (povidone iodine) for an antiseptic
- Alcohol pads to cleanse skin
- Elastic bandage for sprains
- Knife with scissors and tweezers (tweezers are needed to remove ticks and splinters)
- Space blanket for emergency warmth
- First-aid instruction booklet

Remember that no matter how well stocked your first-aid kit is, the contents are worthless unless you know how to use them. A first-aid course will give you experience in using many of the materials listed above.

Bicycle Repair Kit

Always carry a bicycle repair kit that includes the following:

- Two or three tire irons (preferably plastic or aluminum)
- Patch kit for repairing punctured tubes
- Two spare tubes
- Six-inch adjustable wrench
- Small screwdriver

It is also advisable to carry a frame-mounted pump for flats.

The Ten "Plus" Essentials: A Checklist for Safe Hiking and Biking

Use the following checklist before departing on any outing. It includes the Ten Essentials compiled by The Mountaineers, plus a few extra essentials specific to the needs of children and to the Tahoe area. Bringing these items will prepare you for emergencies due to weather, injuries, or other unforeseen circumstances.

1. Extra clothing. The extra weight ensures against cold, cranky children and hypothermia. A space blanket is also a useful and lightweight addition.
2. Extra food and water. Extra food is useful as a hiking incentive and essential in emergencies or if a trip takes longer than anticipated.
3. Sunglasses. Hats with visors offer protection to youngsters too young to wear sunglasses.
4. Knife. A knife has multiple uses in emergency situations.
5. Firestarter candle or chemical fuel. In an emergency, you may need to make a fire for warmth or for signaling.
6. First-aid kit. Indispensable (see "First-Aid Kit," above).
7. Matches in a waterproof container. The containers are available at most outdoor supply stores.

Rock climbing near Donner Pass

8. Flashlight. A flashlight will be needed to negotiate trails at night or to prepare a camp at unexpected hours.
9. Map. Carry a current map in a waterproof case.
10. Compass. Know how to use it.
11. Protective sunscreen for adults and children. Test for skin sensitivity before the trip.
12. Whistles; to be used only in the event children become lost.
13. Water purification tablets or filter. These ensure a source of emergency drinking water.
14. Bike repair kit. A necessary item for cyclists (see "Bicycle Repair Kit," above).
15. Bike helmets. One for each rider and passenger.
16. Toilet paper. This becomes an essential when hiking with small children. Also bring a plastic bag for carrying it out. Never attempt to bury soiled paper; it will surely be unearthed by animals.
17. Insect repellent. In midsummer, adequate protection from biting insects is essential.

A Note about Safety

Safety is an important concern in all outdoor activities. No guidebook can alert you to every hazard or anticipate the limitations of every reader. Therefore, the descriptions of roads, trails, routes, and natural features in this book are not representations that a particular place or excursion will be safe for your party. When you follow any of the routes described in this book, you assume responsibility for your own safety. Under normal conditions, such excursions require the usual attention to traffic, road and trail conditions, weather, terrain, the capabilities of your party, and other factors. Keeping informed on current conditions and exercising common sense are the keys to a safe, enjoyable outing.

The Mountaineers Books

Right: A child explores a fallen giant.

CHAPTER I

THE LAKE TAHOE BASIN AN OVERVIEW

Lake Tahoe is an extraordinary lake in an extraordinary setting. Its depth, clarity, and purity are exceptional. It is the second-deepest lake in the United States (only Crater Lake, in Oregon, reaches deeper). Although its legendary clarity has diminished in recent years, one can still see to depths of 75 feet in parts of the lake. At 6225 feet above sea level, Lake Tahoe's famous blue is a reflection of the dark blue sky common at high elevations. Lake Tahoe is also surprisingly large, measuring 22 miles long and 12 miles wide, with 71 miles of shoreline.

Such a large, deep lake holds an immense quantity of water. Although Lake Tahoe is 100 times smaller than Lake Michigan, it holds nearly the same amount of water—more than 37 trillion gallons. If drained, the water of Lake Tahoe could cover the states of California and Nevada to a depth of eight inches. This quantity of water could meet the drinking water needs for the entire country for the next five years.

Lake Tahoe is located at the northern end of the Sierra Nevada mountains. The Lake Tahoe Basin, consisting of the land and water that contribute to the outflow from the lake, measures approximately 500 square miles. Within the basin, sixty-three streams flow into Lake Tahoe and one, the Truckee River, flows out. The crest of the Sierra Nevada towers above the west shore of Lake Tahoe, while the Carson Range rises high above the east shore. The three highest peaks in the basin rise above 10,000 feet, and numerous others top 9000 feet.

Although more than 78 percent of the land in the basin is publicly owned, the holdings are spread in a checkerboard pattern around the lake. Three federally designated wilderness areas border the lake: the glacier-carved Desolation Wilderness to the southwest; the volcanic Mount Rose Wilderness which overlooks the northeast shore; and the Granite Chief Wilderness to the west. National forests and numerous smaller California and Nevada state parks make up the rest of the public recreation lands. Because several authorities (including two states, six counties, and the federal government) oversee the park and forest lands, it is often difficult to obtain information about the area as a whole. The information in this chapter provides an overview of the parks, campgrounds, beaches, and cultural and recreational facilities that rim the entire lake.

LAKE TAHOE INFORMATION

For general information on the Lake Tahoe Basin, including weather, lodging and activities, check out the websites *www.tahoefun.org* or *www.virtualtahoe.com*.

Important Phone Numbers

General Information for all California State Parks at Lake Tahoe (530) 525-3345

D. L. Bliss State Park (530) 525-7277

Emerald Bay State Park (530) 541-3030

Lake Tahoe–Nevada State Park (775) 831-0494

Sugar Pine Point State Park (530) 525-7982

USFS Desolation Wilderness Permits (530) 573-2600

USFS Visitor Information Center (530) 573-2674

TART (Tahoe Area Regional Transit) (530) 581-1212 or 1-800-736-6365

STAGE (South Tahoe Area Ground Express) (530) 542-6077

How to Get There

The Lake Tahoe Basin is easily reached by car, bus, plane, and train. Lake Tahoe is located 193 miles from San Francisco and 54 miles from Reno. A major international airport in Reno services North Lake Tahoe, and a small airport in South Lake Tahoe services the lake's south shore. Passenger train service from San Francisco and Sacramento via Amtrak runs to Truckee, 15 miles from Tahoe City. Greyhound Bus Lines services both North and South Lake Tahoe. Taxi, limousine, and airport shuttle services are also available.

Getting around the Basin

In the basin, bus and trolley lines service the north, west, and south shores and can be used to great advantage by both bicyclists and hikers. The Tahoe Area Regional Transit (TART) bus runs from Incline Village, Nevada, on the north shore to Meeks Bay, California, on the west shore, serving 30 miles of shoreline, seven days a week. TART also offers "The Bus," which runs between Tahoe City and Truckee. For information on TART schedules and routes, call (530) 550-1212 or 1-800-736-6365. In addition, the Tahoe Trolley services Tahoe City and Squaw Valley. For Tahoe Trolley information, call (530) 581-3922. For general information on all Tahoe Basin transit, call 1-800-COMMUTE.

South Shore visitors have a choice of the Nifty 50 Trolley, (530) 541-7548, or STAGE (South Tahoe Area Ground Express), (530) 542-6077. South Lake Tahoe's Area Transit Management runs a "beach bus" in the summer that services south and west shore beaches and links up with the TART bus at Meeks Bay. STAGE services the city of South Lake Tahoe. Most buses and trolleys have bike racks and are wheelchair-equipped.

Visitors are strongly encouraged to ride the buses whenever possible, as each year South Lake Tahoe violates state and federal air-quality standards due to automobile-generated pollution. A greater reliance on public transportation could ease Tahoe's congested highways and clear its smog.

The Sierra Nevada Climate

The climate of the Sierra is mild in comparison with other mountain ranges. It is characterized by warm, dry summers and mild snowy winters. The following descriptions reflect an average year.

Spring. Snow at the higher elevations may persist through April. At lake level, the first spring flowers appear in May. Ice on subalpine lakes begins to break up in mid-May, but floating icebergs persist until June. Trails are uncrowded, but could be muddy. Check with rangers for trail conditions at higher elevations.

Summer. June days can still be quite brisk, and evenings are cool. Snow remains on most of the higher trails, though wildflowers bloom at lake level. July is the warmest month, with average daytime temperatures in the mid-80s (Fahrenheit) at lake level. July also marks the height of the Sierra wildflower season and peak populations of mosquitoes. August brings a slight decline in temperature and a noticeable drop in biting insects. Subalpine lakes warm to their best swimming temperatures, and even Emerald Bay can reach 70 degrees. In July and August, afternoons are punctuated by occasional brief thunderstorms, and high-elevation hikers must watch the skies for gathering storms. By late summer, snow has melted from all but the highest peaks.

Fall. Autumn brings superb weather for hiking and biking. The days are sunny and mild, with occasional warm days occurring through October. Night temperatures, however, drop steadily. Fall colors and crystal-clear days replace summer flowers. Snow generally begins in earnest in November.

Winter. Sierra winter temperatures are generally moderate, particularly near the lake, where the temperature rarely drops below 0 degrees Fahrenheit. Upper elevations are cooler and may receive considerable snowfall from November through April.

Camping

The Lake Tahoe Basin offers a multitude of camping opportunities. Most campgrounds are open from May to September. The majority require reservations, and the best of them may be booked eight weeks in advance. For U.S. Forest Service camping reservations, call BIOSPHERE at 800-280-CAMP (1-800-280-2267). For reservations at California state parks, call DESTINET at 1-800-444-PARK (1-800-444-7275) or log-in at *www.reserveamerica.com*. To avoid disappointment, consult the listing below carefully and plan ahead. For campground locations, see the map of campgrounds and beaches under "Lake Tahoe's Beaches" later in this chapter.

North Shore of Lake Tahoe and Truckee

- Donner Memorial State Park: East shore of Donner Lake, 3 miles west of Truckee off I-80. Campfire, junior ranger, and interpretive programs. Adjacent to the Emigrant Trail Museum (see "Museums and Cultural Attractions" later in this chapter) and hiking and biking trails. Reservations required. 149 sites. (530) 582-7892 or 1-800-444-7275.
- Granite Flat Campground (USFS): 3 miles south of Truckee on Highway 89. Reservations required. 75 sites. (530) 587-3558 or 1-800-280-2267.
- Goose Meadows Campground (USFS): 5 miles south of Truckee on Highway 89. Reservations required. 24 sites. (530) 587-3558 or 1-800-280-2267.
- Silver Creek Campground (USFS): 8 miles south of Truckee on Highway 89. Reservations required. 28 sites. (530) 587-3558 or 1-800-280-2267.

A ranger leads an interpretive program.

- Lake Forest Campground: 2 miles east of Tahoe City along Highway 28. First come, first served. 20 sites. (530) 581-4017.
- Mount Rose Campground (USFS): 7 miles northeast of Incline Village on Highway 431, near Mount Rose Summit. Reservations required. 24 sites. (775) 882-2766 or 1-800-280-2267.
- Sandy Beach Campground: In Tahoe City. Reservations required. 44 sites. (530) 546-7682.
- Tahoe State Recreation Area: In Tahoe City. Reservations required. 36 sites. (530) 583-3074 or 1-800-444-7275.

West Shore of Lake Tahoe

- William Kent Campground (USFS): 2 miles south of Tahoe City on Highway 89. Reservations required. 95 sites. (530) 583-3642 or 1-800-280-2267.
- Kaspian Campground (USFS): 5 miles south of Tahoe City on Highway 89. Reservations required. Walk or bike in only; 10 sites. (530) 544-5994 or 1-800-280-2267.
- Meeks Bay Resort: 10 miles south of Tahoe City on Highway 89. 28 sites. (530) 525-6946.
- Meeks Bay Campground (USFS): At Meeks Bay. Reservations required. 40 sites. (530) 544-5994 or 1-800-280-2267.
- Sugar Pine Point State Park (General Creek Campground): Between Meeks Bay and Emerald Bay on Highway 89. Campfire, junior ranger, and interpretive programs. Adjacent hiking and biking trails. Reservations required. 175 sites. 1-800-444-7275.
- D. L. Bliss State Park: 11 miles south of Homewood on Highway 89. Prime lakefront and hiking trails. Campfire, junior ranger, and interpretive programs. Reservations required. 168 sites. (530) 525-7277 or 1-800-444-7275.
- Emerald Bay State Park at Eagle Point: Off Highway 89. Prime lakefront. Campfire programs and hiking trails. Reservations required. 100 sites. (530) 541-3030 or 1-800-444-7275.
- Emerald Bay Boat Camp: North shore of Emerald Bay. Prime lakefront and hiking. First come, first served. 20 sites. (530) 541-3030.
- Bayview Campground (USFS): Above Emerald Bay on Highway 89. One-day limit in summer. Adjacent to hiking trails. First come, first served. 10 sites. (530) 544-5994.

South Shore of Lake Tahoe

- Fallen Leaf Campground (USFS): Between Highway 89 and Fallen Leaf Lake. Campfire, junior ranger, and interpretive programs. Adjacent to hiking and biking trails. Reservations required. 205 sites. (530) 544-5994 or 1-800-280-2267.

- Camp Shelly: 1.5 miles west of Camp Richardson. Hiking and biking trails nearby. 26 sites. (530) 541-6985.
- Camp Richardson: 2 miles west of South Lake Tahoe on Highway 89. Reservations required. Adjacent to bike trails. 333 sites. (530) 541-1801.
- Campground by the Lake: Off Highway 50 in South Lake Tahoe. 160 sites. (530) 542-6096.
- Tahoe Valley Campground: South Lake Tahoe at "C" Street and Highway 50. 413 sites. (530) 541-2222.
- Tahoe Pines Campground: In Meyers on Highway 50. 60 sites. (530) 577-3693.

East Shore of Lake Tahoe

- Nevada Beach Campground (USFS): 1.5 miles northeast of Stateline on Highway 50. Reservations required. 63 sites. (775) 573-2600 or 1-800-280-2267.
- Zephyr Cove Campground: At Zephyr Cove on Highway 50. Reservations required. 180 sites. (775) 588-6644.

Day Hiking

Permits are required for some day hike trips. Day hikers entering the Desolation Wilderness need a wilderness permit. Hikers can almost always register at the trailhead for these free permits. In rare cases, such as on extremely busy holiday weekends, the allotted number of wilderness permits may run out. Permits are not currently required for the Granite Chief or Mount Rose Wilderness Areas.

Backpacking

The Tahoe Basin offers myriad opportunities for backpackers. Described below are three nationally designated wilderness areas and a state park. Backcountry camping is also allowed in the Tahoe, Eldorado, and Toiyabe National Forests.

Check for restrictions in the area you plan to visit. In general, on national forest lands, the following rules apply: Camping is prohibited in meadows and within 100 feet of a lake, stream, or trail. Cutting or harming trees and shrubs is also prohibited. Campfire permits are required for fires outside of an improved camp or picnic ground. Permits are available at any Forest Service office. While traveling, smoking is prohibited unless smokers are in an enclosed vehicle equipped with an ashtray. Check with Forest Service rangers for additional seasonal fire restrictions, and note that further restrictions apply in wilderness areas.

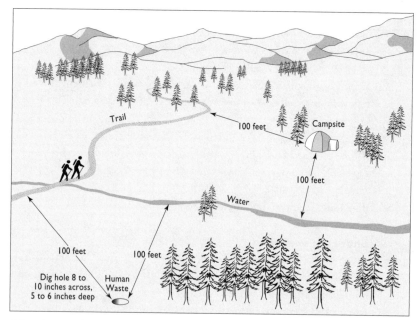

Follow these guidelines to camp responsibly.

Desolation Wilderness

Desolation Wilderness covers more than 63,000 acres of subalpine forest, granite peaks, and glacier-sculptured valleys at the southwest end of Lake Tahoe. The area is renowned for its many clear subalpine lakes. The dramatic beauty of its landscape makes Desolation Wilderness an extremely popular destination for backpackers.

Consequently, the National Forest Service requires permits and imposes a quota system that limits access to 700 overnight users per day from June 15 to Labor Day. For backpackers, 50 percent of quota permits may be reserved up to 90 days in advance. The other 50 percent are issued on a first-come, first-served basis on the day of entry. Permits may be obtained in person, by phone, or by mail. If you are planning to backpack on a busy summer weekend, it is wise to reserve a permit. Make a reservation within 90 days of your trip by writing or calling the Eldorado National Forest Information Center at 3070 Camino Heights Drive, Camino, CA 95709, (530) 644-6048. Note that campfires are not allowed in Desolation Wilderness, and remember that due to heavy use, it is preferable to backpack during the week and to avoid busy holiday weekends. Because of the fragility of this wilderness area, it is essential that backpackers practice minimum-impact camping. For more information, write the Lake Tahoe Basin Management Unit, 870 Emerald Bay Road (Highway 89), South Lake Tahoe, California 96150, or phone (530) 573-2600.

Granite Chief Wilderness

Granite Chief Wilderness is located on the western shore of Lake Tahoe, behind the Alpine Meadows and Squaw Valley ski areas. A spectacular portion of the Pacific Crest Trail runs along its rugged granite peaks. Granite Chief is more heavily forested and hosts fewer lakes than Desolation Wilderness. Because it is not as heavily used, quotas are not imposed at Granite Chief. Overnight users do, however, need a campfire permit if a stove or fire will be used. For permits, write or visit the Lake Tahoe Basin Management Unit, 870 Emerald Bay Road (Highway 89), South Lake Tahoe, California 96150, or phone (530) 573-2600; or contact the Truckee Ranger District, 10342 Highway 89 North, Truckee, California 96161, (530) 587-3558.

Mokelumne Wilderness

Mokelumne Wilderness, located between Highway 88 and Highway 4 south of Lake Tahoe, occupies more than 105,000 acres and ranges from 4000 feet elevation near Salt Springs Reservoir to more than 10,000 feet at Round Top. There are no quotas, but overnight users must obtain permits at the Lake Tahoe Basin Management Unit, 870 Emerald Bay Road (Highway 89), South Lake Tahoe, California 96150, or phone (530) 573-2600; or contact the Forest Service Visitor Center, 3070 Camino Heights (Highway 50), Camino, California 95733, (530) 644-6048.

Lake Tahoe–Nevada State Park

Lake Tahoe–Nevada State Park, on the lake's east shore, contains more than 13,000 acres of forests and peaks at elevations ranging from lake level to 8856 feet. Backcountry camping is permitted in two small designated campgrounds. Campsites must be reserved in advance, and camping outside of these areas is prohibited. For information and reservations, contact the park headquarters at (775) 831-0494 or write Lake Tahoe–Nevada State Park, Box 3283, Incline Village, Nevada 89450.

Mount Rose Wilderness

Mount Rose Wilderness Area was established northeast of Lake Tahoe in 1989. A wilderness permit is not required at this time, but campers must obtain a campfire permit. For information about trails and maps, contact the Carson Ranger District, 1536 South Carson Street., Carson City, Nevada 89701, or call (775) 882-2766.

Lodging

Lake Tahoe offers accommodations of all types, from rustic cabins to full-service resorts. During peak summer months, most establishments are fully booked, so plan ahead. For information on south and east shore lodging, contact the Lake Tahoe Visitors Authority, 1-800-AT-TAHOE or (530) 544-5050. For north and west shore lodging, call 1-800-GO-TAHOE, (530) 583-3494, or visit the website *www.tahoefun.org*.

Emergency Medical Services

Two medical facilities are located near Lake Tahoe. On the north shore, there is Tahoe Forest Hospital, Pine Avenue and Donner Pass Road, Truckee, California, (530) 587-6011 or 1-800-733-9953. On the south shore, the primary facility is Barton Memorial Hospital, South Avenue and 3rd Street, South Lake Tahoe, California, (530) 541-3420. The Incline Village Health Center also offers 24-hour emergency services at 880 Alder Avenue, Incline Village, Nevada, or call (775) 833-4100.

Museums and Cultural Attractions

Several museums and historical sites are located in the Tahoe Basin. Since hours of operation change seasonally, it is necessary to call ahead. Some museums also conduct special programs or cultural festivals during the summer. Inquire about these during your visit.

North Shore

Emigrant Trail Museum. This small but fascinating museum is filled with artifacts of the emigrant movement of the mid-1800s. The collection includes a fully loaded covered wagon and an authentic emigrant homestead. Visitors can also view a slide show of the Donner Party tragedy, participate in a ranger-led nature hike, or visit the dramatic Emigrant Monument (where a 22-foot pedestal marks the height of the snow in the tragic winter of 1846–47). The museum also hosts special lectures on regional history. Located at Donner Memorial State Park, near the eastern end of Donner Lake, just off Interstate 80 at the Donner Lake exit west of Truckee. Open daily. (530) 587-3841.

Cal-Neva Indian Room. The Cal-Neva Lodge at Crystal Bay hosts an "Indian Room" that contains exhibits dedicated to the Washo tribe. The display includes photographs, mounted animals, and cultural artifacts. This small but interesting collection highlights the need in Lake Tahoe for an independent cultural center for the Washo. Open daily, 24 hours. Free admission. (775) 832-4000.

West Shore

Watson Cabin Living Museum. In this authentic log cabin, circa 1909, museum staff in period costume demonstrate how pioneer families lived at the turn of the century. Open daily in summer; weekends and holidays only throughout the

Discovering an old pine

rest of the year. Free admission. Located at 560 North Lake Boulevard, Tahoe City, California. (530) 583-8717.

Gatekeeper's Cabin Museum. This hand-carved log cabin houses a collection of Washo baskets and other artifacts of nineteenth- and early twentieth-century Lake Tahoe. The Gatekeeper's Cabin Museum includes tools, clothing, vintage newspapers, photographs, and a natural history display. Open daily June 15 through Labor Day; open Wednesday through Sunday May 14 through June 14 and Labor Day through October 1. Free admission. Located at the south end of Fanny Bridge in Tahoe City. (530) 583-1762.

Nature Center and Historic Ehrman Mansion. The nature center, housed in an old water tower, contains interactive exhibits on birds, mammals, fish, and trees. Adjacent to the nature center is the Ehrman Mansion, where the lifestyles of the wealthy circa 1900 can be examined. Rangers in period dress give tours of the mansion. The mansion's grounds also contain a log cabin built in 1860 by one of the first white residents of Lake Tahoe. Located at Sugar Pine Point State Park, 10 miles south of Tahoe City on Highway 89 (see Trip 23 for adjacent hiking trails). Open daily, June through Labor Day. (530) 525-7982.

South Shore

Lake Tahoe Visitor Center (USFS Lake Tahoe Basin Management Unit). The Lake Tahoe Visitor Center offers a wide range of free nature activities, lectures, and evening programs. Self-guided hiking trails emanating from the center teach

Artist Adam Fortunate Eagle demonstrates sculpturing at Tallac Historic Site.

youngsters about natural history, Native Americans, and fire prevention (see Trip 34). In inclement weather, visit the Stream Profile Chamber to watch rainbow trout, kokanee salmon, and other aquatic life through the windows of an underground viewing chamber. The center also sells an extensive Stream Profile Chamber collection of books, maps, and brochures. The well-trained staff is equipped to answer most of your Tahoe questions. Located on Highway 89, 3 miles north of the junction of State Highways 89 and 50 in South Lake Tahoe.

Open Tuesday through Sunday, June through Labor Day; weekends only in the fall. (530) 573-2674.

Tallac Historic Site. The beautiful Tallac Historic Site offers guided tours through historic homesteads and resorts dating from the late 1800s. The Baldwin-McGonagle House Tallac Historic Site contains excellent exhibits on the Washo, and a small arboretum provides a beautiful place to picnic and learn about native plants. Throughout the summer, there are biweekly art workshops for children and an impressive array of concerts and cultural events. The Tallac Historic Site is located 0.75 mile south of the Lake Tahoe Visitor Center on Highway 89. (530) 541-5227.

Lake Tahoe Museum. The small Lake Tahoe Museum is filled with artifacts of Tahoe's Native Americans and early settlers. On display are Indian baskets, spear tips, hands-on grinding stones, and displays on logging, ice cutting, and pioneer farming. Located at 3058 Highway 50 in South Lake Tahoe. (530) 541-5458.

Outside the Tahoe Basin

Virginia City. Virginia City, a thriving mining metropolis in the late 1800s, is now nearly a ghost town. Visitors to Virginia City can ride a century-old steam train past abandoned mines, inspect an underground mine, tour Victorian mansions, and stroll the historic boardwalk. The most compelling reason to visit Virginia City, however, is to see "the tomb of the Sierra forest." The building of the Comstock mines and adjacent towns was made possible by thirty years of devastating lumbering that permanently changed Lake Tahoe's forests. The gold and silver discovered near Virginia City was the catalyst that began the exploitation of the Tahoe Basin. To reach Virginia City, take Highway 431 from Incline Village to its intersection with Highway 395. Then take Highway 341 over the Geiger Grade to Virginia City, approximately 1 hour from North Lake Tahoe.

Horseback Riding

The following stables offer guided trail rides within the Lake Tahoe Basin. Many also offer pony and hay rides. Reservations are recommended.

North Shore

- Cold Stream Corral, Cold Stream Road, Donner Lake, CA. (530) 541-4121.
- Northstar Stables, 910 Northstar Drive, Northstar, CA. (530) 562-2480, *www.skinorthstar.com.*
- Ponderosa Ranch, 100 Ponderosa Ranch Road, Incline Village, NV. (775) 831-2154.
- Tahoe Donner Equestrian, 15275 Alder Creek Rd, Truckee, CA. (530) 587-9470, *www.tahoedonner.com.*

West Shore
- Squaw Valley Stables, 1525 Squaw Valley Road, Olympic Valley, CA. (530) 583-7433.
- Alpine Meadows Stables, Alpine Meadows, CA. (530) 583-3905.

South Shore
- Camp Richardson's Corral, Emerald Bay at Fallen Leaf Road, South Lake Tahoe, CA. (530) 541-3113.
- Cascade Stables, 2199 Cascade Road, South Lake Tahoe, CA. Six miles north of the South Lake Tahoe Y junction off Highway 89. (530) 541-2055.
- Sunset Ranch, P.O. Box 10728, South Lake Tahoe, CA. (530) 541-9001.

East Shore
- Zephyr Cove Stables, 760 Highway 50, Zephyr Cove, NV. (775) 588-5664.

Boating

At most major marinas on Lake Tahoe, there are concessions that rent canoes and kayaks. Canoeing or kayaking on Lake Tahoe is not to be missed. The Sand Harbor area by kayak is especially beautiful. Rentals and guided tours are available at many locations. For the best trips, paddle in the morning when wind and boat traffic are light. On most afternoons, the wind creates significant chop. On any day, check the forecast before setting out, because severe storms can develop suddenly. Consider also paddling on one of the basin's smaller lakes, especially Fallen Leaf or Echo Lakes.

Try one of the concessions below for kayak rentals and/or guided tours:
- A Current Adventure Kayak School and Trips, P.O. Box 828, Lotus, CA. 888-452-9254, *www.kayaking.com.*
- Cut-Rite, 7062 West Lake Blvd., Tahoma, CA. (530) 525-7704.
- Enviro-Rents, 6873 North Lake Blvd., Tahoe Vista, CA. (530) 546-2780.
- Kayak Cafe, 5166 North Lake Blvd., Cinnamon Bay, CA. (530) 546-9337.
- Kayak Tahoe, 3411 Lake Tahoe Blvd., South Lake Tahoe, CA. (530) 544-2011.
- Patton Landing, 5166 North Lake Blvd., Cinnamon Bay, CA. (530) 546-9337.
- Sunsports, 3564 Lake Tahoe Blvd., South Lake Tahoe, CA. (530) 541-6095.
- Tahoe City Kayak Shop, 265 North Lake Blvd., Tahoe City, CA. (530) 581-4336.

Rafting

Summer days are perfect for rafting the gentle Truckee River. Rent a family-sized raft at Tahoe City and float lazily 4 miles to the historic River Ranch Lodge. Transportation back to Tahoe City is provided by shuttle. The rapids are few and far between, but the river is clean, cold, and refreshing on a hot summer day. Bring drinks, bathing suits, and plenty of sunscreen.

The following outfitters provide rafts and pick-up:

■ Truckee River Raft Rentals, 185 River Road, Tahoe City, CA. (530) 583-0123.

■ Fanny Bridge Raft Rentals, 125 West Lake Blvd., Tahoe City, CA. (530) 583-3021.

■ Mountain Air Sports, 205 River Road, Tahoe City, CA. (530) 583-7238.

For a more challenging, professionally guided trip, contact Tahoe Whitewater Tours, Tahoe City, CA, (530) 581-2441. They offer 1-day trips on the South Fork of the American River, East Fork of the Carson River, and on the Truckee River from Boca to Floristan.

Fishing

Lake Tahoe and the many lakes and streams in the Tahoe Basin offer a multitude of fishing opportunities. Sport fish in the Tahoe area include rainbow, brook, golden, lake, brown, and cutthroat trout, kokanee salmon, and mountain whitefish. Due to historic overfishing, catching fish is a challenge, but die-hard anglers should not be discouraged.

Numerous regulations in the Tahoe Basin protect the integrity of the region's fish population. Some lakes and streams are closed to fishing; other areas are catch and release. Seasonal restrictions may also apply. In addition, all persons sixteen years of age and older must possess a California or Nevada fishing license when fishing in the basin. For information on regulations, contact the California Department of Fish and Game, (530) 355-7040; the Nevada Department of Wildlife, (775) 465-2242; or the U.S. Forest Service, Lake Tahoe Basin Management Unit, (530) 544-6420.

A good place to take children for their first fishing experience is Saw Mill Pond in South Lake Tahoe. Fishing in this stocked, man-made pond is prohibited to anyone over the age of fourteen. The pond was created by the State of California for the purpose of teaching children "the art of angling." The pond is conveniently, although not scenically, located on Tahoe Boulevard, 2 miles south of the junction of Highways 50 and 89 in South Lake Tahoe. Two other great spots to try are beautiful Sand Harbor State Park (located on Highway 28 about 5 miles south of Incline Village) and Echo Lake (see Trip 47) where one can rent canoes and fishing boats. If a fish must be caught, there is always a trip to the Tahoe Trout Farm, a stocked pond where anglers pay per pound for their catch (located at 1023 Blue Lake Ave., South Lake Tahoe, CA).

Bicycling and Mountain Biking

There are numerous bike rental concessions throughout the Tahoe Basin. On summer weekends, call ahead to reserve or arrive early to ensure availability. Many of the larger outlets offer children's bikes, carriers, tandems, or baby trailers. Concessions that are located next to bike trails are so noted and are more fully described.

North Shore

- Northstar at Tahoe, Highway 267, Truckee, CA. (530) 562-2268.
- Tahoe Bike & Ski, 8499 North Lake Boulevard, Kings Beach, CA. (530) 546-7437.
- Shoreline Ski and Snowboards, 259 Kingsbury Grade, Stateline, NV. (775) 588-8777.
- Village Bicycles, 800 Tahoe Boulevard, Incline Village, NV. (775) 831-3537. Near bike trail. Rents child carriers and children's bikes.

West Shore

- The Back Country, 255 N. Lake Boulevard, Tahoe City, CA. (530) 581-5861, 1-888-625-8444.
- Granite Chief, 1602 Squaw Valley Road, Olympic Valley, CA. (530) 583-2832.
- Cyclepaths, 1785 West Lake Boulevard, Tahoe City, CA. (530) 581-1171. Adjacent to bike trail. Rents baby trailers, tandems, and children's bikes.
- Enviro-Rents, 6873 North Lake Boulevard, Tahoe Vista, CA. (530) 546-2780.
- Olympic Bike Shop, 620 North Lake Boulevard, Tahoe City, CA. (530) 581-2500. Adjacent to bike trail. Rents children's bikes and tandems.
- Squaw Valley Sport Shop, 201 Squaw Valley Road, Olympic Valley, CA. (530) 583-3356. Located next to bike path and tram.
- Squaw Valley Mountain Bike Rental, Squaw Valley USA, Olympic Valley, CA. (530) 583-7675. Located next to bike path and tram.
- Tahoe Gear, 5095 West Lake Boulevard, Homewood, CA. (530) 525-5233. Adjacent to bike trail. Rents children's bikes and baby trailers.
- T.S.R. Bike Rentals, Highway 89, Tahoe City, CA. (530) 583-0123.

Adjacent to bike trail. Rents baby trailers, child seats, children's bikes, and tandems.

■ West Side Sports, 5395 West Lake Tahoe Boulevard, Homestead, CA. (530) 525-0310.

South Shore

■ Anderson's Bicycle Rental, 645 Emerald Bay Road, South Lake Tahoe, CA. (530) 541-0500. Adjacent to bike trails. Rents children's bikes and baby trailers.

■ Cutting Edge Sports, 3930 Lake Tahoe Blvd., South Lake Tahoe, CA. (530) 544-5881.

■ Mountain Bike Rentals, 3979 Lake Tahoe Blvd., South Lake Tahoe, CA. (530) 541-2823. Adjacent to bike path.

■ Richardson's Resort and Marina, Highway 89 at Camp Richardson, South Lake Tahoe, CA. (530) 542-6584. Adjacent to bike trails. Rents children's bikes, baby trailers, and four-person surreys.

■ Tahoe Bike Shop, 2277 Lake Tahoe Blvd., South Lake Tahoe, CA. (530) 544-8060.

Ice Skating

Squaw Valley's High Camp Bath and Tennis Club offers an outdoor, Olympic-size ice rink that is open year-round. The rink, perched at 8200 feet, offers spectacular views of Lake Tahoe and Squaw Valley. The views are particularly nice at sunset; visit after a day of hiking in the Squaw Valley area (see Trips 12, 13, and 14). Open daily, 10:00 a.m. to 9:00 p.m. Entrance and skate rental fees.

Lake Tahoe's Beaches

Summer visitors flock in great number to Lake Tahoe's lovely beaches. Although the water rarely warms above 60 degrees, its color, clarity, and scenic setting entice swimmers all summer long. A few extraordinary beaches are highlighted in the following pages, and a complete listing of Tahoe beaches is found in Appendix B; locations are indicated on the following map. Beach goers are cautioned against choosing beaches close to large marinas, which may rent motorized personal watercraft that destroy the peace for beachcombers, swimmers, and oar-powered boaters. Regulation of these noisy machines may limit their use to appropriate areas in the future. The following beaches are highly recommended.

North Shore

Speedboat Beach. This small, sandy beach is tucked away beneath the Cal-Neva monolith near Stateline where the commotion of the gambling strip seems worlds

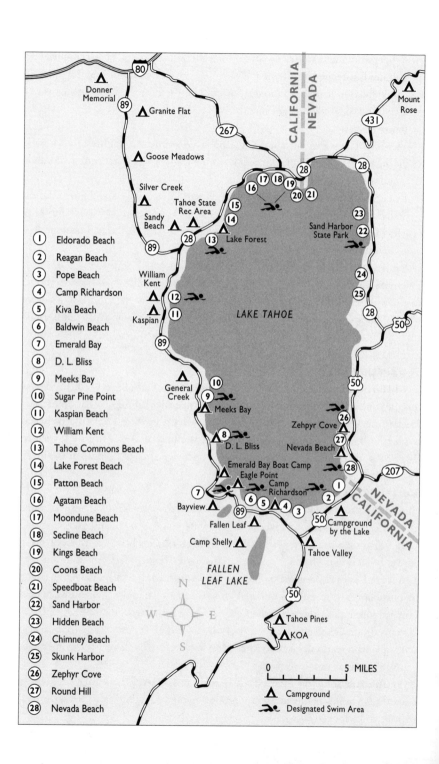

① Eldorado Beach
② Reagan Beach
③ Pope Beach
④ Camp Richardson
⑤ Kiva Beach
⑥ Baldwin Beach
⑦ Emerald Bay
⑧ D. L. Bliss
⑨ Meeks Bay
⑩ Sugar Pine Point
⑪ Kaspian Beach
⑫ William Kent
⑬ Tahoe Commons Beach
⑭ Lake Forest Beach
⑮ Patton Beach
⑯ Agatam Beach
⑰ Moondune Beach
⑱ Secline Beach
⑲ Kings Beach
⑳ Coons Beach
㉑ Speedboat Beach
㉒ Sand Harbor
㉓ Hidden Beach
㉔ Chimney Beach
㉕ Skunk Harbor
㉖ Zephyr Cove
㉗ Round Hill
㉘ Nevada Beach

Donner Memorial
Granite Flat
Goose Meadows
Silver Creek
Sandy Beach
Tahoe State Rec Area
Lake Forest
William Kent
Kaspian
LAKE TAHOE
General Creek
Meeks Bay
D. L. Bliss
Emerald Bay Boat Camp
Eagle Point
Camp Richardson
Bayview
Fallen Leaf
Camp Shelly
FALLEN LEAF LAKE
Zehpyr Cove
Nevada Beach
Campground by the Lake
Tahoe Valley
Tahoe Pines
KOA
Sand Harbor State Park
Mount Rose

CALIFORNIA
NEVADA
NEVADA
CALIFORNIA

N
W   E
S

0   5 MILES

▲ Campground
🏊 Designated Swim Area

away. Large boulders attract snorkelers and crayfish catchers. From Highway 28 northbound, turn right on Speedboat Avenue, 0.25 mile before Stateline. Follow Speedboat to its end; a closed, sandy road leads to the beach. Parking is extremely limited; abide by parking restrictions.

West Shore

Meeks Bay. The white sand beach stretches for a mile in a sheltered cove with all the amenities, including food and sundry concessions and rest rooms. Located 10.7 miles south of Tahoe City on Highway 89. Parking fee.

D. L. Bliss State Park. This is perhaps the finest beach on Lake Tahoe. Enjoy crystal-clear water, white sand, boulder-lined coves, and beautiful hiking trails nearby (Trips 21, 22, and 23). Parking is limited, so arrive early. Located 16.5 miles south of Tahoe City on Highway 89. Entrance fee.

South Shore

Baldwin Beach. The sandy shore is magnificent for miles on the south shore. Baldwin Beach is an excellent beach for young children due to its very shallow water. Majestically dark Mount Tallac is a dramatic backdrop. Restrooms available. Located 0.7 mile west of the Lake Tahoe Visitor Center on Highway 89; turn right on Baldwin Beach Road. Parking fee.

East Shore

Sand Harbor. Located in Lake Tahoe–Nevada State Park, Sand Harbor offers a long, exquisite, white sand beach, plus a nature trail, ample picnic areas, and rest rooms. The setting is superb; crowds are the only drawback. Still, the beach is worth it. Escape the hordes by snorkeling off its rocky point or try shore fishing off its boulders. Located 2.6 miles south of Incline Village on Highway 28. Arrive early on weekends, for the parking lot fills before noon. Parking fee.

Hidden Beach. Take a short hike from Highway 28 to a mostly rocky cove located approximately 2 miles north of Sand Harbor and 0.7 mile south of Incline Village. Popular with swimmers, boaters, and sunbathers. Parking along Highway 28 is very limited.

Secret Cove/Chimney Beach. Escape the crowds by hiking down to a string of lovely coves. Located 2.5 miles south of Sand Harbor on Highway 28. Park in the lot (where the only rest rooms are) and start down the gated, unpaved road. A narrow path on the right winds steeply down to the "clothing-optional" beaches. Once the path levels, hike north to find the cove of your choice. (If the above lot is full, there is a second parking lot 0.25 mile north.)

Skunk Harbor. Hike a closed road for 1.4 miles to reach a lovely sandy cove. Located 5.4 miles south of Sand Harbor on Highway 28. Watch for a parking pullout and a locked gate (see Trip 52).

Natural History of the Lake Tahoe Basin

Geology

Lake Tahoe's fascinating geologic history is etched on its distinctive topography. The deep basin of Lake Tahoe was formed during the uplifting of the Sierra Nevada block five to ten million years ago. Two parallel faults occurred in the upthrown block, and a valley sank to a great depth between the fault lines. The blocks on either side continued to rise, creating the Carson Range to the east and the crest of the Sierra Nevada to the west.

The next important event occurred two million years ago, when a volcanic eruption sent lava to block the northern end of the valley. Rivers and streams flowing into the valley then filled the basin to nearly 7000 feet. Evidence of Lake Tahoe's former level can be seen in the small caves above Cave Rock on the east shore. These caves were made by the action of waves when the lake level was 140 feet higher than its present level.

The third critical event shaping the basin occurred over the past million years. The Ice Age spawned 1000-foot-thick glaciers that covered all but the highest peaks on the west side of the basin. As these rivers of ice slid down the moun-

Golden-mantled ground squirrel

tains to Lake Tahoe, they carved ∪-shaped valleys. From the east shore, glacially carved valleys are clearly visible above Emerald Bay, Cascade Lake, and Fallen Leaf Lake. On their downward course, the glaciers also carved out numerous depressions. These depressions are now the 130-plus lakes of Desolation Wilderness. Stones and rubble that were pushed aside by the advancing glaciers created the lateral moraines, now forested ridges, that cradle Emerald Bay, Fallen Leaf Lake, and Cascade Lake.

Throughout the Sierra Nevada, the glaciers' paths are strewn with glacial erratics, boulders that were broken off by glaciers and dropped miles from their origin. The great tongues of moving ice carried multiton, house-size boulders, then left them stranded as they retreated. The glaciers also left a distinctive gleam on the area's granite. Glaciers carrying sand and stone passed over the granite and burnished it to a high sheen. This glacial polish and the mirrorlike quality of its many subalpine lakes inspired John Muir to call the Sierra Nevada "the range of light."

Plant and Animal Communities

The Lake Tahoe Basin is composed of several distinct communities. The summaries below highlight the flora and fauna found in each habitat.

The **upper montane zone** is found between 6000 feet (lake level) and 8000 feet. It is usually dominated by Jeffrey pine and red fir. Ponderosa pine, lodgepole pine, and white fir also play large roles, while incense cedar and sugar pine are present in smaller numbers. In well-watered areas, quaking aspen form dense stands. On the eastern slopes of the Carson Range, open forests of western white pine are common.

The typical Jeffrey pine forest occupies a sunny slope with widely spaced, parklike stands. Its extremely deep roots make it drought resistant. Understory vegetation includes greenleaf and pinemat manzanita, serviceberry, sagebrush, and rabbitbrush. The forests are often interrupted by dry meadows.

The lush undergrowth of a Jeffrey pine forest attracts a wide variety of wildlife. Mule deer graze on grass and shrubs beneath the trees. Pine seeds attract chipmunks, golden-mantled ground squirrels, Steller's jays, and dark-eyed juncos. Mountain chickadees are year-round residents, and snags attract hairy woodpeckers. The reptile population includes the western fence lizard in rocky areas and garter snakes. Raccoons and black bears are among the larger omnivores. Near meadows, coyotes, red-tailed hawks, pine martens, pocket gophers, and Belding's ground squirrels can be found. At night, bats are abundant.

The red fir forest occurs at the same elevation as the Jeffrey pine forest, but the two are vastly different. While the pine forest is sunny, diverse, and bursting

Playing in the pines

with life, the red fir forest is dark, somber, and silent. Dense stands of red fir shut out most sunlight, preventing the growth of ground cover. As a result, wildlife is scarce because there is little to eat. An exception is the chickaree, or Douglas squirrel, who harvests the cones of the red fir.

The Lake Tahoe Basin contains vast forests of fir due to past logging practices. In the late 1800s, timbermen stripped the basin of the more marketable pine. In many areas, only immature firs were left. The firs flourished in the absence of competition, and the second-growth forest that today covers the basin is primarily fir. Gone are the extensive park-like stands of pine that dominated the basin for centuries before the arrival of white settlers.

Forests of lodgepole pine also occur in the upper montane zone. Appropriately named, these pines are tall, straight, and slender. Plains Indians used their trunks to build teepees. Like red fir, lodgepole frequently grows in dark, dense stands. Understory vegetation is consequently sparse and wildlife meager.

The **subalpine zone** lies roughly between 8000 feet and 10,000 feet. Trees in this zone include lodgepole pine, whitebark pine, and mountain hemlock. Western white pine occurs in smaller numbers, and wind-sculpted western juniper is common in Desolation Wilderness. Groves of aspen make occasional appearances. The subalpine forest is characterized by small stands of trees interspersed with meadows, lakes, or rocky slopes.

Weather conditions are severe in this zone. Fierce winds batter plants and strip the slopes of soil. The growing season is limited to only two months. Snow is heavy and may blanket the subalpine zone for nine months of the year. In the upper reaches of the zone, whitebark pine grows only in ground-hugging, waist-high thickets of krummholz.

Birds of the subalpine zone include Clark's nutcracker, hermit thrush, mountain bluebird, and the pine grosbeak. Mammals such as the yellow-bellied marmot and tiny pika inhabit rocky environs. In addition, many of the birds and mammals of the upper montane zone frequent the subalpine zone during summer months.

Particularly rich in their variety of wildlife are the so-called edge environments, where subalpine forest meets meadows or riparian areas. Here, predators such as coyotes, weasels, and pine martens enjoy a wide assortment of prey, including northern pocket gophers, marmots, shrews, and voles. Mule deer also frequent the edge environment, taking advantage of grazing near protective cover.

The **alpine zone** is found above tree line, but only a few peaks in the Tahoe Basin enter this zone. Near the summits of these peaks, krummholz woodland drops away to reveal a rocky, windy, frigid environment. The alpine zone features meadows, grasslands, and rocky fell fields in a mosaic of communities collectively known as tundra. Vegetation on the tundra must survive hurricane-force winds, arctic temperatures, and an extremely short growing season. Animals inhabiting the alpine zone include pikas, marmots, and pocket gophers. In the summer, rosy finches are found.

Human History in the Tahoe Basin

Prior to the arrival of white settlers, the Tahoe Basin was inhabited for thousands of years by Native Americans. The small tribe of the Washo migrated each spring to the shores of Lake Tahoe from its winter home in the Pine Nut Mountains east of the lake. Lake Tahoe was the spiritual center of the Washo world. The tribe lived in harmony with the natural rhythms of its seasons. The Washo drew their livelihood from the lake, its streams, and the mountains, but did not alter, deplete, or exploit them.

Until the 1840s, the basin remained wholly the Washos'. In 1848, gold was discovered at Sutter's Mill and in Auburn, California. With this discovery, thousands rushed over the Sierra to reach the Sacramento Valley. The traffic intensified in 1859 when the Comstock Lode was discovered near Virginia City. Tens of thousands traveled through the basin to reach the mines. The resources of the basin suddenly were in great demand to house and feed the travelers, to shore up the mines, and to build a railroad.

When white settlers turned to the forests, fish, and game of the basin, the Washo quietly resisted, but their lands, including the sacred lake, were rapidly taken from them. In the hands of the settlers, the resources of the basin were pillaged. Commercial fishermen drained the lake of fish, hunters cleared the forests of game, and huge mills turned trees into millions of board feet of lumber. Sacred places of the Washo were altered beyond recognition.

Today, one can learn about the Washo by visiting several local museums. Their beautiful willow baskets and other cultural artifacts are on display. Washo legends about the origin and natural history of the basin have also survived. The Washo used legends to teach their children about their world. Through entertaining stories, Washo children learned about animals, geography, wilderness survival, and the tribe's place in the natural world. Parents today are encouraged to read these legends to their children (see "Books for Parents" in Appendix C). They speak of a wise people who lived in harmony with nature and knew how to pass that knowledge to future generations.

Right: *Mount Rose*

CHAPTER 2

THE NORTH LAKE TAHOE BASIN

T he North Lake Tahoe Basin offers a variety of hiking and biking routes, from meadow walking to summit climbs. Although the north basin may lack the subalpine lakes and dramatic topography found in the south and west Lake Tahoe Basin, its routes usually offer   more solitude and a greater opportunity to view wildlife.

The trips described in this chapter are located on the north shore of Lake Tahoe in the area bordered on the east by Highway 431, on the north by Interstate 80, and loosely to the west by Donner Pass and Highway 89. The trips include two very challenging hikes. Trip 1 climbs to the summit of Mount Rose, and peak-bagging Trip 7 ascends Mount Judah, Mount Lincoln, and Anderson Peak. For a more moderate family outing, choose the hike to the lovely Loch Leven Lakes (Trip 8) or hike the Tahoe Rim Trail from Watson Lake to Lava Cliffs (Trip 6). For families with young children, the nature strolls in Tahoe Meadows and Ophir Creek (Trips 3, 4, and 5) are ideal. Children will also enjoy visiting the Stateline Fire Lookout (Trip 9). Those accompanied by strollers or wheelchairs should try the specially constructed segment of the Tahoe Rim Trail (Trip 3).

For family mountain biking, Ophir Creek is an excellent choice (Trip 5). Wildlife enthusiasts may see coyote and deer there in early-morning hours. For a more urban flavor, with beaches and pools nearby, choose the paved bike trail through Incline Village (Trip 10). More advanced riders can ride the first 2.5 miles of the Mount Rose climb (Trip 1) for a scenic workout. For more views and greater challenge, try biking to the Mount Rose Relay Station (Trip 2).

▌ MOUNT ROSE

Difficulty: strenuous
Distance: 5.9 miles one way; mountain bikers first 2.5 miles only
Usage: moderate
Starting elevation: 8840 feet
Elevation gain: 1886 feet
Season: summer
Map: USGS Mount Rose

Mount Rose (10,776 feet) is the third-highest peak in the Tahoe Basin and a fine mountain to climb. Although the trail is long, it is seldom excessively steep, and the panoramic view from the summit is well worth the effort. The hike courses through countless gardens, from dry chaparral to subalpine meadow to alpine rock gardens above timberline. For families, there is a scenic meadow at the trail's halfway point where younger members can picnic and explore while older siblings assault the peak. Most of the trail is shadeless, so bring sun protection and plenty of water.

Advanced mountain bikers can ride the trail for the first 2.5 miles, for it follows an unpaved logging road. After 2.5 miles, the trail becomes single track, and its grade steepens considerably. Because the summit of Mount Rose lies in a designated wilderness area, bikes are prohibited on the last leg of the climb.

From the junction of Highways 28 and 431 on the northeastern shore of Lake Tahoe, take Highway 431 north 8 miles. Look to the left for a cinder-block building and a sign indicating "wilderness trailhead." Park on the shoulder in front of the building. The hike begins on the closed road. Approaching from the east on Highway 431, the trailhead is 0.3 mile west of a road sign that says Mount Rose Summit.

Begin with a gentle ascent on the dusty logging road. Enjoy views to the south of Tahoe Meadows framed by lodgepole pines. To the southwest, Lake Tahoe appears with the peaks of Desolation Wilderness rising behind it. To the southeast, the Virginia Range is purple in the morning sun.

Trailside flowers are abundant. Watch for mule's ears and arrow-leaved balsamroot, two very similar yellow composites. Children quickly learn to distinguish the "mule's ear," whose long, rounded, gray-green leaves are "furry" to the touch and shaped like a mule's ear. In contrast, the leaves of the balsamroot are pointed, like an arrow. Red Indian paintbrush and purple lupine are also plentiful along the trail.

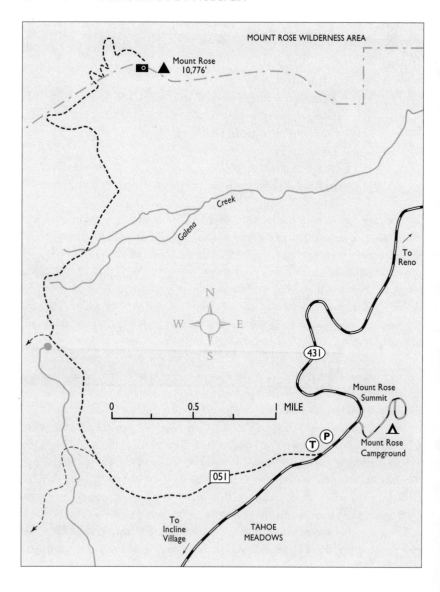

Pass over a creek, and the good views increase. After 1.2 miles, the road curves north, eventually passing a small pond at 2.5 miles. Make a short detour to check for Pacific tree frogs. Most likely you will hear these raucous carolers before you see their tiny, well-camouflaged bodies along the edges of the pond. The croaking is made by the male frogs inflating their throat pouches in the water. The sound can be quite impressive, especially given their

Yellow-bellied marmot

size (1 to 2 inches). Contrary to its name, the tree frog shows no particular preference for living or breeding in trees.

While at the pond, admire the many flowers blooming in the adjoining meadow. Look particularly for pink elephant's heads, whose blossoms resemble the heads of elephants with gracefully upturned trunks.

Just after the pond, arrive at a junction. Take the trail on the right heading north, marked by a large sign indicating the Mount Rose Trail. Rise briefly, then descend to a meadow. The trail heads across the meadow and soon regains the road. Turn right on the road, descending and paralleling power lines through a flowered meadow. Corn lilies are tall and conspicuous. Early in the season, the corn lily's thick flowerless stalk and wide leaves resemble a corn plant. The corn lily, however, is poisonous to humans and animals. The Washo Indians, in fact, made a tea from the roots of the corn lily to aid birth control.

Descend north on the road and cross a stream. Beyond the stream, the trail and ascent begin. Those not planning to reach the summit can choose a picnic spot beside the inviting stream and explore the flowers in the surrounding meadows.

Hikers assaulting the summit climb north on a progressively steeper and narrower path. On the rocky slopes beside the trail, look for sunbathing marmots, a Western relative of the woodchuck. These plump rodents, also called "whistle pigs," whistle in alarm at passing hikers. Marmots are commonly seen basking on sun-warmed rocks while munching incessantly. By fall, they build up a rotund physique to survive their long winter hibernation. In July, the wildflowers, particularly lupines, are spectacular on this portion of trail.

The view east is quite scenic. The green valley is walled by two steep slopes, the one to the north is the dark volcanic hulk of Mount Rose. Beyond the valley, waves of blue mountains extend to the horizon.

At 3.9 miles, head northwest up a steep gully. The trail crosses the stream and climbs to a saddle, entering Mount Rose Wilderness, where the trail forks. Stay right and resume the climb in a northeasterly direction.

Switchback up the western flank of Mount Rose. The environment changes noticeably. This trail is one of the few in the Tahoe Basin that climbs to the alpine zone, and you can feel the difference. The temperature drops; the air is thinner.

The plants in the alpine zone are adapted to a severe environment. The whitebark pines stand barely waist high. Due to high winds, severe cold, and a short growing season, the trees grow no higher than shrubs. Note the alpine cushion plants that hug the trailside rocks. All alpine vegetation struggles to survive by growing close to the ground to avoid the ripping, desiccating winds. Hikers, too, may wish to lay low and huddle together to avoid the wind, even in midsummer.

In this zone, it is critical to stay on the trail. Hiking boots easily destroy fragile alpine flowers. A trampled alpine garden could take a century to grow back. Growth is slow when the growing season is only a few weeks long. For example, the fist-size cushion plant beside the trail might be twenty-five years old! Even the waist-high pines may be more than a hundred years old.

Breaking from the switchbacks, the trail appears to climb to the sky. The summit looms ominously. Strangely eroded rock formations come into view to the north. Atop the summit are spectacular views in all directions. To the northeast is Reno and the desert ranges, to the southeast lies the Carson Range, and to the south is Lake Tahoe with the craggy peaks of Desolation Wilderness beyond. Facing west, look down upon the reservoirs of Stampede, Boca, and Prosser Creek, which lie north of Truckee. To the north, on the clearest of days, you may see the lovely volcanic peak of Mount Lassen, 115 miles away.

2 MOUNT ROSE RELAY STATION

Difficulty: strenuous
Distance: 4 miles one way
Usage: moderate
Starting elevation: 8800 feet
Elevation gain: 1260 feet
Season: summer, early fall
Map: USGS Mount Rose

This challenging ride along a rocky dirt road takes mountain bikers to fabulous views at the Radio Relay Station near the peak of Mount Rose. The high starting altitude of this route makes this a tough climb. Because this route offers no shade, watch the weather, bring plenty of water and wear adequate sun protection.

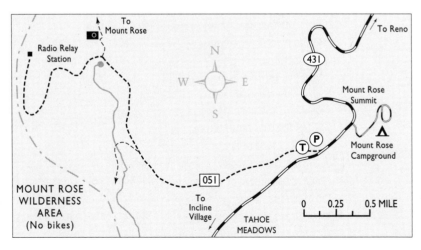

From the junction of Highways 28 and 431 on the northeastern shore of Lake Tahoe, take Highway 431 north 8 miles. Look to the left for a cinder-block building and a sign indicating "wilderness trailhead." Park on the shoulder in front of the building. The hike begins on the closed road. Approaching from the east on Highway 431, the trailhead is 0.3 mile west of a road sign that says Mount Rose Summit.

Start your ride at this trailhead, following the dirt road (Forest Road 051) for 2.5 miles to the junction with the trail to the Mount Rose summit (bikes are prohibited past this point on the summit trail). Find this junction shortly after passing a small pond. To reach the relay station, mountain bikers should continue climbing on the road. The goal is clearly visible above you. The grade is moderate until the final 0.1 mile, where you may have to push your bike the final yards to the station.

Views from the station reward your efforts. Settle down with a picnic and enjoy the panorama. Wonderful views of Lake Tahoe lie to the south. To the northeast are the desert ranges and city of Reno, directly north is the dark hulk of Mount Rose, and to the west are the reservoirs of Stampede, Boca, and Prosser Creeks. To return to your car, simply retrace your route and enjoy the long coast back to Highway 431.

Option: If you've got energy to burn after returning to the junction with the Mount Rose summit trail, hide your bike and hike the demanding 3.4 miles to the dramatic peak of Mount Rose. To try this exhilarating hike, see Trip 1.

3 TAHOE RIM TRAIL: TAHOE MEADOWS INTERPRETIVE TRAIL

Difficulty: easy, handicapped access
Distance: 1.25-mile loop
Usage: low
Starting elevation: 8600 feet
Elevation gain: none
Season: spring, summer, fall
Map: USGS Mount Rose
See Trip 5 for map.

This easy loop trail courses through a scenic meadow in the western shadow of impressive Mount Rose. In early to mid-summer, colorful flowers bloom beside clear creeks. Early-morning hikers can spy coyotes and red-tailed hawks hunting

Creek-jumping at Tahoe Meadows

in the rodent-rich meadow. The level hike is effortless and fully handicapped-accessible. Interpretive signs describe the flora and fauna.

To reach the Tahoe Meadows Trailhead, drive 7.4 miles north on Highway 431 from its intersection with Highway 28 near Incline Village. Look to the right for a large fenced meadow and paved parking lot. Reach the lower parking lot, head past the warming hut, and find the trail at the northeast end.

With your back to busy Highway 431, head east on the paved trail. Early in the summer, when the creeks are flowing and the meadow is still wet, deep yellow buttercups bloom in fragrant abundance. Since wet meadows are very susceptible to damage, it is critical to stay on the trail. Later in the summer you'll find yellow and white marsh marigolds, purple penstemons, bright pink elephant's heads, and tall white corn lilies.

The wealth of flowers attracts a rich variety of insects, including lovely butterflies, pesky mosquitoes, and hovering bees. One of the noisiest inhabitants is the flying grasshopper. Common in the meadows of the Tahoe Basin, these grasshoppers were collected by the Washo Indians and considered a gastronomic delicacy. In flight, they emit a loud clicking noise. When resting on the trail, they look deceptively easy to capture. Children will enjoy trying, and a "bug bottle" and magnifying glass will add to their adventure. Be sure to release all prisoners unharmed. These days, the coyotes enjoy this delicacy.

To view coyotes, arrive at the meadow at dawn or dusk. Look in edge environments, where meadows meet shrubby areas or forest. Coyotes control the rodent population, preying on rabbits, squirrels, gophers, and other small rodents that, unchecked, might nibble a meadow bare. Coyotes, the size of a large dog, have buff, gray, and black fur with a lighter belly and black-tipped tail. Watch for doglike droppings and tracks.

Coyotes are handsome, extremely resourceful animals. Native Americans held coyotes in high regard; some attributed to them supernatural powers. One California tribe, the Miwok, believed that the coyote was a god who had modeled man in clay and had breathed life into him at dawn. To the Miwok, the coyote's howls at daybreak were cries of joy at the act of creation.

Follow the trail as it curves south, heading toward a creek. Cross the creek on the first of several well-made bridges. Enter a shady stretch at the east end of the meadow amid lodgepole and silver pines. Birds such as the blue Steller's jay and the gray and black Clark's nutcracker compete with the chickarees and golden-mantled ground squirrels for the seeds of the pine cones.

Sierra Nevada golden-mantled ground squirrels are common in the Tahoe Basin, and are usually found in open forests and shrubby meadows. They spend the summer collecting seeds, bulbs, and roots for storage until spring. The squirrels begin their long hibernation in October in tunnels or burrows filled with shredded bark. The squirrels subsist on layers of fat gained during the summer. With a body temperature near freezing, breathing slowed from 200 breaths per minute to 4, and heartbeats reduced from 200 to 400 beats per minute to 5, the squirrels sleep in furry balls until spring. In April, the squirrels emerge and survive on their stored treasures.

When you arrive at a long, low bridge, you are three-quarters of the way around the loop. From this bridge the trail takes you directly back to the parking lot.

If you want to do some additional exploring around Tahoe Meadows, try the informal trail to the right of the parking lot (Trip 4) or the wooded trail at the south end of the meadow at Ophir Creek (Trip 5). For a totally different experience of the meadow, return on a starry evening. The level path provides a safe walkway for night hiking and stargazing.

4 TAHOE MEADOWS

Difficulty: easy
Distance: 0.25 to 0.75 mile one way
Usage: low
Starting elevation: 8600 feet
Elevation gain: none
Season: spring, summer, fall
Map: USGS Mount Rose
See Trip 5 for map.

A walk through Tahoe Meadows is a gentle excursion. Wildflower enthusiasts appreciate this colorful meadow in June and July, while youngsters enjoy the effortless level path. Arrive in the early morning or at dusk to see the coyotes and deer that frequent this meadow.

To reach the Tahoe Meadows Trailhead, drive 7.4 miles north on Highway 431 from its intersection with Highway 28 near Incline Village. Look to the right for a large fenced meadow and paved parking lot.

From the parking lot, head right (southwest) along the trail paralleling Highway 431. The Forest Service and the Tahoe Rim Trail Association recently built this trail in order to protect the fragile meadows from overuse.

Stay on the trail because off trail hiking can severely damage meadow vegetation and wipe out fragile flowers for years, particularly when the meadow is wet.

Examining rodent burrows in Tahoe Meadows

Because of the proximity of the highway, it is best to arrive in the early morning so that traffic noise will not be intrusive.

Early in the summer, golden buttercups, yellow marsh marigolds, and pink elephant's heads are plentiful. Children enjoy the unique elephant's head blossoms because they actually resemble their namesake: the petals form large floppy ears, a protruding forehead, and an uplifted trunk. The "heads" are arranged on a tall stalk like a totem pole. Later in the summer, purple penstemons appear, along with delightfully colorful skyrocket gilias. Near the summer's end, look for purple asters, tall pink Anderson thistles with their sharp thorns, huge orange Indian paintbrush, big pink ranger buttons, and white yarrow. You can recognize the plentiful yarrow by its cluster of white flower heads on a stalk covered with grayish hairs, graced with fernlike leaves.

Throughout the meadow, "gopher garlands" mark the winter routes of the pocket gophers. The gophers tunnel under the snow to eat the shoots of snow-covered plants. Later they fill these tunnels with soil when they excavate the roots of the plants. When the snow melts, the soil that the gophers packed into their snow tunnels survives as above-ground coils.

The elusive but ubiquitous pocket gopher is probably busy tunneling as you admire his winter work. As an earth-mover, this gopher is almost unequaled. In a single night, the pocket gopher can tunnel more than 100 feet. The unusual name derives from the gopher's external cheek pockets, in which it stores bits of roots and seeds. The gopher empties its fur-lined pockets by turning them inside out, as we would a pants pocket.

Look for mule deer and coyotes in the edge environments, where the meadow meets the forest or shrubs. Wildlife is most populous in these areas, because they offer both food and cover from predators. Mule deer are the Sierra Nevada's only species of deer. The deer are reddish brown in summer, grayish brown in winter. Their long ears flicker constantly to detect intruders. Each ear moves independently, endowing the deer with extraordinary hearing.

Coyotes rarely prey on mule deer, unless a fawn or an old, diseased deer is found. Half of the coyote's diet consists of small rodents, a quarter is carrion, and the remainder consists of grasshoppers and other large insects, berries, frogs, fish, snakes, and occasional ducks. Coyotes are swift, intelligent, and exemplary fathers. Males care for their pregnant mates, play with and teach their pups, and build the family den. Both Native American and Mexican cultures have long held the coyote in high esteem.

Ambitious hikers can walk 0.9 mile to junction with the Ophir Creek Trail (Trip 5) and then continue east to explore Ophir Creek. The entire scene is park-like and perfect for an early-morning summer stroll.

OPHIR CREEK

Difficulty: easy
Distance: 2 miles one way
Usage: low
Starting elevation: 8600 feet
Elevation gain: 200 feet
Season: spring, summer, fall
Map: USGS Mount Rose

This trail offers young hikers and bikers an easy route through beautiful and varied terrain. The trail begins along Ophir Creek, travels through open forest, passes flowered meadows, and arrives after 1.5 miles at a superb natural playground

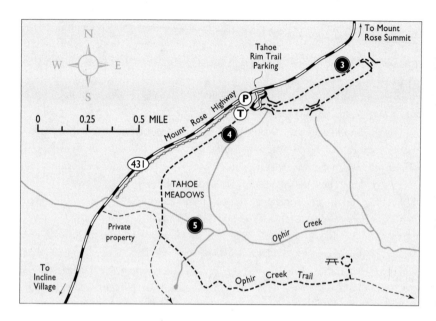

and picnic area. It is a great route for beginning mountain bikers. Start in the early morning or at dusk to view coyote and deer.

To reach the Ophir Creek Trailhead, drive 7.4 miles north on Highway 431 from its intersection with Highway 28 near Incline Village. Look to the right for the paved parking lot at Tahoe Meadows.

Find the trail that heads southwest from the parking lot, paralleling Highway 431. Enjoy the expanse of beautiful Tahoe Meadows as you walk 0.9 mile southwest to the trail's junction with the Ophir Creek Trail.

In the meadow, pause to watch the Belding's ground squirrels, better known as "picket pins." These lively squirrels got their name because of their habit of standing upright on their hind feet to survey the area for predators. They rapidly pop up and down, whistle shrilly at trouble, and then disappear into nearby burrows. Picket pins are abundant at Tahoe Meadows. You'll see them throughout the summer until late September or October, when they hibernate until spring.

Trailside, note the plentiful lavender Brewer's lupine and white gangly yarrow. Both plants were used by Native Americans. Lupine leaves were steamed, the roots were roasted, and the seeds steeped for tea. Don't try the lupine, however, since some species are highly poisonous. Indians used the yarrow plant medicinally. They placed the crushed plant on painful areas, because it was thought to have anesthetic value. Early settlers used it to stop bleeding and dubbed it the "nosebleed plant."

Cross Ophir Creek at 0.75 mile. From the creek the trail rises gently. At 0.9 mile, reach the Ophir Creek Trail. Leave the Tahoe Rim Trail and head left. Continue traveling southeast. Pass the northern edge of another attractive meadow on your right. Look for red-tailed hawks hunting the many rodents that populate the meadow. Next cross a creek that sports moisture-loving flowers in spring to midsummer.

Beyond the creek, the lupine-lined road climbs again gently, then soon levels. After a level stretch of approximately 0.5 mile, the road veers to the left and terminates in a loop 100 yards to the north. The end of this road lies on the western slope of a beautiful forested canyon. Large boulders to the northeast form a natural playground, providing forts or climbing obstacles for children's games. The open country also makes for safe exploring. This wonderful picnic area occupies an edge environment, where open meadow meets the forest, creating an ideal habitat for wildlife such as coyotes and mule deer. Watch carefully.

To lengthen your route, continue east on the trail where you turned left for the loop road. The surface becomes rougher as it descends. Enter a cool, shady fir forest. A wet meadow to the left sports corn lilies and willow thickets. Rocks on its edge make this secluded meadow another fine picnic stop, if the earlier meadow is occupied.

Continuing eastward, the trail becomes more rugged. Beginning bikers and small hikers may want to turn back to the main road 0.25 mile down the primitive trail. There is plenty of easy exploring on the road back.

6 TAHOE RIM TRAIL: WATSON LAKE TO LAVA CLIFFS

Difficulty: easy
Distance: 1.5 miles one way
Usage: low
Starting elevation: 7800 feet
Elevation gain: 140 feet
Season: summer, fall
Map: USGS Tahoe City

This short section of the Tahoe Rim Trail takes hikers through open forest to a scenic overlook atop Lava Cliffs, high above Tahoe City. It is an easy, pleasant walk. Take a picnic and enjoy the view.

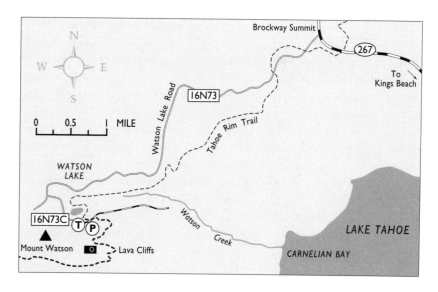

To reach Watson Lake, take Highway 267 northwest 3.1 miles from its intersection with Highway 28 in Kings Beach. Turn left onto unpaved Watson Lake Road (Road 16N73). If you're approaching from the west on Highway 267, Watson Lake Road is 0.1 mile east of Brockway Summit. Drive 5.9 miles on Watson Lake Road (the road becomes rough after 4 miles), then turn left on Road 16N73C. After 0.7 mile, turn left again to reach Watson Lake. Park in a turnout near the lake, but do not block access, because logging trucks pump water from Watson Lake. The trail is located to the right of the road.

Walk east on the path along the south shore of Watson Lake. In about 100 yards, near the east end of the lake, where some fallen logs block the trail, look to the right for a Tahoe Rim Trail marker. After climbing over the logs, you're on the Tahoe Rim Trail. Take the right fork, which heads south. The left fork continues around the lake and then travels north to Watson Creek, where wildflowers are spectacular in midsummer.

The trail south soon intersects a narrow road. Turn left on the road and hike approximately 0.2 mile to a blue trail marker on the right. Head east (right) on a trail up a forested slope. The forest of pine and fir is open and pleasant, with abundant ground cover of manzanita and other shrubs. Bright green staghorn lichen hangs from the fir, providing brilliant color as well as nourishment for mule deer.

As you climb, the terrain becomes rockier and views of Lake Tahoe begin to appear through the trees. At a fork, keep right, following the blue markers. Cross another logging road, and continue to ascend gently through parklike forest. The trail next turns sharply to the east, narrows, and descends briefly before climbing again.

Panoramic views commence as the rocky peaks of Desolation Wilderness appear to the south above forested slopes. Arrive at the top of Lava Cliffs and enjoy splendid views of Carnelian Bay and the southern half of Lake Tahoe. Lava from volcanic eruptions in this area hardened into rough, dark rock. The lava cooled into amorphous, rounded forms that differ dramatically from the sharp-angled, glacier-carved topography farther south. A perch atop the cliffs is an excellent place to enjoy a quiet picnic and spectacular views. From here, the Tahoe Rim Trail descends on a scenic path through forest for approximately 10 miles to Tahoe City.

To return, retrace your steps to the trailhead. Hikers with energy to spare can take a short side trip from Watson Lake to view fabulous wildflowers in mid-summer. From the fork on the southeast shore of Watson Lake, travel north on the Tahoe Rim Trail around the east end of the lake. Then hike briefly along the lake's north shore before the trail leaves the lake to travel north to Watson Creek. For approximately 0.5 mile, the trail follows the creek amid moisture-loving, wildly colorful flowers. In June and July, be sure to pack insect repellent and your camera.

Jeffrey pine needles

7 PACIFIC CREST TRAIL TO MOUNT JUDAH, MOUNT LINCOLN, AND ANDERSON PEAK

Difficulty: moderate (strenuous to Anderson Peak)
Distance: 2.3 miles one way to Mount Judah; 2.5 miles one way to Mount Lincoln; 6.2 miles one way to Anderson Peak, 5.2 miles round trip on Mount Judah Loop Trail
Usage: moderate
Starting elevation: 7060 feet
Elevation gain: 1183 feet to Mount Judah, 1323 feet to Mount Lincoln, 1633 feet to Anderson Peak
Season: summer, fall
Map: USGS Norden

Fabulous panoramic views are less than an hour from the trailhead on this magnificent and challenging trail. After climbing through forest and scrub-lined slopes, horizons explode to breathtaking vistas atop a treeless crest. Following the crest for 3.7 miles brings you to Anderson Peak, an ambitious but worthwhile goal. Hikers who find the distance to the peak daunting can hike for any distance along the inspiring ridgeline south of Mount Lincoln, where extraordinary scenery abounds. In the 1990s, trail builders created a third popular option, the 5.2-mile Mount Judah Loop Trail. Any route on this section of the Pacific Crest Trail (PCT) offers dazzling and awe-inspiring vistas.

Approaching from the east on I-80, take the second Donner Lake exit west of Truckee. Turn left under the highway and then right on the road along the shore of Donner Lake (Donner Pass Road). At the west end of Donner Lake, continue straight ahead and ascend old Highway 40 for 3.5 miles toward Donner Pass. Turn left on a pole-line road 0.4 mile west of the bridge on old Highway 40. A private road immediately forks right. Park near the start of the private road near the Pacific Crest Trail sign.

Through July, there may be snow on sections of this trail, particularly on the eastern flank of Mount Lincoln, approximately 3 miles from the trailhead. Therefore, before hiking, check with the ranger station in Truckee to determine snow conditions. Hikers, especially youngsters, should not traverse a snow-covered slope without proper equipment, including ropes.

The trail starts in a fragrant and colorful forest bursting with flowers in July and August. Watch for yellow monkey flowers and bright pink fireweed. Very shortly, ascend an open rocky slope on steep switchbacks. Purple and pink pen-

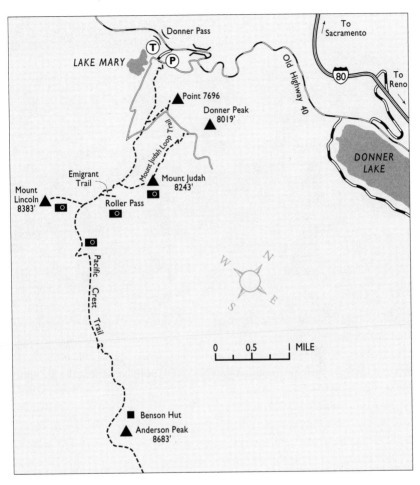

stemons appear; trumpet-shaped blossoms adorn nearly every crevasse. Look for yellow-bellied marmots, too, among the rocks. Marmots are commonly seen sunning themselves or lazily munching on greenery. Their goal in summer is to build up a thick layer of fat to see them through their winter hibernation. (Please do not feed them, however.) Sedges, grasses, and occasional insects are the keys to their survival.

After about seven switchbacks, the trail traverses a west-facing slope, offering views and a chance to catch your breath. Next enter a shady red fir forest. At 1.1 miles from the trailhead, the trail crosses a logging road. Stay on the ascending Pacific Crest Trail (PCT). Patches of snow are likely to remain in the forest through July, followed by mud. Flowers thrive where the trees let in sufficient

View from the Pacific Crest Trail

sunlight. In this moist environment look for giant cow parsnip. This conspicuous flower can grow to 5 feet by late summer and sports clusters of small white flowers in a compound umbel. A member of the parsley family, its aromatic leaves and stem were gathered by the area's Native Americans for food.

At 1 mile from the trailhead, just before the logging road crosses your path, another trail enters from the left (east). This is the north end of the Mount Judah Loop Trail, a highly scenic detour that offers hikers the chance to summit not only Mount Judah (8243 feet), but Point 7696 as well. Experienced climbers can also scramble to the top of Donner Peak (8019 feet) via the loop. Those hiking the loop head left. The trail climbs 0.2 mile through forest to a gully. Just after the gully, a spur trail to Point 7696 enters on the left. For superb views of Donner Pass, take the 0.1 mile path northeast to the summit.

Returning to the loop trail, continue southeast where the trail joins an old logging road and gently climbs. After 0.4 mile, meet a faint path to the north (left) that approaches the summit of Donner Peak. Shear drop-offs and a vague trail make this a very dangerous peak to climb, and thus it is not recommended for children, amateurs, or those who have a fear of heights.

Continue south on the loop trail, which next switchbacks up the east-facing slope of Mount Judah. At the summit, the views are fantastic in all directions. From the summit, the loop trail descends via switchbacks 0.75 mile to the Pacific Crest Trail. To return to the trailhead for a round trip hike of 5.2 miles, head north (right). To continue to Mount Lincoln and Anderson Peak, turn south (left).

For those who didn't take the loop trail, continue on the PCT hiking south. The trail gently traverses the west side of Mount Judah. To climb this peak, follow the trail south of the peak to a crest saddle, then hike northeast along a ridge to reach the peak, a climb of 320 feet. Mount Judah offers great views to the north. Look to the northwest for the dramatic turrets of Castle Peak (9102 feet).

Approximately 2 miles from the trailhead, the PCT crosses the Emigrant Trail. Walk a short distance to the left to the sign indicating Roller Pass. There, in 1846, the pioneers pulled their wagons out of the valley to cross the Sierra. Through the use of oxen, chains, and log rollers, wagons were hoisted more than 1500 vertical feet. Far below is a meadow that was used as a staging area when the emigrants pulled their wagons one by one up the pass. An emigrant named Elisha Perkins recorded the arrival at Roller Pass in his diary: "As we came up to it the appearances [sic] was exactly like marching up to some immense wall built directly across our path, so perpendicular is this dividing ridge." Look below the pass for rust-scarred boulders where iron wagon wheels left their mark.

Roller Pass has been called the most spectacular pass in the Sierra. The sheer difficulty of the route is awe-inspiring. Not surprisingly, soon after Roller Pass was opened, the emigrants found an easier route between Donner Pass and Mount Judah. To learn more about the Emigrant Trail and view historical artifacts, including a loaded covered wagon, visit the Emigrant Museum at Donner Memorial State Park (see "Museums and Cultural Attractions" in Chapter 1).

Return to the main trail and climb moderately. Cross a small stream, then gain beautiful views as the traverse begins on the eastern slope of Mount Lincoln (8383 feet). To climb to the peak of Mount Lincoln, ascend southwest cross-country up its steep, denuded slope. Arrive at an unpaved road and follow the road to the peak, a climb of about 300 feet from the trail. The peak offers marvelous views, including an excellent view of Royal Gorge to the west.

Continuing on the main trail, traverse the eastern slope of Mount Lincoln. On the south side of Mount Lincoln, begin a long descent on switchbacks through gardens rich with red columbines, pink elephant's heads, and scarlet gilias. Reach a crest saddle, and in late July delight in slopes covered with purple lupine, orange Indian paintbrush, and yellow mule's ears. Spectacular views abound.

A natural archway on the Pacific Crest Trail

Next begin a gentle ascent with excellent views to the forested canyons of the southwest. The wind can be ferocious on the ridge. Evidence of this constant west wind is seen in the "banner" trees, whose branches only grow on their leeward eastern sides.

Enter a stand of conifers and temporarily lose the marvelous views. Soon regain the ridgeline. Look for strange volcanic rock formations. Anderson Peak (8693 feet), which now dominates the southern skyline, is the remnant of an ancient volcano. To reach its peak, climbers can ascend its forested northern slopes on a spur trail, or follow the main trail across the western slopes to the southern side of the mountain and hike cross-country to the summit. Views from the trail are superlative also. A logical turnaround point is the Benson Hut, a cabin on the north slope, 5.6 miles from the trailhead. Sierra Club members can reserve the cabin for an overnight stay—a real treat.

8   LOCH LEVEN LAKES

Difficulty: moderate
Distance: 2 miles one way to Lower Loch Leven Lake; 2.6 miles one way to Middle Loch Leven Lake; 2.7 miles one way to Salmon Lake; 3.5 miles one way to High Loch Leven Lake
Usage: moderate
Starting elevation: 5720 feet
Elevation gain: 1040 feet to Lower and Middle Loch Leven Lakes and Salmon Lake, 1150 feet to High Loch Leven Lake
Season: spring, summer, fall
Map: USGS Soda Springs and Cisco Grove

Loch Leven Lakes is an excellent summer hike. Its flower-lined trail climbs to a trio of fine swimming lakes. For younger hikers, the hike to Middle Loch Leven Lake (formerly Upper Loch Leven Lake) is ideal. For the more ambitious, a 1.4-mile detour brings hikers to a fourth scenic lake that attracts anglers and rock climbers. This trail offers many wonderful options.

Approaching from the east, leave I-80 at the Big Bend exit, 6 miles west of the Soda Springs exit (almost 20 miles west of Truckee). Turn left under the freeway, then right onto Hampshire Rocks Road (old Highway 40). Approaching from the west on I-80, the Big Bend exit is 1.5 miles east of the Cisco Grove exit. Drive 1.5 miles to the Big Bend Visitor Center, and park 0.1 mile past the center. The trailhead is on the south side of the road at a sign that marks a private road/public trail.

Walk 0.2 mile on a private road that passes several homes. At a sign for the Loch Leven Trail, turn west and climb through lodgepole and Jeffrey pines. About 0.3 mile past the trailhead, arrive at an overlook with clear views of I-80. Descend to the welcome company of a gurgling creek bordered by alder. Along the creek are boulders that provide pleasant rest stops in dappled sunshine.

Take a small wooden bridge across the creek, then ascend a moderate slope. Carefully cross a set of railroad tracks near overhead lights. The trail resumes on the opposite side. Follow switchbacks on a wide, shady trail through lodgepole, Jeffrey, and western white pines, incense cedars, and white firs. This is a good time to learn the different trees. Count the bunched needles and note the changes in the color, texture, and smell of their bark.

The trees provide homes for countless squirrels and birds, their voices thankfully replacing the buzz of I-80. Listen for the sharp chattering of the Douglas

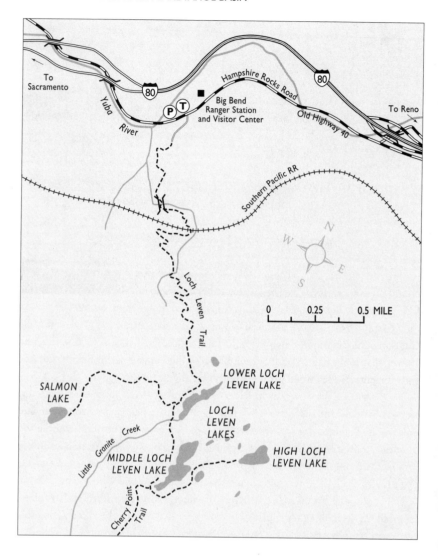

squirrel, or Sierra chickaree. If you hear one, sit down and try imitating its squeak to attract it. Do not feed it or allow it to approach too close, however. The squirrels are wild and may bite.

From June through July, the trail is brightened by lovely red-and-yellow columbines, which flourish in moist soil. The distinctive flower arches gracefully down, while its five red petals turn back and skyward, revealing bright yellow petals inside. The columbine is a favorite of hummingbirds, whose long, tubular tongues enter the flower to retrieve its nectar. Look, too, for the abundant and

Middle Loch Leven Lake

fragrant lavender lupine. In July, you will also find red Indian paintbrush, the flower that looks like a scruffy green brush dipped in red paint. In July and August, bright pink fireweed grows profusely along the trail.

As you rise, the terrain becomes drier. Follow a wide trail, bordered by stones, that winds through open landscape studded with blooming shrubs in June and July. White flowers adorn the serviceberry and bitter cherry bushes. Later in the summer, numerous mammals and birds feed on the sweet purple berries of the serviceberry. In earlier times, settlers and Native Americans gathered and ate the berries.

The trail rises through this lovely, gardenlike landscape until, at 2.3 miles, the trail descends 0.1 mile to the shoreline of Lower Loch Leven Lake. The lakes improve with distance from the trailhead, so after a short rest stop, travel on.

At the southwestern end of Lower Loch Leven Lake, a trail heads west to Salmon Lake, a 1.4-mile detour (round trip) from the main trail. To visit Salmon Lake, take the trail west, hook around to the southwest, then turn northwest to climb a low ridge. Cross the ridge, then head southwest down a gully to Salmon Lake. Rock slabs and sparse pines surround this warm lake. Rock climbers are attracted to the impressive cliffs to the northwest. The lake is an excellent spot for secluded picnicking, fishing, and swimming.

To reach the more popular Middle and High Loch Leven Lakes, continue south at the junction with the Salmon Lake trail. Cross the small outlet creek and climb through the rocky landscape. In rock crevasses, watch for stunning pink mountain pride, one of Tahoe's prettiest blossoms. At 2.6 miles, reach lovely Middle Loch Leven Lake. The lake is dotted with islands and framed by granite slabs. The shoreline is garnished with delicate pink mountain heather, whose bright blossoms and needle-like leaves adorn the gray granite. In late summer, the lake's water is warm, so take time to frolic amid the picturesque islands. Lay a picnic atop a convenient granite tabletop. There are few more inviting spots for a warm, sunny afternoon.

Head south along the lake's western shore to continue on to High Loch Leven Lake. At Middle Loch Leven Lake's south end, come to the junction with the Cherry Point Trail, which heads west. Stay on the Loch Leven Trail, which turns northeast, following orange blazes on rocks. Travel through a landscape of glacial erratics and wind-stunted trees, then cross a small creek. After the creek, climb briefly and arrive at High Loch Leven Lake.

High Loch Leven Lake is just as wonderful as Middle Loch Leven and probably hosts fewer admirers because of the extra effort required to reach it. It, too, boasts a tree-studded island and granite-lined shores. The high granite walls that rise steeply from its shore lend drama to its beauty. Pastel phlox, violet penstemon, and red paintbrush create delightful gardens among the rocks. If the day is especially cool or windy, High Loch Leven can be a chilly spot, so retreat to one of the lower lakes for swimming or picnicking.

9 STATELINE FIRE LOOKOUT TRAIL

Difficulty: easy
Distance: 0.4 mile one way
Usage: moderate
Starting elevation: 6920 feet
Elevation gain: 100 feet
Season: spring, summer, fall
Map: USGS Kings Beach

A short but steep walk up a dirt road leads to a Forest Service fire lookout. Learn how fires are discovered, how their positions are determined, and how help is summoned. Adjacent to the lookout is a short, self-guided nature trail and a picnic area with splendid views of Lake Tahoe.

From Highway 28 in Crystal Bay, turn left on Reservoir Drive (the road between the Tahoe Biltmore and the Tahoe Mariner Casinos) and drive 0.3 mile.

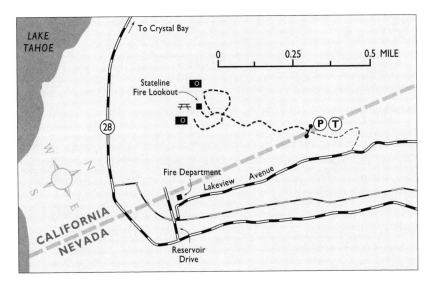

Then turn right on Lakeview Avenue (after the firehouse) and drive 0.6 mile to a gravel road ascending on the left. Drive 0.3 mile up the gravel road to a parking lot at its end. Hike up the closed road. (If the gate is open, you can drive to the lookout station.)

The closed road leads directly to the lookout. Between 8:00 a.m. and noon, the station is open to the public. During those hours, forest service personnel will answer questions, and children can look at their equipment.

The threat of devastating wildfire in the Tahoe Basin is very real. Under normal conditions, periodic wildfires are beneficial to a forest ecosystem. Tahoe's forests, however, could generate destructive and uncontrolled fires. From the lookout, observe the many dead and dying conifers. These trees could quickly fuel an intense fire that would burn the forests down to mineral soil.

What happened to Tahoe's forests? The original forests of the basin differed dramatically from the dense fir forests that prevail today. The native forest consisted of widely spaced, drought-resistant Jeffrey, ponderosa, and sugar pines with a diverse understory of grasses and wildflowers. Periodic low-intensity natural fires kept the meadows open and the forests free from excessive litter, and prevented the stands from becoming too dense.

Tahoe's problems can be traced to the logging practices of a century ago. When lumber was needed to fuel the mining industry and build the transcontinental railroad, Tahoe's forests were the nearest source. Lumbermen stripped the slopes of the more valuable pines and left only firs and smaller pines. Fir grows at greater densities than pine and is shade tolerant. As a result, a dense forest of fir replaced the parklike pine stands. To make matters worse, the fire-suppression policies of the last 100 years allowed fire-sensitive firs to flourish unchecked and created an unnatural accumulation of fuel within the forests.

Unfortunately, years of severe drought in the early 1990s weakened the vulnerable fir forests. The trees' weakened condition has ushered in an invasion by bark beetles. While healthy trees can often fend off pests, weakened trees cannot. Bark beetles are responsible for many of the dead trees visible from the lookout.

A high-intensity wildfire would endanger wildlife, private property, human life, stream environments, and ultimately Lake Tahoe. Intense fire would destroy the ground cover that controls erosion. Without such cover, sedimentation of the basin's lakes and streams would dramatically increase.

To reduce the threat of intensely destructive fires, the National Forest Service promotes the removal of dead and dying trees on both public and private land. Thinning live trees has also been proposed. Restoration of the balanced ecosystem that existed prior to human intervention is clearly very difficult. Basin visitors must do their part by exercising extreme caution when building campfires. The best practice is to camp without a fire and use a portable stove. To introduce children to fire safety, visit Smokey's Trail at the Lake Tahoe Visitor Center (see Trip 34).

Starting from the Stateline Fire Lookout station, hikers can meander on the self-guided nature trails, enjoying truly spectacular views. Interpretive signs describe vegetation and identify mountain peaks. Benches for picnicking are set along the trail.

10 INCLINE VILLAGE BIKE TRAIL

Difficulty: easy
Distance: 2.5 miles one way
Starting elevation: 6240 feet
Elevation gain: none
Usage: high
Season: spring, summer, fall
Map: USGS Marlette Lake

This popular bike path passes lakeside mansions in opulent Incline Village. Sandy beaches are within reach, but riders must be residents or guests of Incline Village to use them. The path is shady and attractive, but riders see far more real estate than nature on this paved trail.

Lending a helping hand

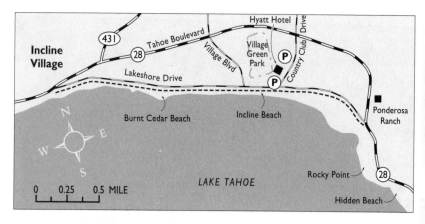

At the intersection of Highway 28 and Lakeshore Drive, at the west end of Incline Village (approximately 2 miles from Stateline), turn onto Lakeshore Drive. The bike path runs 2.5 miles along Lakeshore Drive to the east end of Incline Village, where it again intersects Highway 28. Free parking is available off Lakeshore Drive between Village Boulevard and Country Club Drive. Alternately, park in the multi-acre Hyatt Hotel lot on Country Club Drive. Find both off Lakeshore Drive about 1.7 miles from the west end of Incline Village.

From the parking lot, cross the street to the bike path, then ride either way to the bike path's end. Burnt Cedar Beach, located 0.8 mile west, has beautifully manicured grounds, including a playground, barbecue pits, picnic tables, a lovely outdoor pool, a volleyball court, and a rocky beach.

Incline Beach is located across the street from the parking lot. It offers all of the above except the swimming pool. Swimmers can enjoy Incline's sandy beach and rent boats from the Hyatt Hotel next door. Both beaches have snack concessions.

The trail to the east arrives at Highway 28 in approximately 1 mile. In the early morning, when traffic is light, riders can pleasantly tour the lake's east shore by following the highway south. However, heavy traffic and narrow shoulders discourage most from riding along the highway during the day. Note informal trails to rocky coves along the highway. Look for the well-worn trail to Hidden Beach 0.7 mile after leaving Incline Village. The steep walk down to the beach is a worthwhile side trip.

Several bike rental shops are convenient to the bike path. Incline Village concessions are listed under "Bicycling and Mountain Biking" in Chapter 1.

Right: *Lake Tahoe from the Rubicon Trail*

CHAPTER 3

THE WEST LAKE TAHOE BASIN

This chapter describes hiking and biking trips in the area bordered on the north by the Truckee River and on the south by Emerald Bay. Included are hikes in two designated wilderness areas, Desolation Wilderness and Granite Chief Wilderness. The National Forest Service requires permits for day hikes in Desolation Wilderness, but not for Granite Chief. Hikers can obtain self-issued permits at the trailheads. Those camping in Desolation Wilderness must obtain a camping permit and those camping in Granite Chief Wilderness must obtain a campfire permit; both are available at the National Forest Service Lake Tahoe Basin Management Unit in South Lake Tahoe and at the William Kent Visitor Center, located at the entrance to the William Kent Campground, 2.25 miles south of Tahoe City (see "Desolation Wilderness" in Chapter 1).

For families hiking with young children, try the following easy trips: 12, 13, 19, 23, 25, 27, 28, 30, and 31. Trips 23 and 28 are accessible by stroller and wheelchairs. Youngsters with more developed hiking skills will enjoy Trips 16, 24, 26, 32, and 33. A challenging, but rewarding, summit climb for experienced hikers is described in Trip 14.

Families looking for bike trips should try Trips 17 through 21. Trip 19 along General Creek is particularly recommended for beginning mountain bikers. Trip 21 is recommended only for strong off-road cyclists. The West Lake Tahoe Basin also offers two paved bike paths, described in Trips 17 and 18. Trip 17, along the Truckee River, is especially scenic in the fall. Please note that mountain biking is prohibited on trails in designated wilderness areas and on the Pacific Crest Trail.

Many of the hikes in this chapter are popular, particularly those entering Desolation Wilderness and D. L. Bliss State Park. These two areas offer some of the most beautiful scenery in the Tahoe Basin. Desolation Wilderness is unequaled for its dramatic peaks and lovely subalpine lakes. For full enjoyment of these areas, arrive at the trailhead early, hike midweek or off-season, and avoid holiday weekends.

NORTHSTAR-AT-TAHOE MOUNTAIN BIKING

Difficulty: easy and moderate
Distance: 3 miles round trip to Sawmill Flat; 9 miles round trip to Watson Lake (using chairlifts on both routes)
Usage: high
Starting elevation: 6800 feet
Elevation gain: 200 feet and 890 feet, respectively
Season: summer, fall
Map: USGS Martis Peak and Tahoe City

At Northstar's Mountain Bike Park, cyclists ride the chairlift to access high mountain trails and thus eliminate hundreds of feet of climbing. While the scen-

Northstar Reservoir

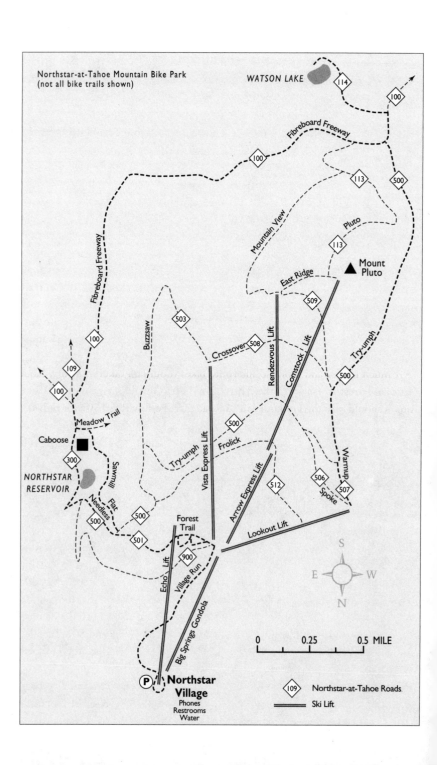

Northstar-at-Tahoe Mountain Bike Park
(not all bike trails shown)

WATSON LAKE

114

100

Fibreboard Freeway

100

113

500

Mountain View

Pluto

113

Mount
Pluto

East Ridge

509

Fibreboard Freeway

Buzzsaw

503

Crossover 508

Rendezvous Lift

Comstock Lift

Try-umph

100

100

109

100

Meadow Trail

Caboose

300

NORTHSTAR
RESERVOIR

Sawmill

500

Try-umph

Vista Express Lift

500

Frolick

Arrow Express Lift

512

500

Warmup

506

507

Spoke

Flat
Needless

500

500

501

Forest
Trail

Lookout Lift

Echo Lift

900

Village Run

Big Springs Gondola

S

E   W

N

0   0.25   0.5 MILE

P

Northstar
Village
Phones
Restrooms
Water

109 Northstar-at-Tahoe Roads

——— Ski Lift

ery is not as fine as at other Tahoe destinations, many appreciate Northstar's convenience. This popular summer resort offers on-site bike rentals, guided trips, instruction, a bike camp for youngsters, and a practice park to introduce novices to mountain biking. If you don't mind the crowds and cheating a bit by skipping the grunt work, give Northstar a try. The following two beginner trips are a good introduction to the area.

Find the Northstar-at-Tahoe Resort by driving 6 miles south of Truckee on Highway 267. For information on lift tickets and times of operation, call (530) 562-1010, 1-800-GO-NORTH, or visit *www.skinorthstar.com*.

For those seeking the easiest route on the mountain, Sawmill Flat is a fine destination. After the chairlift ride, it requires only a gain of 200 feet and round trip mileage of 3 miles. The destination offers views of Northstar Reservoir and pleasant picnicking. Riders should take the Echo Lift to Road 501. From Road 501, turn right on Road 500, then turn left immediately on the Sawmill Flat Trail. Ride the trail until you see a caboose in a meadow. Northstar Reservoir is soon visible to the left and is a nice spot for a picnic. To return, follow the route back to the Echo Lift. To descend to the base, take Forest Trail to Village Run, a bumpy, sometimes sandy, 1.24-mile coast down.

A much longer and more scenic route takes mountain bikers through Tahoe National Forest to Watson Lake. This 9.2-mile trip involves a gain of 890 feet. Riders should take the Lookout Lift to Road 507. Follow Road 507 for only 0.3 mile to the intersection of Road 507 with Road 500. Turn right and follow Road 500 about 1.6 miles across Mount Pluto to the junction of the "Fibreboard Freeway." Turn right.

After only 0.2 mile, turn left at Watson Lake Road (Road 114). Ride Watson Lake Road, and reach Watson Lake after 0.7 mile. Picnic at the lake, then prepare to complete the long and scenic route around the mountain. Retrace your route up the Watson Lake Road to the Fibreboard Freeway (Road 100). Turn right, climb a short hill and then ride the Fibreboard Freeway 3.4 miles down to Road 300. Enjoy nice views on this mountain traverse.

When you reach Road 300, turn left and follow it 0.25 mile to the Meadow Trail. Turn left onto the Meadow Trail and ride a short distance past the caboose and Northstar Reservoir to the Sawmill Flat Trail. Turn right onto the Sawmill Flat Trail and follow it 0.8 mile to the junction of Roads 500 and 501. Turn left onto Road 501 and ride about 0.75 mile to the Echo Lift. From Echo Lift, return to the base via the Forest Trail and Village Run.

Maps and additional information on trails in the area are available from the well-informed staff at Northstar-at-Tahoe's Mountain Bike Shop at Northstar Village. For rental information and reservations, call (530) 562-2268.

12 SQUAW CREEK TRAILS

Difficulty: easy
Distance: 0.5 to 1.5 miles one way
Usage: moderate
Starting elevation: 6240 feet
Elevation gain: 400 feet
Season: summer, fall
Map: USGS Tahoe City and Granite Chief

These trails explore the pools and waterfalls of pretty Squaw Creek. On a hot August day when the creek is nearly dry, hikers can boulder hop up the creek bed. Squaw Creek's tiny waterfalls and pools of water are perfect for late-summer sunbathing and swimming. In any season, picnic by the sparkling creek on wide granite ledges beneath towering cliffs. This hike is for exploring—there is no set destination. Children especially enjoy the freedom this trail affords.

From Tahoe City, drive to Squaw Valley Road, 5.2 miles northwest on Highway 89 from its junction with Highway 28. Turn left on Squaw Valley Road and drive 2.2 miles to the Squaw Valley ski complex. Between the Squaw Valley Inn and the cement building housing the tram, turn right on Squaw Peak Way, winding around to the right through condos to a parking area at the north end.

Find the wide, sandy trail heading northwest from the parking lot. Enjoy level

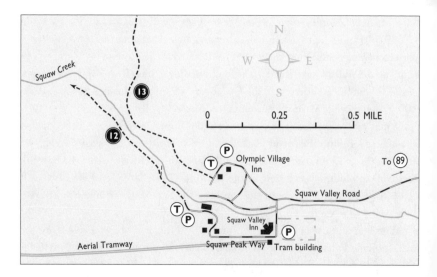

A natural table in Squaw Creek

walking amid sagebrush, yellow mule's ears, and aspen. Dark cliffs rise steeply to the left. At a fork in the trail, stay left. Squaw Creek is just minutes away.

Once the trail reaches Squaw Creek, you have several options. Attractive trails flank the creek bed. To the far left, ducks on granite slabs lead one north on sunny, open slopes. (A "duck" is a type of trail marker that consists of a small rock on top of a larger one; the effect is ducklike.) Alternatively, a narrow, shady trail parallels the creek to the west through dense trees. An easy trail also travels nicely along the east bank. In late summer, the creek bed itself is climbable.

Regardless of the route chosen, it is unlikely it can be retraced on the way down. There is no need to worry, however. Follow the direction of the creek; trails on either bank lead back to the Squaw Valley complex. To avoid unnecessary walking through the condo developments, do try to cross to a west-bank trail shortly before the trail's end.

The trails are enjoyable in any season. In early summer, melting snow swells the creek to white rushing cascades. In midsummer, creekside flowers peak in brilliant color. In fall, the bright foliage of the quaking aspen, alder, and willow delights hikers.

In any season, watch for the highly entertaining dippers in Squaw Creek. These chunky brown birds, which resemble wrens, dive in the rushing water in search of small fish and insects. The superbly adapted dippers are able to walk on the bottoms of streams, swim underwater, and fly behind waterfalls. They build their nests on rocky ledges, often within the spray of a waterfall, where their eggs are safe from predators. Dippers are year-round residents of the Sierra.

Young children especially love this hike in late summer. The creek diminishes to bathtub-size pools and lazy trickles. Waterbugs and an occasional fish inhabit the clear basins. Water-eroded boulders in the creek bed provide thrones, tables, forts, and playhouses for imaginative youngsters. Bring bathing suits, towels, and an extra pair of socks or aqua shoes for the kids. In August, look also for sweet scarlet thimbleberries beside the trail. The berry's shape resembles a thimble when picked, and it tastes similar to a raspberry. Look for the thimbleberry in partial shade. It is easily recognized by its large, lobed leaves that resemble huge maple leaves.

After climbing gently for approximately 1 mile, the grade steepens considerably, and it is advisable to return to the trailhead.

13   SQUAW CREEK MEADOW   🐾

Difficulty: easy
Distance: 1 mile one way
Usage: moderate
Starting elevation: 6240 feet
Elevation gain: 280 feet
Season: spring, summer, fall
Map: USGS Tahoe City
See Trip 12 for map.

For truly amazing fields of flowers, hike to the lovely meadows above Squaw Creek. Along the way, visit cool pools and waterfalls. Even the youngest hikers in your group will be able to complete this short excursion. For peak flowers, visit the meadows in early to mid-July.

Squaw Creek Trail

From Tahoe City, drive to Squaw Valley Road, 5.2 miles northwest on Highway 89 from its junction with Highway 28. Turn left on Squaw Valley Road and drive 2.2 miles to the Squaw Valley ski complex. Request permission to park behind the Olympic Village Inn, located to the right of the main complex just beyond the Squaw Valley Fire Station. The trailhead is found behind the inn at the end of the paved fire lane.

The trail rises steeply, but briefly, through a wooded area. Several minor trails run through this area (including one heading left); stay on the main trail and continue to climb. The well-established trail is sunny, for little shade is offered by the scattered lodgepole and Jeffrey pines.

In these dry environs, look for the western fence lizard. This lizard is commonly found on rock outcrops and in dry, open areas throughout the Sierras. The lizard is grayish, 6 to 9 inches long, with blue on its throat and on the sides of its belly. Its cousin, the smaller sagebrush lizard, has smoother scales and rusty spots along its sides. Hikers are more likely to encounter the fence lizard, since the sagebrush lizard is shyer and tends to hide under brush.

Cross over a creeklet. Above and to the left, a high rock wall attracts experienced rock climbers. Surrounding the trail, greenleaf and pinemat manzanita are abundant. In spring they sport delicate bell-shaped flowers, much loved by Sierra chipmunks. In the fall, the manzanita's tiny fruit resembles golden apples; Native Americans used them to make a type of cider. Ignore the spur trails to the left, which lead to Squaw Creek or to the Squaw Valley complex.

Lively chipmunks are plentiful along the trail. Eight species of chipmunks inhabit the Sierra Nevada. Although all have the characteristic stripe from their eyes to their haunches, they differ subtly in color. The brightness of their stripes changes with the chipmunk's habitat. For instance, the lodgepole chipmunk, found primarily in lodgepole pine forests, sports stripes with higher contrast than the sagebrush chipmunk, who must blend with the muted colors of the scrub ecotone. All need protective coloring to evade their chief predator, the weasel. In the fall, the chipmunk gathers seeds of the manzanita, stuffing them into its expandable cheek pouches. Chipmunks have been found with more than a thousand seeds in their cheeks!

At a little less than 0.5 mile from the trailhead, arrive at the banks of Squaw Creek. In spring, the creek is full of snow runoff, and its cascades are fast and frothy. In late summer, when the creek slows to a trickle, the creek bed is safe for exploring, with clear, tempting pools. Trails run up and down both banks. (To hike Squaw Creek, see directions in Trip 12.)

The trail veers north away from the creek and enters the meadow. More than thirty million years ago, this area was covered by volcanic lava. Squaw Peak, towering to the west, is an old volcano. The breakdown of the volcanic rock to soil left mineral-rich deposits on these slopes. Sun-loving flowers, particularly mule's ears, thrive under these conditions.

If the hike is timed right (early July in most years) the slopes are blanketed with dramatic color. Yellow woolly mule's ears are the most conspicuous. Sometimes called wild sunflowers, they have bright yellow flowers that may reach 3 inches in diameter. Their long, distinctive leaves are covered with short white hairs that make them fuzzy to the touch, giving the flower its colorful name.

Blue lupine is also abundant in the meadow, as is red-orange Indian paintbrush. Pink sidalceas are prominent, and delicate mariposa lilies can also be found. The lilies have three large white petals, usually creamy white with a yellow center. Mariposa means "butterfly" in Spanish, and alludes to the ephemeral beauty of the flower. The lilies' bulbs were an important source of food for many Indian tribes. The Yosemite tribe roasted the bulbs and considered the delicacy a gift from the gods.

Late in the summer, the meadow is laced with the small white flowers of yampah, whose umbrellalike clusters of flowers wave on spindly, leafless stems.

The yampah has an edible root that was much prized by Native Americans. Its tuber is said to resemble a sweet potato, and the yampah, in fact, is sometimes called "squaw potato."

Please remember that these flowers are to be enjoyed by all, thus picking is prohibited. Removing flowers from the meadow reduces the seed stock for the next year.

The variety of plants in these meadows attracted the Washo Indians to this area during their summers at Lake Tahoe. They used the level meadow of Squaw Valley as a permanent summer settlement. Women and children of the tribe gathered plants for food and medicine while Washo men hunted large game in the surrounding mountains.

As the trail climbs, it enters an area of bare granite. Hikers who wish to continue should see Trip 14. Those who came to view the flowers should leisurely retrace their steps to the trailhead.

14 GRANITE CHIEF PEAK

Difficulty: strenuous
Distance: 5.6 miles one way (aerial tram riders subtract 4 miles one way)
Usage: low
Starting elevation: 6240 feet at Squaw Valley, 8080 feet at top of tram
Elevation gain: 926 feet from top of tram
Season: summer, fall
Map: USGS Tahoe City and Granite Chief

Spectacular views are abundant on the trail to Granite Chief Peak. Most hikers let the Squaw Valley aerial tram pull them most of the way up the mountain. Then it's an exhilarating scramble up to the rocky summit of Granite Chief Peak (9006 feet) and a leisurely walk down through flower-filled meadows. Although development has marred some portions of Squaw Valley, its natural beauty is indomitable. This is a truly fabulous hike.

From Tahoe City, drive to Squaw Valley Road, 5.2 miles northwest on Highway 89 from its junction with Highway 28. Turn left on Squaw Valley Road and drive 2.2 miles to the Squaw Valley ski complex and the vast parking lot at the base of the mountain. If you're riding the tram, park in the main lot near the

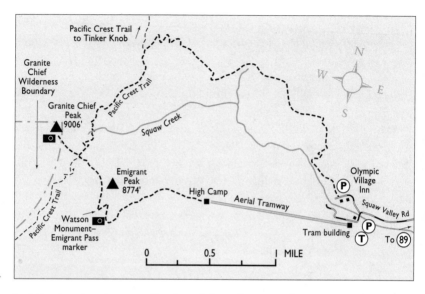

building housing the tram. For those hiking the entire distance, park behind the Olympic Village Inn, located to the right of the main complex just beyond the Squaw Valley Fire Station. The trailhead is found behind the inn at the end of the paved fire lane.

To gain nearly 2000 vertical feet and avoid 4 miles of uphill hiking, purchase tickets and ride the aerial tram. The cable car dangles dramatically over colorful rock formations and provides spectacular views of the immense ski complex. Those hiking the entire distance should follow the trail description in reverse to the junction of the Pacific Crest Trail with the summit route.

White settlers named this area Squaw Valley when they discovered an encampment of Washo women and children settled in the meadow. Apparently, the men of the tribe were away hunting or fishing. The Washo used this rich valley annually as a summer retreat. Its creeks were rich with trout, its meadows lush with plants to gather, and its forests populated with abundant deer, bear, and cougar.

Since the late 1800s, this beautiful and fragile valley has been irreparably altered by logging, cattle grazing, and, most recently, ski and resort development. Fortunately, by hiking the Squaw Creek trails (Trips 12 and 13) and the Pacific Crest Trail (PCT) above the valley, it is still possible to experience the area's natural beauty.

After exiting the cable car, hike west on a dirt road. Set your sights on the highest lift terminal on Emigrant Peak (8774 feet) and climb toward it. Ascend approximately 1 mile via a network of roads and trails through the ski complex, bearing right at most junctions. On the rocky slopes, look for yellow-bellied

Watson Monument–Emigrant Pass marker, Granite Chief Peak Trail

marmots, a relative of the eastern woodchuck. Marmots spend their summers dozing on sun-warmed rocks and eating mountain greenery. By fall, the well-rounded marmots are ready for their winter hibernation in burrows beneath the talus slopes. During hibernation, the marmot's body temperature drops to near freezing (34 degrees) and it breathes only once or twice a day. You are likely to see at least a few marmots sunbathing on warm sunny days.

Finally, switchback steeply on a dusty road and gain the ridgeline. To the east is a superlative view of Lake Tahoe. Look south for the peaks of Desolation Wilderness. The protected lands of Granite Chief Wilderness lie to the west. Granite Chief Peak sits almost directly west among the gorgeous array of peaks and wooded valleys extending as far as one can see. It is a strikingly beautiful scene, powerful enough to conjure up an image of the beauty that must once have graced Squaw Valley before the arrival of white settlers 150 years ago.

On your left is the Watson Monument–Emigrant Pass marker. Descend to the right, on the trail heading northwest. A multitude of flowers, including pastel phlox and Indian paintbrush and, later in the summer, radiant red California fuchsia and blue lupine, brighten the slopes. Shrubs such as greenleaf manzanita, currant, and tobacco brush line the trail. Look for soaring hawks riding updrafts created by the strong west winds.

The distinctive Tinker Knob (8949 feet) looms directly to the north. Thirty-three million years ago, Granite Chief Wilderness was covered with volcanic lava,

Granite Chief Peak

and Tinker Knob is a remnant of a once great volcano. Much of the volcanic rock has eroded from today's landscape to reveal the underlying granite, thanks to the scouring power of the glaciers that moved through this area.

The trail descends in 0.3 mile to the base of Granite Chief Peak. Ascend gently west to the junction with the Pacific Crest Trail. The PCT heads north and south; the trail continuing west climbs steeply to the summit of Granite Chief Peak. Those hiking the entire distance from Squaw Valley meet the summit trail here.

Enter Granite Chief Wilderness and begin a rocky ascent up the peak's east slope on an often indistinct trail. The trail swings slightly south to find a more gradual grade. After much effort, but only 0.3 mile, arrive at the rocky peak.

The reward is a superlative view in all directions. To the west, gaze at the singular pinnacle of Needle Peak, the throat of an ancient volcano. Below it lies the deep canyon of Royal Gorge. To the south, view the rugged peaks of Desolation Wilderness's Crystal Range. Tinker Knob and Anderson Peak dominate the view to the north. To the east, Lake Tahoe lies beyond squarish Squaw Peak.

Descend via the route of ascent to the junction with the Pacific Crest Trail. Head north (left) on the PCT, crossing under chair lifts. Descend on steep switchbacks through rocky terrain. Snow may remain on this ridgeline until well into the summer. Pass a subalpine meadow (please stay on the trail) and cross a creek, the beginning of Squaw Creek. Then rise briefly to a level, sandy area rich with pines. Next descend on switchbacks through beautiful woods with abundant mountain hemlock. The rocky, open landscape provides pleasant hiking with beautiful views to the east.

After traveling 1.4 miles north on the PCT, arrive at a junction with the trail to Squaw Valley. The PCT continues north, reaching Tinker Knob after 3 scenic miles. To return to the trailhead, turn right. Squaw Valley is 4 miles away.

Descend quickly on switchbacks. Magnificent canyon views unfold. The trail crosses wide granite benches; look for ducks (cairns) to guide the descent. Nearby, 50-foot cliffs attract intrepid rock climbers. In July, pink mountain pride bursts from cracks in the granite. In late summer, bright red California fuchsia takes its place.

Below the granite benches, the remaining miles of the trail are enchanting in midsummer. Follow the trail as it turns south and crosses a small stream twice. Again watch for ducks and painted blazes on the rocks. After the third stream crossing, pass through the middle of a dry meadow. A multitude of colorful flowers, dominated by yellow mule's ears, blankets the open area. The effect of the flowers is quite dramatic and beautiful (see Trip 13).

Next, meet, but don't cross, Squaw Creek. Take a moment to appreciate its pools and waterfalls, framed by green ferns and white granite slabs. The trail travels briefly along the north side of the creek. It then heads east and slopes gently back to the Squaw Valley complex. Look for a trail descending to the right that takes you to the parking area behind the Olympic Village Inn.

15 SQUAW VALLEY MOUNTAIN BIKING AT HIGH CAMP

Difficulty: easy and moderate (downhill to mountain base for advanced riders only)
Distance: High Camp Loop: 1 mile; Gold Coast Loop: 3 miles
Usage: high
Starting elevation: 8200 feet
Elevation gain: 100 feet and 300 feet, respectively
Season: summer, early fall
Map: USGS Granite Chief

The Squaw Valley USA Mountain Bike Park offers some of the most exciting mountain biking in the Tahoe area amid stunningly beautiful surroundings. Most of the mountain bike routes require advanced skills and nerves of steel. Bikers ride the aerial tram 2000 feet up the mountain to charge down its steep and

Squaw Valley Summit, Gold Coast Loop

rock-strewn slopes. For the less intrepid, two easier bike routes sit just above High Camp where riders can pedal on narrow trails through beautiful meadows of subalpine flowers, avoiding excessively steep downhill runs. While it is expensive to ride the tram for just a few miles of moderate mountain biking, this rugged setting is so inspiring that it is worth it. One can easily spend a glorious day atop the mountain. From Squaw Valley's High Camp, there are fabulous hikes (see Trips 12, 13, 14) as well as an ice skating rink, spa, and swimming pool.

From Tahoe City, drive to Squaw Valley Road, 5.2 miles northwest on Highway 89 from its junction with Highway 28. Turn left on Squaw Valley Road and drive 2.2 miles to the Squaw Valley ski complex and park in the main lot near the base of the tram. After purchasing your tickets and choosing from the wealth of activities available at High Camp, ride the tram to the top.

Upon exiting the tram, there are two options for intermediate mountain bikers. To ride the very short "High Camp Loop" (approximately 1 mile loop), bear right on Ridge Road after leaving the tram building. Follow signs for High Camp Loop, which will be the first left off the road. Ride this singletrack trail through meadows that sparkle with vibrant color in late July. Stay on the singletrack to

Squaw Valley bike park

preserve the lush carpet of flowers, including purple lupine, yellow mule's ears and orange Indian paintbrush.

For a slightly longer ride, with more climbing and faster descents, try the "Gold Coast Loop." From the tram, turn right on Ridge Road and then left on High Camp Loop. When High Camp Loop meets Ridge Road again, turn right and then immediately left for Gold Coast. Climb on Gold Coast, traversing the mountainside between Emigrant and Squaw Peaks. The trail eventually loops back and drops to Ridge Road, where one can take either the road or High Camp Loop back to the tram building. Spectacular views to the valley and surrounding mountains are seen from this moderately challenging trail.

Options: Back at the base of the mountain, it is very pleasant to ride the 2.3-mile bike path around the Olympic (Squaw) Valley floor. The paved, gently rolling path is perfect for younger cyclists. Starting at the tram, head north along the west edge of the valley, passing the Squaw Valley stables along the way. At the end of the valley, the trail curves to the east, passes over a small bridge, then terminates at the road leading to Highway 89. To return to your car, retrace your route.

To reserve rental bikes, call the Squaw Valley Sport Shop, (530) 583-3356.

16   FIVE LAKES TRAIL

Difficulty: moderate
Distance: 2.1 miles one way
Usage: high
Starting elevation: 6560 feet
Elevation gain: 960 feet
Season: spring, summer, fall
Map: USGS Tahoe City

The hike to Five Lakes is sunny, festive, and short. Colorful flowers and unusual rock formations guide the way to five small lakes where families can picnic, fish, and swim. Due to its proximity to the trailhead, Five Lakes is a very popular destination and should be avoided on summer weekends. Also, bring plenty of water, sunscreen, and bug repellent.

From the junction of Highways 89 and 28 in Tahoe City, drive 3.8 miles west on Highway 89 to reach Alpine Meadows Road. From Truckee, drive 10 miles south on Highway 89 (1.4 miles south of the Squaw Valley entrance) to reach

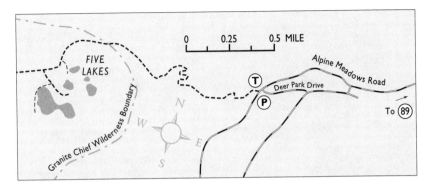

Alpine Meadows Road. Turn west onto Alpine Meadows Road and drive 2.1 miles to the Five Lakes Trailhead on the right side of the road, opposite Deer Park Drive. Park along the shoulder.

The trail begins by climbing steeply through abundant bitterbrush and huckleberry oak. Bountiful hillside flowers include yellow furry-leafed mule's ears, orange Indian paintbrush, and brilliant scarlet gilia. Also known as skyrocket gilia, its bright red tubular flowers have lobes that flare backward and long stamens that burst forward like fireworks. The midmorning sun can be hot and brilliant on this south-facing hillside.

Enter briefly the welcome shade of red fir and gaze left to Alpine Meadow's forested ski slopes. Climb out of the shade to a trail that becomes rockier and switchbacks up through tall, fragrant shrubs that bloom profusely in midsummer. Keep a lookout for the swift western fence lizard, which enjoys these dry, rocky environs. The lizard is 6 to 9 inches long and is likely to be seen darting across the trail. The abundantly flowered landscape attracts hordes of lovely butterflies as well.

At 1.1 miles, the trail turns abruptly northwest and continues to climb moderately. The thin, rocky soil of the ridge supports stunted but picturesque pines. Follow the trail along the side of a small, beautiful canyon. Thankfully, most of the climb is over now. Enjoy the marvelous shapes and colors of the dramatic cliffs. Below you, a small waterfall cascades to the floor of the canyon, where handsome, majestic firs stand in parklike formation. High on the canyon walls, the pink rock, like molded wet Bermuda sand, is cast in rounded, amorphous shapes. Observe the groping fingers and leaning, globular creatures. Be sure to stay on the trail. Short-cutting damages these beautiful, erosion-prone slopes.

At 1.6 miles, enter Granite Chief Wilderness and the shade of a red fir forest. The yellow-green staghorn lichen on the trees appears almost fluorescent against

Cliffs above Five Lakes Trail

the deep purplish bark and forest green needles. The height of the lichen is said to measure the depth of snow during the previous winter.

Hike on a moist, level trail into the forest, ignoring the first spur trail to the left. Proceed to a second fork, signed for Five Lakes, and take the trail to the left. In 0.2 mile, arrive at the largest of the area's lakes. For hikers who wish to explore all the lakes (three are grassy ponds), spur trails circle the lake area.

The large, westernmost lake is by far the most attractive and popular. Due to its popularity, vegetation on its shores is stressed, so stay on the trails to allow for regrowth. Choose some rocks for picnicking and enjoy fishing or swimming in the lake's warm and shallow waters. The Forest Service does not recommend camping in the Five Lakes area due to the area's heavy use and the environmental damage already sustained. Camping is prohibited within 600 feet of the lake to protect water quality.

17 TRUCKEE RIVER BIKE TRAIL

Difficulty: easy, handicapped accessible with assistance
Distance: 5 miles one way (add 2.3 miles one way for Squaw Valley extension)
Usage: high
Starting elevation: 6240 feet;
Elevation gain: none
Season: spring, summer, fall
Map: USGS Tahoe City

This popular paved trail parallels the Truckee River for 5 scenic miles through a steep-walled canyon. There are numerous places to picnic and fish for trout. The prettiest and least crowded times to ride the trail are the spring and fall. In spring, the river swells with frothy rapids. In autumn, bright foliage embraces the path along the river. In any season, this is an easy and scenic ride that is perfect for a family outing. Don't forget a picnic!

The trail starts on the south side of westbound Highway 89, about 0.3 mile west of the intersection of Highways 28 and 89 in Tahoe City. If riding from Tahoe City, park in the large lot signed "Truckee River Access Bike Trail Parking"

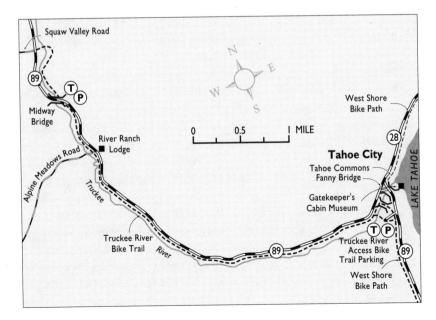

located just 0.25 mile south of the intersection of Highways 89 and 28 (the Tahoe City Y junction) on Highway 89. The trail terminates at the intersection of Highway 89 and Squaw Valley Road. Approaching from Truckee on Highway 89, find the northwest end of the bike path at Squaw Valley Road (about 9.3 miles south of Truckee). Look for a parking lot on the left side of the road.

Cyclists can ride the trail in either direction. Most riders start in Tahoe City, so this description assumes the same. At the start of your trip, pass several rafting outfitters that provide small rubber rafts for floating the gentle river. A good deal of whooping and hollering ensues on summer afternoons, when the river is clogged with floating funseekers (see "Rafting" in Chapter 1). Good picnic spots abound along the route, as well as places to fish and wade.

From the bike trail parking lot in Tahoe City, ride across the little bridge at the end of the lot and turn left onto the bike path. The path quickly drops down to the river, away from busy Highway 89, and rolls gently beside it. Frequent clearings along the river provide places to wade, picnic, and fish. Although there are sixty-three streams flowing into Lake Tahoe, the Truckee River is the lake's only outlet. A dam built in 1910 at its mouth controls its flow.

The Truckee River has a rich history. For centuries, it was the life-blood of the Washo Indians. The spring spawning of trout triggered the Washo's annual migration from winter homes in the Pine Nut Mountains to the shores of Lake Tahoe. The Washo camped in the area where the Truckee River meets the lake, where they caught abundant trout. The Truckee River was named for an elderly Indian who directed a party of emigrants to the river in 1844. Following a tributary of the river, the emigrant party discovered Donner Pass and made the first successful wagon crossing of the Sierra Nevada.

Fishing was extraordinary before the settlement of the basin. Cutthroat trout by the thousands swam in side streams during the spawning runs. Silver bodies filled the streams from bank to bank. By the 1930s, however, clear-cutting, water diversion, pollution, and commercial fishing brought the virtual extinction of the cutthroat in Lake Tahoe and the Truckee River.

The U.S. Forest Service, in conjunction with the California Department of Fish and Game and the Nevada Department of Wildlife, is working to reintroduce the cutthroat trout through spawning and stocking programs. To learn more about native fish, visit the Stream Profile Chamber at the Lake Tahoe Visitor Center (see Trip 34) and the fish spawning station at Marlette Lake (see Trip 54). To help the resurgence of Tahoe Basin fish, observe all fishing regulations and prohibitions.

At about 4 miles from Tahoe City, cyclists arrive at the historic River Ranch Lodge. This marks the end for the commercial raft trips, so the river is substantially quieter north of the lodge. The River Ranch has a pleasant patio overlooking the river where lunch and dinner are served. A summer music series adds to the festivity.

Beyond the River Ranch, cyclists must cross Alpine Meadows Road and ride the path's newest section to Squaw Valley Road. This is my favorite part. The riverbed is rockier and the river noisier. Anglers outnumber the rollerbladers and rafters, and the trail winds scenically along the river. Choose from several good picnic spots. Choose quickly, nevertheless, for in just 0.7 mile, the trail terminates at Squaw Valley Road.

To lengthen your trip at the path's northwest end, take a fun, uncrowded, and very scenic detour through Squaw Valley to the base of the ski resort. The valley is a quiet alternative to the sometimes overwhelming summer crowds of West Lake Tahoe. A 2.3-mile bike path extends down the entire length of the valley, paralleling Squaw Valley Road and terminating at the Squaw Valley USA Ski Resort. At the base of the mountain, you can catch the tram and visit the summit (and even take your bikes for some exhilarating mountain biking! See Trip 15). To visit Squaw Valley, cross Highway 89 at the traffic light and ride Squaw Valley Road to pick up the bike path on the left side of the road. The path crosses a small bridge, then heads left into the valley.

To extend the trip from the trail's east end, ride the scenic West Shore Bike Path north to Dollar Point (2.5 miles) or south to Sugar Pine Point State Park (9 miles) (see Trip 18). For information on bike rentals near the trail, see "Bicycling and Mountain Biking" in Chapter 1. To ride a portion of the Truckee River Bike Trail one way, inquire about shuttle service from a variety of points along the path. Call the Tahoe City Trolley at (530) 581-6365 or 1-800-COMMUTE.

18 WEST SHORE BIKE PATH

Difficulty: easy, handicapped accessible with assistance
Distance: 11.5 miles one way
Usage: high
Starting elevation: 6238 feet
Elevation gain: 60 feet
Season: spring, summer, fall
Map: USGS Tahoe City and Homewood, CA

The West Shore Bike Path travels 11.5 miles along the scenic shore of Lake Tahoe. It is mostly level and entirely separate from the main highway. Weekend crowds

A young hiker is shown a graffiti-damaged aspen.

and the trail's half-dozen crossings of Highway 89 are its only detractions. Ride it to see the many attractions of the west shore, and leave plenty of time for side trips.

Access the trail at the intersection of Highways 89 and 28 in Tahoe City, or anywhere along its 11.5-mile route from its northern end at Dollar Point (where Old Mill Road intersects Highway 28) to its southern end at Sugar Pine Point State Park. Riders parking at General Creek Campground could combine this trail with Trip 19.

There are several bike rental concessions in Tahoe City and a few along the route in Homewood, Sunnyside, and Lake Forest. On holiday weekends, families must arrive early or reserve bikes by phone to ensure availability (see "Bicycling and Mountain Biking" in Chapter 1).

If you're beginning in Tahoe City, stop first at Fanny Bridge, which spans the Truckee River. The bridge was given its unusual name by a local newspaper columnist who claimed to be able to estimate the number of tourists in the area by the number of backsides he counted at the bridge—numerous large trout are visible if one leans over the railing. Children may feed the fish, but fishing is prohibited here and within 1000 feet of the adjacent dam. A museum located near the bridge contains information on the dam and regional history (see "Museums and Cultural Attractions" in Chapter 1).

North from Tahoe City, the bike path borders Highway 28. Just north of Fanny Bridge is historic Watson Cabin Living Museum (see "Museums and Cultural Attractions" in Chapter 1). Behind the cabin is Tahoe Commons Beach, a popular family destination. Farther north, pass the Tahoe State Recreation Area. Approximately 2.25 miles from Tahoe City is Lake Forest, where there is a rocky public beach and playground next to a campground. To tour the area, turn right at a sign for the U.S. Coast Guard Station. Back on the trail, the path terminates at Old Mill Road, just north of Lake Forest.

Traveling south from Tahoe City, the path parallels Highway 89. The route south of Tahoe City is your best option because a wealth of attractions awaits riders on the 9 miles to Sugar Pine Point State Park. About 1 mile south of Tahoe City, the path crosses to the lake side of the highway. Dismount and use extreme caution when crossing Highway 89. Approximately 2.2 miles south of Tahoe City, arrive at William Kent Campground, just after Sunnyside Resort. A sandy beach at the campground makes a nice picnic stop. A detour to Ward Creek (see Trip 20) can be taken from here.

Cross and recross Highway 89, then at 4.2 miles from Tahoe City arrive at Kaspian Campground, a campground catering to bicyclists. If your group is ready for a break, visit its small rocky beach. Advanced cyclists may try the demanding

Blackwood Canyon ride by turning right at the sign for the campground (see Trip 22).

Shortly after the Blackwood Canyon turnout, arrive at Eagle Rock, a granite cliff towering 250 feet above the highway. A steep trail on the cliff's north side brings hikers to the top of the rock. There are additional trails on the rock's south side, but they are badly eroded. On top, the views are excellent. In fact, the Washo Indians used this rock to watch for their rivals, the Paiutes, and to locate large game.

Continuing from Eagle Rock, travel south about 1 mile and cross Highway 89 for the last time before you reach Sugar Pine Point State Park. Pass the Homewood Ski Area and ride approximately 3 miles to General Creek Campground. A right turn into the campground gives cyclists access to the General Creek Loop Trail (see Trip 19). Another 0.7 mile farther south on the bike path brings cyclists to the trail's end at the entrance of Sugar Pine Point State Park (lakeside). At the park, hikers can tour a historic mansion, swim or picnic on a pebbly beach, visit the nature center, or hike on one of several enticing nature trails (see Trip 23).

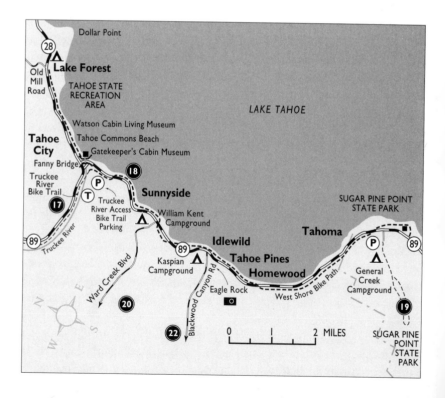

South from Sugar Pine Point State Park, Highway 89 (no bike trail) begins to climb and wind as it works its way past Meeks Bay and Rubicon Bay to D. L. Bliss State Park. The scenery is gorgeous, but the road is not designed for the happy coexistence of bicycles and cars. For that reason, it is not recommended for families. The safer alternative is to retrace your tracks north.

19 GENERAL CREEK LOOP TRAIL

Difficulty: moderate, handicapped access with assistance (easy for mountain bikers)
Distance: 6-mile loop
Usage: moderate
Starting elevation: 6320 feet
Elevation gain: 80 feet
Season: spring, summer, fall
Map: USGS Homewood

The General Creek Loop Trail, once a logging road, is excellent for family biking. As a hiking trail, it is a very pleasant, level stroll with lots of safe diversions for wandering children. In midsummer, the meadows offer abundant flowers, and the creek provides fishing opportunities.

From Tahoe City, drive south 9 miles on Highway 89 to the General Creek Campground on the west side of the highway. From the junction of Highways 89 and 50 in South Lake Tahoe, drive north on Highway 89 approximately 18 miles, 1.6 miles north of Meeks Bay Resort. Enter General Creek Campground and find the visitor parking to the left of the entrance station. Pick up a trail guide when you pay the entrance fee. If you're camping at the General Creek Campground, you can begin the route from campsite 150 and cut 1.1 miles from the total mileage.

Starting at the visitor parking lot, find the trail at the south end of the lot and head south for 0.1 mile, then head west, skirting the edges of the campsites for nearly a mile until the trail joins a logging road just southwest of campsite 150. At the road, turn left and travel southwest. After 0.25 mile, arrive at a junction with a second road. The loop trail begins here. Head left toward General Creek and cross it on a wooden bridge. The clear, slow-moving creek and accessible bank provide lots of area for exploration. After the bridge, turn right.

The Washo Indians, who summered in the Lake Tahoe Basin, fished the mouth of General Creek and camped in this vicinity. Lake Tahoe was the spiritual center of the Washos' world. Each spring the tribe, which had separated into family units for the winter, would reunite on Tahoe's shores. Summer was a time of plenty after the long lean winter. As well as finding abundant fish at General Creek, the Washo gathered the plants of this area for food, medicine, and weaving material. The Washo were expert basket weavers. For their baskets they gathered the shoots of the willows that still grow in abundance on the banks of General Creek.

The trail heads southwest, paralleling General Creek. Pass meadows accented by lavender lupines, yellow mule's ears, and red Indian paintbrush. By the trail are magnificent towering pines and firs. Look for the tallest of the pines, the sugar pine, for which this state park is named. Unfortunately, loggers in the early 1900s nearly cleared the Tahoe Basin of this majestic tree. To identify a sugar pine, look for long pinecones (up to 1½ feet) hanging from its highest branches and needles in groups of five. Sweet sap seeps through the bark of the sugar pine, giving it its name. The Washo and early settlers chewed this sap as a laxative.

At any point along this quiet trail, descend to the creek and explore its banks. If you've brought a sketch pad, collect pieces of charcoal from the charred stumps along the trail and sketch a bit or make some bark rubbings.

The trail becomes drier and sunnier as it veers from the creek. The landscape opens, revealing the moraines that flank the valley north and south. A glacier carved out General Creek's valley, leaving in its wake the mountain of debris that makes up the steep-sloped moraines. The glacier also deposited numerous large granite boulders, or glacial erratics, throughout the valley. Today these erratics scenically punctuate the level trail.

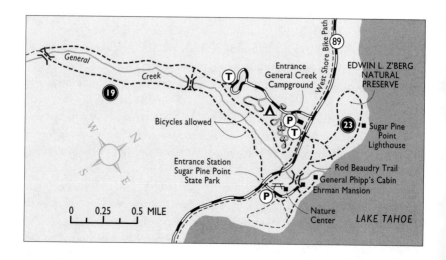

Leaving this sunny expanse, enter a shady forest at about 1.75 miles from the bridge. The terrain changes dramatically to a wetter, more lush environment. Pass waist-high ferns and chin-tickling corn lilies to arrive at a second wooden bridge over General Creek. Cross the bridge, then turn right to return to the trailhead. To visit Lily Pond, a 1-mile diversion, stay left and continue southwest. The small, shallow pond is not terribly scenic, however, and is often plagued with mosquitoes.

The loop trail returns along the north side of General Creek and travels through quite different terrain. The north side is shadier, wetter, and surrounded by lush vegetation. Colorful wet meadows are dazzlingly bright with abundant yellow mule's ears, dark purple penstemon, and red columbines. Don't miss the delightful scent of the huge Jeffrey pines that border the trail. Smell their reddish bark for a sweet, vanilla-like treat.

Travel among the lush meadows for 1.1 miles to reach the junction with the road leading to the first bridge. Continue straight ahead to the junction with the trail to the parking area. If you started at campsite 150, continue straight on the logging road to its termination at the campground road.

Since this is a loop trail, you may, of course, reverse the directions and travel the north leg first.

20 WARD CREEK BIKE TRAIL

Difficulty: easy
Distance: 4 miles one way
Usage: low
Starting elevation: 6250 feet
Elevation gain: 400 feet
Season: spring, summer, fall
Map: USGS Tahoe City and Homewood

This easy bike ride begins on pavement, continues on a logging road past scenic meadows, and ends by a trail at Ward Creek. The creek makes a fine summer or fall picnic spot. Trails radiating from Ward Creek provide lots of uncrowded exploring opportunities.

Start at William Kent Campground, located on Highway 89, 2.2 miles south of the junction of Highways 89 and 28 in Tahoe City.

Bike 0.25 mile south of William Kent Campground on Highway 89 to Pineland

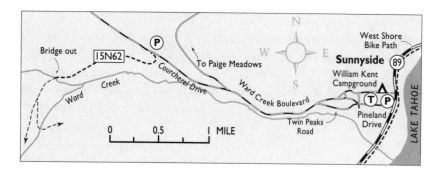

Drive. Turn right on Pineland Drive and pedal for 0.4 mile, then turn left onto Twin Peaks Road. In 0.1 mile, where Twin Peaks Road turns into Ward Creek Boulevard, bear right. Ride west on Ward Creek Boulevard for 1.5 miles, rising moderately. Pass a sign on the right for Paige Meadows and ride just 0.75 mile farther to a logging road signed 15N62 on the left. Turn left onto the unpaved road and descend briefly.

On the logging road, leave all traffic behind and course past flowered meadows. Don't ride off-trail through the meadows; some are undergoing rehabilitation from previous overuse. The trail is gently rolling for the next mile. After 1.1 miles the logging road ends at a disabled bridge at Ward Creek. In late summer, the creek is easily crossed (with or without bikes). On the other side spur trails encourage quiet creekside and meadow exploring.

21 WARD CREEK MOUNTAIN BIKE LOOP (PAIGE MEADOWS)

Difficulty: strenuous
Distance: 13 miles round trip
Usage: moderate
Starting elevation: 6240 feet
Elevation gain: 1040 feet
Season: summer, fall
Map: USGS Tahoe City

This challenging route takes mountain bikers through lush woods and flowered meadows, across view-filled ridges, down and up steep slopes, along gentle paths, and on and off pavement. Good views of surrounding peaks as well as a visit to flower-filled Paige Meadows are the highlights. Bikers ride across ev-

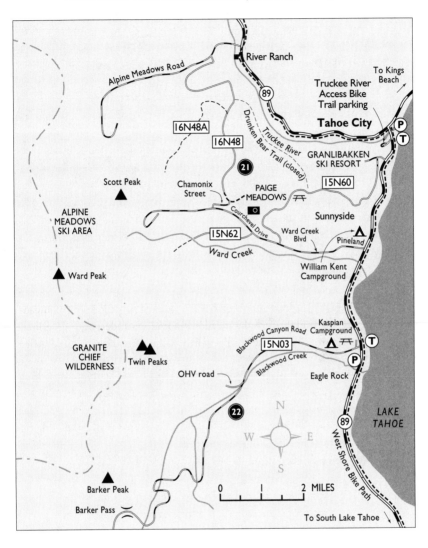

erything from logging roads to singletrack, completing about 5 miles on pavement and 8 miles on dirt. For strong cyclists, it's a beautiful and exciting ride on constantly changing terrain. In summer, flowers fill Paige Meadows; in fall, the foliage is magnificent.

Start by parking in the Truckee River Access Bike Trail parking lot located off Highway 89, 0.25 mile south of the intersection of Highways 89 and 28 in Tahoe City. From the lot, turn right and bike south on the paved bicycle path that runs along the highway. After about 0.25 mile, turn right, following signs for

Granlibakken Ski Resort. Climb the road until almost reaching the resort entrance, then turn left on Rawhide Road and follow the road to its end. Behind a gate find the bike trail.

The trail (Forest Road 15N60) runs through the forest and immediately begins climbing fairly steeply. As you reach intersections, remain on the main trail. At the first major intersection (marked by a large rock), bear right. At most subsequent intersections, keep left.

After almost 3 miles of climbing through dense and fragrant pines, bikers reach lovely Paige Meadows, a series of grassy meadows separated by thin stands of pine and aspen. The meadows are currently in the process of recovering after years of abuse from four-wheel-drive vehicles. If the ground is wet, do not bike through the meadows, instead stay on the trails that run along their border. In dry weather, especially in the fall, enjoy the singletracks that cross the grassy fields. It is a wonderful place to ride. Ward Peak provides the dramatic backdrop, and spectacular wildflowers fill the meadows in summer.

Make your way west from Paige Meadows to the dirt road at their western end. Then begin a steep descent down the road, glimpsing impressive views of surrounding peaks to your right. The road terminates at paved Ward Creek Boulevard, where you turn right to continue the loop.

Ride Ward Creek Boulevard west and regain much of the altitude lost on the trail. Ward Creek Boulevard changes to Courchevel Drive and continues to climb. After 0.5 mile, pass the forest road access to the Ward Creek Trail (Trip 20), marked with a sign for Twin Peaks, on the left side of the road. After another 0.75 mile, arrive (fairly breathless) at Chamonix Street and turn right. Ride this residential street to its end to pick up another dirt trail.

Follow the trail as it heads briefly left, then pick up Forest Road 16N48. The excellent road surface soon narrows. At approximately 1.25 miles from the beginning of 16N48, arrive at a junction with the decommissioned Forest Road 16N48A. Stay right on the main road and in another 0.4 miles, reach the intersection on your right with the singletrack Drunken Bear Trail. In 2000, the forest service closed this poorly designed trail to protect the watershed and to prevent disturbance of endangered species living in the area, such as the spotted owl. Please do not use this trail. Continue straight on the main trail and proceed along the side of the mountain through trees to a few good glimpses of Lake Tahoe to the right. Then arrive at the open slopes of the Alpine Meadows Ski Area. At this point the trail makes a steep and sandy descent to the base of the mountain. Ride carefully on this section. At the end of the trail, proceed around a gate to paved Snow Crest Road. Descend on Snow Crest Road briefly to Alpine Meadows Road and turn right.

Ward Creek Bike Loop Trail, Paige Meadows

Coast down Alpine Meadows Road about ½ mile to its junction with Highway 89 and the Truckee River Bike Trail. To return to Tahoe City and your car, turn right on the bike path and pedal the rolling 4-mile river path to its termination in Tahoe City. Cyclists seeking mid-trip refreshment can stop at the River Ranch, located at the junction of Alpine Meadows Road and Highway 89. Food, drinks, and often music are offered on a patio overlooking the Truckee River. Just before reaching Tahoe City and the end of the bike path, watch for a short cut to the bike trail parking lot via a bridge over the river to the right.

22 BLACKWOOD CANYON BIKE ROUTE

Difficulty: strenuous
Distance: 7 miles one way
Usage: moderate
Starting elevation: 6400 feet
Elevation gain: 1300 feet
Season: spring, summer, fall
Map: USGS Homewood
See Trip 21 for map.

This 7-mile ride up Blackwood Canyon is difficult, but the views are exhilarating. On the return, the 5-mile coast down is tremendous fun. To make the ride a little easier, this route takes you up a paved road. Traffic is usually light, and the excellent road surface lets you enjoy the scenery.

From the junction of Highways 89 and 28 in Tahoe City, drive 4.2 miles south on Highway 89 to the Kaspian Picnic Area at the Kaspian Campground. Turn right on Blackwood Canyon Road (Forest Road 15N03) opposite Kaspian Beach, noting the signs for Blackwood Canyon. Park at the beginning of Forest Road 15N03 or at the Kaspian Picnic Area. Approaching from the south on Highway 89, Forest Road 15N03 is 4.5 miles north of Tahoma.

Ride 2.2 gentle miles on Forest Road 15N03 past intermittent meadows filled with wildflowers to a fork in the road where an unpaved OHV road branches right. Stay on the paved road and cross a bridge over Blackwood Creek 0.1 mile later. After the bridge, the road begins to rise, and over the next 4.7 miles gains 1300 feet in elevation. The grade is tough, but not gruesome.

At 7 miles from Highway 89, the paved road ends, surrounded by a forest of red fir. Barker Pass is 0.2 mile farther, after a gentle descent on the unpaved road. Most riders will want to turn around and reap the delicious reward for all their work. Riders deserve the gorgeous ride down the gently winding road amid spectacular canyon scenery. This is one route that feels like downhill skiing!

23 SUGAR PINE POINT STATE PARK NATURE TRAILS

Difficulty: easy, handicapped access with assistance
Distance: Ehrman Mansion grounds: 0.25 to 0.5 mile one way; Rod Beaudry Trail: 0.5 mile one way; Edwin L. Z'Berg Natural Preserve: 1.25-mile loop from Rod Beaudry Trail
Usage: high
Starting elevation: 6280 feet
Elevation Loss: 40 feet
Season: spring, summer, fall, winter
Map: USGS Meeks Bay
See Trip 19 for map.

Sugar Pine Point State Park offers a variety of easy and interesting trails. One trail winds by a set of historic buildings, another courses through mature forest, and a third makes a scenic loop along the lakeshore. Since the walking is easy, a family outing could include all three. Strolling in Sugar Pine Point State Park is a lovely way to spend an afternoon, especially if you are accompanied by young children or wheelchair hikers. Remember, please, that bikes are prohibited on these hiking trails.

From Tahoe City, drive south 10 miles on Highway 89 to the park entrance on the east side of the highway. From D. L. Bliss State Park on Highway 89, drive north 6.4 miles on Highway 89. Enter Sugar Pine Point State Park, picking up a trail guide at the entrance station. Park in the lowest parking lot, near the water tower and generating plant.

Forest Stroll (Rod Beaudry Trail): 0.5 mile one way (paved), handicapped access with assistance. Walk on the road past the water tower and generating plant (the Nature Center), and take the first left onto the paved Rod Beaudry Trail. Cross a bridge over General Creek behind the Ehrman Mansion, then continue on the paved path. The Rod Beaudry Trail intersects the unpaved path to the Edwin L. Z'Berg Natural Preserve after 0.25 mile. Stay on the paved trail and curve northwest until you meet Highway 89, approximately 0.5 mile from the parking lot.

The paved path travels through a mature mixed conifer forest, leading you on an enjoyable and educational walk. Markers along the trail tell of the Washo Indians, local flora and fauna, and the logging and settlement of the Tahoe Basin. The story is one of loss and recovery. In the late 1800s, loggers cleared this area and built roads through the meadows. In the twentieth century, the healing process began. Now second-growth forest covers many of the scars inflicted during those logging years. Unfortunately, gone forever are the Washo Indians, who were forced from Lake Tahoe; the abundant wildlife, including bear and bobcats, that once thrived here; and the magnificent stands of towering sugar pine.

Edwin L. Z'Berg Natural Preserve: 1.25-mile loop (unpaved). This trail is reached via the Rod Beaudry Trail (see above). Cross the bridge behind the Ehrman Mansion and walk 0.25 mile north to the fork with an unpaved trail. Keep to the right and take the unpaved trail into the nature preserve.

The unpaved trail heads north through mature sugar pine forest and then loops south, paralleling the scenic lakeshore before regaining the paved Rod Beaudry Trail. The coniferous woods are open and breezy. Prime examples of the magnificent sugar pine tower above. The sugar pine is the largest pine in the area and can grow to a height of 240 feet, as tall as a twenty-four-story building. The tree is easily recognized by its 3- to 4-inch-long needles (in bunches of five) and its wonderfully huge tawny pine cones that can grow as long as 18 inches. Native Americans and early settlers used to chew the sap, which extrudes from the dark, deeply furrowed bark. It has a sweet flavor (hence the tree's name) and is known to have laxative properties.

The highest lighthouse in the world stands on the lakeshore at Sugar Pine Point. The relatively modest, 22-foot-tall wooden lighthouse qualifies as the "highest" due to Lake Tahoe's 6229-foot elevation. Boats traveling on Lake Tahoe still use this light as a beacon. It flashes every 5 seconds from dusk until dawn from May 1 to December 1.

The nature preserve is well worth exploring. The sharp contrast between dark forest and sunny beach keeps little hikers interested. The loop trail also provides excellent cross-country skiing in the winter.

Ehrman Mansion Grounds: 0.25 mile to 0.5 mile (paved) one way. A stroll around the grounds of the Ehrman Mansion can fill an interesting afternoon. State park personnel, dressed in period costume, offer tours of the 1901 mansion throughout the summer. The beautifully manicured surroundings and lavish green lawn sloping down to the lakeshore provide pleasant settings for an elegant

A ranger in period costume at the Ehrman Mansion

picnic with grand views of the lake. The path on the lake side of the mansion is paved and handicapped accessible. For a self-guided nature tour along this path, pick up the booklet entitled Path of the Water Babies, available at the Nature Center's bookshop.

In approximately 0.2 mile, the paved path takes you past a pier to General Phipps's Cabin. This hand-hewn log cabin, built by the "general" in 1870, was the home of William Phipps (1813–91), one of the first permanent white settlers in the Lake Tahoe Basin. Mr. Phipps is credited with saving the majestic sugar pines on his 160-acre homestead while all surrounding land was robbed of this valuable and beautiful tree.

While on the grounds, don't miss the Nature Center set up in the old water tower and generating plant. It houses some nice dioramas for children and some hands-on exhibits depicting the plants and animals of the park. Families should inquire at the center about special children's interpretive programs. For information on tours and hours of operation, call (530) 525-7982.

24 LAKE GENEVIEVE AND CRAG LAKE

Difficulty: strenuous
Distance: 4.6 miles one way to Lake Genevieve; 4.9 miles one way to Crag Lake
Usage: moderate
Starting elevation: 6240 feet
Elevation gain: 1230 feet to Crag Lake
Season: spring, summer, fall
Map: USGS Meeks Bay, Homewood, and Rockbound Valley

This pleasant hike along Meeks Creek arrives at two attractive lakes, fine for fishing, swimming, and camping. The best way to reach the lakes is to bike the first third of the way. The trail begins on a logging road, popular among mountain bikers. The first third also makes a good hike for those pushing wheelchairs or strollers. When you reach the Tahoe–Yosemite Trail at 1.3 miles, bikes may be stowed and locked.

From Tahoe City, drive south 10.9 miles on Highway 89 to a small parking area on the west side of the highway just south of Meeks Bay Resort. Approaching from the intersection of Highways 50 and 89 in South Lake Tahoe, drive 16.5 miles north on Highway 89 and find the trailhead just past the Meeks Bay Campground entrance. If the parking area is full, park on the shoulder. Obtain a wilderness permit at the trailhead.

Begin on the sandy, tree-lined road. Pass by numerous meadows blooming with flowers and a wide variety of trees, including incense cedars and sugar, lodgepole, Jeffrey, and ponderosa pines. Pass a wet meadow and pond on the

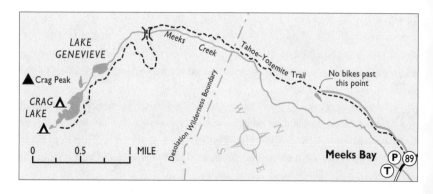

left and look for cruising ducks, with ducklings in tow, in the late spring and early summer. On the right, shortly after the pond, is Desolation Wilderness's Meeks Creek Trail.

If you're riding, secure your bikes here. Mountain bikes are strictly prohibited in Desolation Wilderness. Rise steeply on the shady Meeks Creek Trail (the sign will indicate Phipps Pass). After 0.5 mile of moderate climbing, the trail levels and opens up to good views of a forested canyon. Catch your breath as you hike southwest to the sounds of birds and nearby Meeks Creek. The trail joins the flower-lined creek and enters Desolation Wilderness immediately thereafter. The cool, alder-lined creek offers pleasant rest stops. Meeks Bay, where Meeks Creek empties into Lake Tahoe, was a favorite fishing and camping spot of the Washo Indians who summered in the Tahoe Basin.

Leave the creek as the needle-covered path widens and travels through a forest of red fir. Still on a level grade, pass a boggy area with many standing dead trees. Listen and watch for the many birds among these snags. Dead trees play an important part in the ecosystem of forests, providing homes for birds and small mammals and supplying breeding areas for the insects that support the bird population.

Next, enter a drier meadow where violet lupine and yellow mule's ears abound, then resume your climb. The trail once again joins Meeks Creek, which rises steeply beside you. If the climb makes you weary, pause beside the cascading creek and be cooled by its spray.

At 3.5 miles, cross the creek on a small bridge, then rise again on a path curving east. Manzanita and thimbleberry line the trail and giant red firs tower above. In June, the tiny pinkish "bells" of the manzanita grace the shrubs, and in July the showy white flowers of the thimbleberry brighten the slope. In late summer, sample the raspberrylike thimbleberries. Be forewarned, however, that the small greenish "apples" of the manzanita are edible but quite bitter, although the Washo Indians made a type of cider from them.

The trail seems strangely quiet after leaving behind noisy Meeks Creek, but the silence is soon broken by the inevitable scolding of the Sierra chickaree. This handsome, dark-furred, medium-sized tree squirrel produces raucous bursts of chatter from high in the trees. Despite their obvious calls, the squirrels are surprisingly hard to locate. Search the branches for the flash of their fine, silver-tipped tails.

Next, pass by an area punctuated by glacial erratics, then resume the climb. Reach an open, rocky ridge with views of a tumbling creek and vast forested slopes. To the east is a glimpse of Lake Tahoe.

Hike south through the open forest, the sun-dappled landscape still studded with tremendous boulders. Reach the shore of shallow Lake Genevieve, 4.6 miles from the trailhead. This tree-rimmed lake is nicely sheltered by high rocky ridges. Its shore provides nice picnic spots, and its relatively warm water is good for swimming.

To reach Crag Lake, 0.3 mile farther, follow the trail south along the east side of Lake Genevieve. Rise gently through a lovely open forest of fir and Jeffrey pine and arrive shortly at beautiful Crag Lake, larger and more scenic than its nearest neighbor.

Crag Lake's granite shoreline sports an abundance of good picnic spots, and the setting is delightful. A parklike grassy slope rises gently to the east, while majestic Crag Peak (9054 feet) towers above the lake to the southwest. Crag Lake offers fine fishing, including brook, lake, brown, and rainbow trout. Backpackers should avoid trailside campsites northeast of the lake and proceed southwest around the lake for environmentally sound sites.

25 RUBICON TRAIL TO ROCK PINNACLES

Difficulty: easy
Distance: 0.5 mile one way
Usage: moderate
Starting elevation: 6230 feet
Elevation gain: 300 feet
Season: spring, summer, fall
Map: USGS Emerald Bay

For breathtaking lake views, this short hike is unsurpassed. The trail hugs steep cliffs high above Lake Tahoe's emerald waters. On sunny days the lake shimmers in dazzling blue-green luminescence, framed by the dark boughs of conifers. Hike to an interesting group of rock pinnacles where you can perch on a boulder and picnic amid the unparalleled scenery. This hike is an excellent choice early or late in the season when trails at higher altitudes are snow-covered. The trail is not recommended for youngsters prone to wandering, for there are numerous places where the trail drops off precipitously.

Drive to D. L. Bliss State Park, 11 miles north on Highway 89 from the split of Highways 50 and 89 in South Lake Tahoe, or 16.5 miles south on Highway 89 from Tahoe City. Enter the park and drive north 2.4 miles on the park road to a

D. L. Bliss State Park

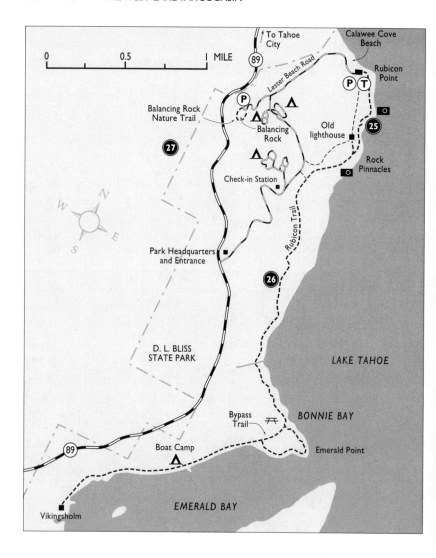

parking area at the east end of Lester Beach Road, following signs saying Beach Area and Rubicon Trail.

Leave the busy parking lot at Calawee Cove Beach for a cool, shady trail at the lot's eastern end. Enter a mixed conifer forest and look for a few giant sugar pines, one of the most distinctive and magnificent trees in the Tahoe Basin. This remarkable tree was once plentiful along the western shore of Lake Tahoe. Unfortunately, most were logged during the mining boom of the late 1800s.

Seek out the few sugar pines that remain. The five-needled sugar pine is easily recognized by its outstanding height and foot-long pendulous cones. The scales of the cones resemble delicate wood inlay. Don't keep this treasure, however, for removing natural objects violates park regulations. Furthermore, the seeds of the cones are a source of food for squirrels, chipmunks, and birds. By removing the cones, you also destroy any chance for the sugar pine to regenerate. Lastly, check the sugar pine's trunk for nodules of whitish sap. Native Americans and early settlers chewed the sweet sap for chewing gum and for its laxative qualities.

The trail climbs moderately, arriving quickly at the edge of an east-facing cliff with dramatic views of the radiant blue lake. For your safety there is a steel cable along the narrowest sections. Hand holding is highly advisable.

Pass several large trees struck by lightning. Next, the path curves slightly to the right and arrives at the rock pinnacles. An imaginative eye can see many strange creatures in these natural sculptures. One large pinnacle resembles a figure sitting with its back to the lake, sternly guarding the trail. Another looks like a fierce prehistoric rhinoceros with large, toothed jaws. A more whimsical eye turns a nearby pinnacle into a koala bear kissing a smiling man.

The Washo Indians, who summered at Lake Tahoe before the arrival of the white settlers, also saw figures in these pinnacles. One surviving legend describes the origin of Balancing Rock, located only a short drive from the trailhead (see Trip 27).

There are many wide boulders on which to spread a picnic. On your perch near Rubicon Point, gaze down to one of the deepest points along the shore of the lake. Lake Tahoe is the third-deepest lake on the continent, with a maximum depth of 1645 feet. Due to the lake's fluctuation in depth, your view reveals a dazzling spectrum of blues.

An additional landmark to explore is the old lighthouse that sits on the cliff north of the pinnacles and to the right of the trail. Watch for an obvious spur path leading steeply up the backside of the cliff. It leads to an old shack that once housed an important lighthouse for the lake. Perched about 900 feet above the lake, the lighthouse operated in the 1920s and 1930s until it was replaced by the lighthouse at Sugar Pine Point (see Trip 23). Trees now obscure the once fabulous view from this spot.

Hike this trail in the early morning to avoid the boisterous gunning of pleasure boats. For supreme scenery and solitude, hike at dawn, when the rising sun lights the eastern sky above the Carson Range.

It is possible to return to the parking lot by way of the Lighthouse Trail, which lies just east of the old lighthouse. This trail takes an inland, viewless route through the forest, so it is advisable to retrace your steps on the cliffs above the shoreline.

26 RUBICON TRAIL TO EMERALD BAY

Difficulty: moderate
Distance: 3.1 miles one way to Emerald Point; 4.5 miles
one way to Emerald Bay
Usage: moderate
Starting elevation: 6230 feet
Elevation gain: 300 feet
Season: spring, summer, fall
Map: USGS Emerald Bay
See Trip 25 for map.

The Rubicon Trail is one of the treasures of the Tahoe Basin. Views of the lake are dramatic, fabulous, and plentiful. The trail climbs high on cliffs near Rubicon Point, then rises and falls along the shoreline, finally descending to Emerald Bay, a superb place to picnic and one of the best swimming spots on Lake Tahoe. Don't miss this one.

Drive to D. L. Bliss State Park, 11 miles north on Highway 89 from the split of Highways 50 and 89 in South Lake Tahoe, or 16.5 miles south on Highway 89 from Tahoe City. Enter the park and drive north 2.4 miles on the park road to a parking area at the east end of Lester Beach Road, following signs to the beach area and Rubicon Trail.

Begin on the Rubicon Trail and hike to the rock pinnacles, as described in Trip 25. Continue past the pinnacles, heading southwest on a smooth, easy path amid superlative scenery. In early summer, flowering shrubs line the trail.

A wide path enters from the right at 0.75 mile. That trail leads west to a parking area off the park's main road. Continue south on the main trail and enter a dark, somewhat gloomy and viewless forest of white fir. Dry, dead branches litter the ground in tangled masses. In this forest, the long descent to the lake begins. Note on your right a burned area where tobacco brush thrives.

Past the burned area, descend the slope via two switchbacks. Pass a lovely stream that feeds Lake Tahoe. In the spring and early summer, the stream cascades delightfully down the rocks. Next, watch for tremendous nests on tall, dead firs on the slopes below you. Ascend briefly, then descend to large boulders from which you have a memorable view of the rocky, undulating shoreline. In 1956, a regional historian described this view eloquently:

> *Here the shore formation is wild and irregular, with deep holes, majestic, grand*
> *and rugged rocks and some trees and shrubbery. . . . These objects and conditions*

all combine to produce a mystic revelation of color gradations and harmonies,
from emerald green and jade to the deepest amethyst or ultra-marine. . . .
The eyes are dazzled with iridescences and living color-changes . . . as exquisite,
glorious and dazzling as revealed in the most perfect peacock's tail-feathers, or
hummingbird's throat. . . . The blue alone is enough to impress it forever upon
the observant mind.

From this viewpoint, descend almost to the shore, then head over a low rise to arrive at boulder-strewn Bonnie Bay. The quiet bay is a nice place for a short rest stop.

Immediately after Bonnie Bay, arrive at a fork. The trail on the right, the Bypass Trail, leads directly over the moraine to Emerald Bay, reaching the bay in 0.25 mile. The trail to the left also reaches Emerald Bay, but it wanders for 0.75 mile along the shoreline of Emerald Point first. If time allows, take one route one way and the other on the return. Both are worth traveling.

Following first the wider and more-traveled Bypass Trail, enter an open forest of giant, magnificent trees dubbed "Avenue of the Giants." Pass lofty incense cedars with deeply furrowed, shaggy orange-brown bark and olive green foliage. The fragrant and durable wood of the incense cedar is used for posts, shingles, and, most

A comparison of bark: platelike Jeffrey pine (left) and shaggy incense cedar (right)

commonly, pencils. Also along this path are towering Jeffrey pines, noted for their large cones and bark that smells like vanilla. In early summer look for bright red snow plants. The leaves and stem of this fleshy-looking plant lack chlorophyll; consequently, this wholly red plant resembles a fat stalk of red asparagus.

After 0.25 mile, you reach the north side of Emerald Bay. This narrow and shallow bay was named for the brilliant emerald green of its clear waters. You may wish to hike all the way to its mouth, to see Vikingsholm and Eagle Falls (Trip 28). Alternatively, there is a wealth of scenic and secluded shoreline to explore along the bay's north side. The shallow waters of the bay warm by late summer to provide fine swimming. Be forewarned that this gorgeous bay draws hundreds of tourists each summer weekend. To see its beauty at its best, arrive early in the day, before the cruising tourist boats.

To return to the trailhead by the alternate route, follow the path that parallels the shoreline on the north side of Emerald Bay. This path leads around the perimeter of Emerald Point, arriving after 0.5 mile at the north shore of the point. The trail then runs east along the shoreline for 0.25 mile to meet the three-way junction with the Bypass Trail. Take the Rubicon Trail north to return to the trailhead at Calawee Cove Beach.

27 BALANCING ROCK NATURE TRAIL

Difficulty: easy
Distance: 0.5-mile loop
Usage: moderate
Starting elevation: 6240 feet
Elevation gain: none
Season: spring, summer, fall
Map: USGS Meeks Bay
See Trip 25 for map.

The fun and informative Balancing Rock Nature Trail is located in D. L. Bliss State Park. This short trail is a must-see for park visitors. Since Bliss State Park offers some of the best beaches, trails, and campsites in the basin, Tahoe visitors are heartily encouraged to spend at least a day there. The self-guided Balancing Rock Nature Trail is a good introduction to the Sierra plant and animal communities and thus is recommended for the beginning of your visit. Since the park is very popular, arrive before 11:00 A.M. on summer days because day-use parking is very limited.

Drive to D. L. Bliss State Park, 16.5 miles south on Highway 89 from Tahoe City. The park is located 11 miles north of the intersection of Highways 89 and 50 in South Lake Tahoe. Enter the park and drive 1.65 miles north to the intersection with Lester Beach Road. Turn left and drive 0.25 mile to the parking area signed for the Balancing Rock Nature Trail. The trail begins just south of the lot.

The park provides a brochure with information keyed to numbers along the nature trail. In a clear and succinct manner, the narrative describes the interrelationship of the trees, rocks, soils, plants, and animals of the upper montane zone.

The highlight of the nature trail is the impressive and unusual Balancing Rock formation. The origin of the name is obvious, as one looks up at the 130-ton granite boulder perched precariously

Balancing Rock

atop a smaller rock pedestal. The formation is also remarkable for its resemblance to the head of a smiling dinosaur.

The Washo Indians who inhabited Lake Tahoe before the arrival of white settlers saw something else in Balancing Rock. According to Washo legend, a tribe of giant Indians inhabited this site long ago. The giant Indians were plagued by a huge sea serpent that lived near the shore and preyed upon the Indians. One day the chief of the giant Indians decided to end his tribe's misery, so he set out in a boat to slay the serpent. The bloody fight that resulted lasted all day and night. The next morning, the tribe found the bodies of their brave chief and the slain evil serpent. In reverence to their beloved chief, the tribe buried him upright in his favorite spot overlooking Lake Tahoe, with his giant head remaining above ground so that he could forevermore gaze at the sacred lake. The chief's head remains there to this day.

The last part of the trail gives children the chance to view more rock formations. As one looks up from the trail, ghoulish and humorous figures can be seen in the cliffs overhead. For more free-standing, phantasmagoric "sculptures," hike 1 mile on the Rubicon Trail, also located in this park (Trip 25).

The Balancing Rock trail is also an excellent trail on which to learn to distinguish the Sierra conifers. Bring along a tree guide and observe the needles, bark, and cones of the trees to determine their species. The descriptions in the park's brochure are also helpful.

28 EMERALD BAY, VIKINGSHOLM, AND EAGLE FALLS

Difficulty: easy, handicapped access with assistance to Emerald Bay and Vikingsholm
Distance: 0.8 mile one way to Emerald Bay; 0.9 mile one way to Vikingsholm; 1.1 miles one way to Eagle Falls
Usage: high
Starting elevation: 6630 feet
Elevation loss: 400 feet
Season: spring, summer, fall
Map: USGS Emerald Bay

Although the first 0.7 mile of this "trail" (a closed, unpaved road) is often crowded, dusty, and noisy, the trip to Emerald Bay is precious in many ways. The lovely path (0.2 mile) from Vikingsholm to impressive Eagle Falls is ideal for the youngest hikers. For beach seekers, there is access to a stretch of wonderfully scenic shoreline and superb swimming spots. For history buffs, the eccentric replica of a Viking castle is a rare treat. Since this is one of Lake Tahoe's most popular spots, visit it on weekdays, early in the day, or in the off-season.

To reach the trailhead, drive 9 miles north on Highway 89 from the split of Highways 50 and 89 in South Lake Tahoe. Approaching from the north, drive 18.5 miles south on Highway 89 from Tahoe City. The trailhead is located at the Emerald Bay Overlook on the lake side of the highway. On summer weekends, the large parking lot often fills. Overflow parking can be found at the Eagle Falls Picnic Area, which is 0.1 mile south of the larger lot.

Before you descend to the lakeshore, climb the boulders at the edge of the parking lot for a dramatic overlook of Emerald Bay. On clear days, Emerald Bay is a radiant, translucent blue-green. The bay was shaped by glaciers that swept west from huge Eagle Canyon behind you. The glaciers advanced in the direction of the lake, carrying with them masses of rock debris. As the glaciers

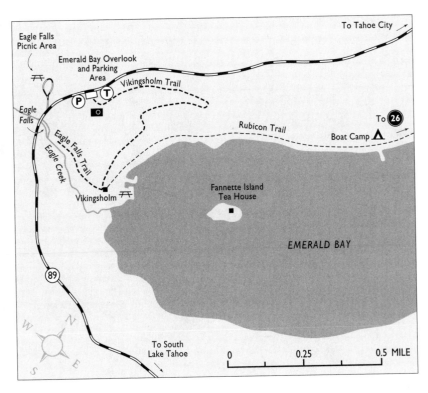

melted, the debris was deposited, forming ridges (glacial moraines) on either side of Emerald Bay. Rock left by the glaciers formed scenic Fannette Island in the center of the bay.

To reach Emerald Bay, Eagle Falls, and Vikingsholm, follow a steep dirt road that winds down 400 feet. After 0.7 mile, the road levels and paths diverge. Go to the left for Emerald Bay. Walk to the bay under immense firs and incense cedars, scattering the plentiful chipmunks and ground squirrels. At the end of the bay are picnic tables, a pier, and a buoy-marked swimming area. The water warms to pleasant swimming temperatures in late summer. If you want to continue hiking along the magnificently scenic shore, follow the path that heads northeast, following the contour of the shore. The farther away from the pier you travel, the more solitude you are likely to find. This is the southern end of the beautiful Rubicon Trail (Trip 26).

Stay on the main road if your goal is Vikingsholm or Eagle Falls. Vikingsholm is reached after 0.1 mile. The curious sod-roofed building is a replica of a Viking castle. It was built in 1929 as an elegant vacation home for a California heiress. From July to Labor Day, daily tours of the castle are given by well-

Picnic at Eagle Falls

trained state park rangers in period costume for a modest fee. The tour is fun for all ages.

Across from the entrance to Vikingsholm is the trail leading to Eagle Falls.

The trail begins under towering firs and incense cedars. The trees change to mountain alder and quaking aspen as you enter the moister environment by Eagle Creek. The staired trail rises gently beside the sparkling creek. Wood plank bridges aid your ascent. Bracken ferns and flowers flank the lush trail. In spring and early summer, look for the unusual leafless red snow plant near the creek. This trail is especially colorful in the fall, for it passes a variety of deciduous trees, including alder, quaking aspen, and Sierra maple.

Arrive at Eagle Falls after only 0.2 mile. In spring and early summer, Eagle Falls is a roaring three-tiered cascade, well worth the short walk. A clearing at the trail's end makes a perfect spot for a picnic.

29 UPPER EAGLE FALLS

Difficulty: easy
Distance: 0.5 mile one way
Usage: high
Starting elevation: 6500 feet
Elevation gain: 160 feet
Season: spring, summer, fall
Map: USGS Emerald Bay

If you're short on time or energy, this very easy hike to a scenic overlook is rich despite its brevity. Pass over roaring Eagle Creek, then climb to a granite bench with fabulous views of Lake Tahoe and Emerald Bay. This is an excellent hike to introduce youngsters to the dramatic work of glaciers.

To reach the trailhead from Tahoe City, take Highway 89 south 18.6 miles to the Eagle Falls Picnic Area. Eagle Falls Picnic Area is 0.1 mile south of the large parking lot above Emerald Bay on the east side of Highway 89. Turn right and park in the lot at the end of the road. Approaching from the south, drive 8.9 miles north on Highway 89 from the junction of Highways 50 and 89 in South Lake Tahoe. The picnic area is approximately 1 mile north of the Bayview Campground on Highway 89. Obtain a wilderness permit at the Eagle Falls–Emerald Bay Trailhead at the west end of the lot. Be sure to lock your car and conceal valuables in your trunk prior to arrival at the trailhead. There have been numerous vehicle break-ins.

The well-worn Emerald Bay–Eagle Falls trail begins gently. This trail leads to popular Eagle Lake (Trip 30) and the beautiful Velma Lakes (Trip 33). Because

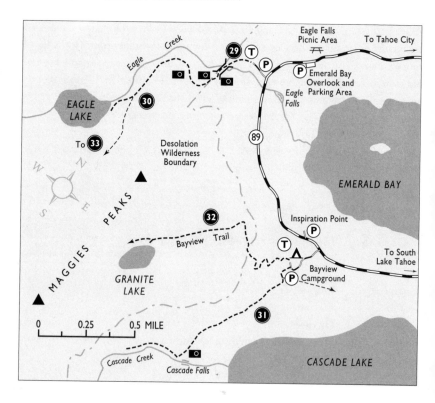

of its popularity, this portion of the trail is often littered. Bring extra litter bags and initiate a trail pickup game for your youngsters. (Don't forget the rewards!)

Head west through quaking aspen and wildflowers. The wealth of aspen and Sierra maple makes this trail a wonderful fall hike. Pass a steep cliff on your right and rise on granite steps. Youngsters may need a helping hand. In very little time, arrive at a substantial steel bridge over Eagle Creek. Early in the season, Eagle Creek tumbles down the rocky bed in white torrents. The creek feeds the very impressive and beautiful Eagle Falls, which can be seen from above (across the highway from the Eagle Falls Picnic Area) or from below (Trip 28). A leaf or twig dropped from the bridge will float rapidly away, eventually reaching Lake Tahoe.

On the opposite side of Eagle Creek, the trail rises more steeply. At a point where the rocky path turns slightly to the left, a granite bench is visible to the right. Leave the trail, and go to the bench. You'll soon discover a fabulous view northeast to Emerald Bay and Lake Tahoe, and beyond to the Carson Range on the lake's east side.

A second bench is found on the trail about 0.2 mile above this spot. To reach the higher bench, return to the trail. After rising 120 feet, the trail turns west, traversing the granite. The views are better from this bench, but the spot attracts more people because it is on the trail. On either bench, you stand on the edge of Desolation Wilderness, named for its large expanses of exposed granite and wind-swept peaks. Three million years ago, glaciers began to transform the mountains lying west and south of Lake Tahoe. Two million years ago, the largest glaciers, rising almost 1000 feet from lake level, flowed down this canyon, scouring the rock on which you stand. Although Lake Tahoe was never filled by glaciers, immense icy tongues extended into the lake from its western and southwestern shores, filling Emerald Bay.

The last glaciers retreated 10,000 years ago, but their work can still be clearly seen. Glaciers pushed rock and soil to the side as they advanced, then left these mounds in place when they melted. These mounds of debris, called moraines, are the rocky hills that flank Emerald Bay. The bay's picturesque little Fannette Island is a pile of rock left by a glacier. Since Desolation Wilderness is made up largely of granitic, erosion-resistant rock, the sculpting accomplished by the glaciers remains largely unchanged. Large boulders quarried by glaciers were carried from their source, then left by the glaciers in odd positions. These errant boulders, called glacial erratics, can be seen on the scenic bench and throughout Desolation Wilderness.

Bridge over Eagle Creek

The vegetation of Desolation Wilderness is also dramatic. It bursts onto the scene in robust triumph against the wind and rock. In the crevices of the bench, where small amounts of soil accumulate, deep pink mountain pride grows profusely. Despite the scanty soil, trees also grow on the bench. Twisted pines, firs, and junipers grow seemingly straight out of bedrock, gnarled and stunted from the barrages of wind and snow.

Picnic at this fine viewpoint. Choose this trail for a sunrise hike, so you can breakfast at dawn as you watch the sun rise over the Carson Range and Emerald Bay. At any time, it is a wonderful introduction to the dramatic glaciated scenery of the Desolation Wilderness.

30   EAGLE LAKE

Difficulty: easy
Distance: 1 mile one way
Usage: high
Starting elevation: 6500 feet
Elevation gain: 460 feet
Season: spring, summer, fall
Map: USGS Emerald Bay
See Trip 29 for map.

Eagle Lake is a good hike for destination-oriented hikers. The trail is short (though steep), has great views, and arrives quickly at a lake that is fine for picnicking and fishing. Eagle Lake draws crowds, however, so it's best to save this hike for fall or midweek.

To reach the trailhead from Tahoe City, take Highway 89 south 18.6 miles to the Eagle Falls Picnic Area, 0.1 mile south of the large parking lot above Emerald Bay on the east side of Highway 89. Turn right and park in the lot at the end of the road. Approaching from the south, drive 8.9 miles north on Highway 89 from the junction of Highways 50 and 89 in South Lake Tahoe. The picnic area is approximately 1 mile north of the Bayview Campground on Highway 89. Obtain a wilderness permit at the Eagle Falls–Emerald Bay Trailhead at the west end of the lot. Be sure to lock your car and conceal valuables in your trunk prior to arrival at the trailhead. There have been numerous vehicle break-ins.

Walk the Upper Eagle Falls Trail (Trip 29) to the second granite bench. Following cairns, head west across the bench, regaining the trail as it turns south

Eagle Lake

and enters a stand of lodgepole pine. The stand has many dead trees. With the trees stripped of their bark, the origin of the lodgepole pine's name becomes clear. Their tall, straight trunks were used by Indians as supporting poles in their lodges. The lodgepole pine is easily recognized because it is the only two-needled pine in Desolation Wilderness.

Before leaving the flat, look closely at the dead, barkless trees. On the exposed wood, observe the wriggly paths bored by bark beetles. The Tahoe Basin is experiencing an epidemic infestation of bark beetles, which feed and reproduce in the inner bark (cambium) of pine and fir trees, between the outer bark and the wood of the tree. The tunnels bored by beetles and their larvae kill a tree by girdling it, thereby choking the tree to death. Large numbers of dead trees, displaying telltale orange-brown needles, can be seen along the roadways and in the backcountry.

The dead and dying lodgepoles are a boon to wildlife. Hairy woodpeckers pry off the bark and feast on juicy beetle larvae. Snags provide hunting perches for hawks and homes for squirrels, owls, woodpeckers, and mountain chickadees. Decomposing fallen trees shelter small animals such as voles, salamanders, toads, and snakes.

As you pass through the pines, listen for the scolding of the Sierra chickaree. This tree-dwelling squirrel enjoys the seeds from the lodgepole cones. In late summer and fall, chickarees bury large numbers of pine cones in one location. When snow blankets the forest, the chickarees have to uncover only one cache, unlike gray squirrels, which bury nuts singly. If you can locate the source of the chatter, you'll see a medium-size, handsome squirrel with a whitish belly whose distinctive, furry tail is trimmed in grayish white.

Continue around a headwall whose cracks are bursting from June through August with pink mountain pride. Then start through a stand of mature Jeffrey pine and incense cedar. The shaggy cinnamon bark of the majestic incense cedar contrasts pleasingly with its rich green foliage. Children may recognize that the cedar supplies the wood for most pencils. For thousands of years before the arrival of white settlers, Washo Indians used the bark of the cedar to build their homes in the Tahoe Basin.

Let youngsters also discover the secrets of the beautiful Jeffrey pine. Notice the long, graceful needles (up to 10 inches) that resemble the tuft of a lion's tail and the huge football-shaped cones. Best of all, the bark smells like vanilla! On warm summer days it smells as if cookies are baking within the tree.

The trail turns south and soon arrives at an overlook above Eagle Creek, the outlet for Eagle Lake. The trail then climbs through a wide variety of shrubs and flowers. At 0.6 mile, enter a lovely, shady forest of white pine, lodgepole fir and pine. The trail moderates as it runs roughly parallel to Eagle Creek. Pine needles carpet the forest floor, and granite boulders provide places for a shady rest stop.

After this relaxing stretch of trail, resume your ascent on a rocky path. Above to the east, the jagged cliffs of the west side of Maggies Peaks (8688 feet) loom impressively. Below are the noisy cascades of Eagle Creek.

Arrive at a fork in the trail at 0.9 mile. The trail to the Velma Lakes continues to rise on the left (Trip 33). Take the right-hand fork, which descends briefly to Eagle Lake.

Arrive at the lake's northeastern end. Granite cliffs surround the small lake on three sides. Picnic on the lake's rocky shore, wade in its clear water, or try for brook and rainbow trout. If you've avoided the crowds that flock to this lake, you'll be well rewarded with the lovely setting.

31 CASCADE FALLS

Difficulty: easy
Distance: 0.7 mile one way
Usage: high
Starting elevation: 6800 feet
Elevation gain: 80 feet
Season: spring, summer, fall
Map: USGS Emerald Bay
See Trip 29 for map.

The short hike to Cascade Falls is bursting with views and flowers. Best of all, it ends with a marvelously dramatic waterfall. The trail traverses a steep, open slope high above Cascade Lake. Because parts of the trail are exceedingly narrow and the slope near the falls is very steep, children must be watched very carefully.

From Highway 89, enter the Bayview Campground, located 1 mile south of the Eagle Falls–Emerald Bay Trailhead (see Trip 28). Drive past the campground to the upper parking area. If this lot is full, there is additional parking across Highway 89 at Inspiration Point.

At the trailhead, take the left-hand fork; the one to the right leads to Granite Lake (Trip 32). Shortly after, the trail divides again. Stay right. Hike the smooth, sandy trail pine, to a third fork at 0.2 mile, where you bear left to climb a rocky knoll.

Atop the crest, lovely views appear. The graceful, tiered Cascade Falls are visible to the south. Below lies Cascade Lake, large and deep blue and surrounded by high forested moraines. Like Emerald Bay, Cascade Lake was carved by glaciers that scooped out the lake's basin as they moved northeast. Glacial debris forms the high slopes around it.

Cascade Lake was once a favorite summer camping site for the Washo Indians. Prior to white settlement, the Washo occupied a territory in which Lake Tahoe was the spiritual and nearly geographic center. The Washo annually migrated to the Tahoe Basin each spring from their winter homes east of the Sierra. The purpose of the spring migration was to partake of the bountiful fishing and to renew contact with the rest of the tribe. The tribe congregated in large communal camps at the shore of Lake Tahoe to capture spawning trout from its streams and celebrate reunification. After the spawning runs were over, the tribe split into smaller family groups and left Lake Tahoe's shores to set up camps at higher mountain lakes.

Cascade Lake was known to the Washo as "Wa-su-sha-te," translated as "good fishing lake." The lake is said to be the site of a fierce territorial battle between the Washo and the Paiutes, a neighboring tribe to the west. Numerous arrowheads were found here in the 1800s.

Cascade Lake gets its present-day name from the falls that tumble from granite terraces at its southwestern end. The falls were formerly known as White Cloud Falls, named for the billowing mist created by the water falling 100 feet down the granite steps. Spring runoff creates gorgeous showy cascades, the magic of which can be glimpsed as one is negotiating the hairpin curves of Highway 89 south of Emerald Bay.

Traverse the brushy slope on the narrow trail. In early summer, the manzanita lining the trail is generously adorned with tiny white bells. Watch for brightly striped chipmunks; the tiny rodents are especially fond of the fruits of this shrub. In spring, hungry chipmunks fill their stomachs with the fragrant bells. In fall, they stuff their cheek pouches with large quantities of seeds to stow underground for winter. The chipmunks' forgotten seeds will become new manzanita plants come springtime. Another fan of the flowers is the black bear. Due to the bear's decline in this area, however, chipmunks today have little competition.

Other trailside flowers are also abundant. In the summer, plentiful broadleaf lupines cover the slopes with delicate purple blossoms. From June through July, the trumpet-shaped blossoms of bright pink mountain pride burst from rock crevices. This lovely flower grows throughout the Tahoe Sierra, from lake level to 10,000 feet.

Next, the trail descends gently. Pines and firs are widely spaced, framing but not obscuring the views. At 0.5 mile from the trailhead, the trail begins to climb again gently. Just before the falls, ascend a series of granite slabs. Keep a close watch on children.

The trail disappears on a granite slope. Continue south, following the roar of the falls, and arrive at the edge of Cascade Creek. This expanse of granite, beside the creek and above the lake, makes a great picnic spot.

Cascade Falls are below you, so to get a truly inspiring view, carefully descend alongside the falls. For intrepid and surefooted climbers, the view of the powerful early-summer cascade is awesome. The water falls in swift, sinuous rivulets to Cascade Lake, where it erupts in a cloud of mist. Do not bring children too close to the falls. The footing is too difficult.

For a safer walk with better footing, head west, upriver from the falls, along Cascade Creek to its tumbling rapids. Walk farther west to find deep emerald pools and flat granite perfect for picnicking.

Most of Cascade Lake is privately owned, but fortunately it has not been extensively developed. Vacation homes dot the northeastern shore. The southwest shore and falls are owned by the Forest Service.

The admirers of this lovely scene are many. As a college student, John Steinbeck once summered at the lake. Mark Twain and John Muir also stayed on its shore. On July 1, 1888, Muir wrote about his trip to Cascade Lake: "Snowy mountains and a fall and a grand glacier basin, and well-timbered lateral moraines, make a fine setting for Cascade Lake. I saw a duck with her young sailing and running on the lake, a fine, wild, happy sight." Cascade Lake is indeed still a fine, wild, and happy place.

32 GRANITE LAKE 🦆

Difficulty: moderate
Distance: 1.1 miles one way
Usage: high
Starting elevation: 6800 feet
Elevation gain: 880 feet
Season: summer, fall
Map: USGS Emerald Bay
See Trip 29 for map.

It is a tough climb to modest Granite Lake, but there are good views and plentiful flowers along the way. Granite Lake boasts large boulders at its shore for picnicking, relatively warm water for swimming, and some brook trout for anglers.

To reach the campground from Tahoe City, take Highway 89 south 19.6 miles

to the Bayview Campground, which is 1 mile south of the Emerald Bay–Eagle Falls Trailhead (see Trip 29). Approaching from the south, drive 7.9 miles north on Highway 89 from the junction of Highways 50 and 89 in South Lake Tahoe. Drive past the campground to the upper parking area, where there is parking for hikers. If this lot is full, there is additional parking across Highway 89 at Inspiration Point. Obtain a wilderness permit at the trailhead.

At the trailhead, the trail forks immediately. The left fork arrives at lovely Cascade Falls in 0.7 mile (Trip 31). Take the right fork (the Bayview Trail), which climbs steadily through a forest of white fir. Bordering the trail is a thick undergrowth of chinquapin and manzanita. Ground-nesting birds, such as blue grouse, fox sparrows, and colorful finches, take shelter under these shrubs. The birds feed on the fruit of the manzanita and the nutlike burrs of the chinquapin. Look closely at the branches of the manzanita. It is rumored that a $100 reward was once offered for a 12-inch-long straight section. It is a good bet that no one ever collected.

At 0.5 mile from the trailhead, enter Desolation Wilderness and cross a small stream. The forest becomes less dense, the granite boulders more numerous, and delightful vistas abound. The handsome boulders are glacial erratics, stones ripped from their source by an advancing glacier two million years ago. The boulders were left here when the glacier melted. Erratics weighing thousands of pounds are scattered throughout Desolation Wilderness. Take advantage of the boulders for a prime perch to catch your breath and take inventory of the impressive scenery. To the east, directly below, is Cascade Lake; to the north is Emerald Bay and Fannette Island; and to the southwest is Fallen Leaf Lake.

Continue rising through a sun-dappled, granite-studded landscape. At 0.9 mile, enter the shade of red firs and travel alongside the lake's outlet creek. Look for the grandiose California corn lilies that grow in the moist soil along the stream bank. The showy white flowers grow on stalks 3 to 6 feet tall. Although the leaves and stem of the corn lily resemble an edible corn plant, young corn lilies are poisonous. When mature, however, the lily is no longer toxic and parts of the plant are used in the manufacture of medicines to slow the heart and lower blood pressure. Take a whiff of the plant; it is commonly called "skunk cabbage" because of its strong aroma.

The trail levels as it heads south, traveling along the alder-lined creek. Alder grow in impenetrable thickets on the banks of streams and in moist gullies. The dense thickets provide excellent habitat for small mammals and birds. Deep within the alder thickets are scores of shrews. The Sierra support at least six species of shrew, the world's smallest mammal. You are unlikely to see these tiny, beady-eyed insectivores, but they are surely darting along hidden paths under logs and

Glacial erratic

leaves within the thicket. The shrews follow their long pointed noses to hunt spiders, termites, and earthworms. Crouch down and listen for their high-pitched squeaks.

As you walk beside the creek, note the contrasting environments on either side of the trail. On the left, the creek and saturated soil support an abundance of lush greenery, including bracken fern, thimbleberry, and willow. To the right the slope is drier, rockier, and more sparsely vegetated, supporting very different plant life.

The trail climbs again briefly, then the first view of Granite Lake appears to the left. A spur trail on the left descends steeply down to the lakeshore. High moraine walls surround the lake, giving it a pleasant sense of isolation despite its proximity to the trailhead. The shoreline provides a lot of areas to explore. Hike around to the east side of the lake to view North and South Maggies peaks (8499 feet and 8699 feet, respectively) rising to the west, 1000 feet above the lake. In late summer, this lake is a good place for a refreshing swim, since the water may warm to 70 degrees, toasty for a lake within Desolation Wilderness. Due to its popularity and proximity to the trailhead, the lake is not recommended for camping.

33 VELMA LAKES

Difficulty: strenuous
Distance: 4.5 miles to Upper Velma Lake
Usage: moderate
Starting elevation: 6500 feet
Elevation gain: 1650 feet
Season: summer, fall
Map: USGS Emerald Bay and Rockbound Valley

The hike to the Velma Lakes reaches some of the most outstanding scenery accessible on a day hike in the Tahoe Basin. The lakes are set high in Desolation Wilderness, and it is hard work to visit them. The rewards are rich, nevertheless. The trip encompasses fabulous views and three beautiful lakes set in a stark and breathtakingly desolate setting. This strenuous hike is recommended only for those youngsters who enjoy a long, difficult trail.

From Tahoe City, take Highway 89 south 18.6 miles to the Eagle Falls Picnic Area, 0.1 mile south of the large parking lot above Emerald Bay on the east side

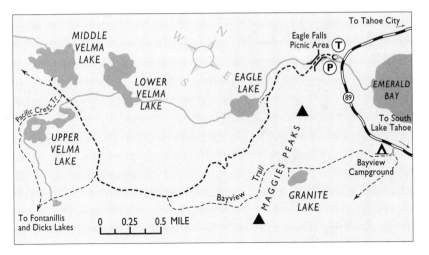

of Highway 89. Turn right and park in the lot at the end of the road. Approaching from the south, drive 8.9 miles north on Highway 89 from the junction of Highways 50 and 89 in South Lake Tahoe. Beginning at the Emerald Bay–Eagle Falls Trailhead, hike to the fork leading to the Velma Lakes, 0.1 mile before reaching Eagle Lake, as described in Trip 30. Take the left fork.

The trail to the Velmas rises steeply after leaving the Eagle Lake Trail. Climbing the steep, rocky trail, watch for excellent views of Eagle Lake below you. The path is bordered by manzanita, a shrub that thrives in poor, dry, and rocky soil. Manzanita sports distinctive pink or white flowers that are shaped like tiny bells. Later in the season, manzanita bears fruit that looks like miniature apples. In fact, in Spanish manzanita means "little apple."

Hike under a sheer granite wall that is the west side of North Maggies Peak. Briefly enter the shade of pines and firs, crossing a small creek, 1.3 miles from the trailhead. Then ascend steeply once again, following switchbacks up a shady slope. Climb steeply for 0.3 mile, then emerge from the trees onto a granite slab. Follow ducks (cairns) to the top of the slab and enjoy a fabulous view. Then again enter a stand of lodgepole pine for an almost level walk. Appreciate this short, shady respite, for the ascent begins shortly thereafter.

Easy hiking ends as the trail turns south to climb a steep slope at 2.1 miles. Reach a granite bench between North and South Maggies Peaks. Celebrate your ascent and enjoy spectacular views from this saddle.

The trail is pleasant as it leaves the saddle to traverse the west side of South Maggies Peak, heading south. Enjoy the abundant, beautiful red heather that brightens open rocky areas of Desolation Wilderness. The dainty, cup-shaped flowers have prominent stamens and needle-like leaves. Enjoy also the views to the

Sculptural Sierra juniper

stark and formidable valley below.

After 2.5 miles, resume your climb. Ascend 0.3 mile to reach a junction with the Bayview Trail. Stay right for Velma Lakes, heading west. At this point, the climbing is almost over. Rejoice while hiking through lovely Jeffrey pines and manzanita. Travel in and out of trees, up a granite slab following ducks, and then through trees again. At 0.8 mile past the junction with the Bayview Trail, reach a second junction. Stay right and head north.

Enter an enchanting area where the almost level trail courses through the dry, rocky landscape. Widely spaced pines create magnificent silhouettes against the blue sky. In early summer, look for dainty, pastel phlox clinging to rocks beside the trail. Pass a small pond on the right. Look to the northeast for a view of large Middle Velma Lake, the most scenic of the Velma Lakes.

From this viewpoint, begin the descent to Middle Velma. Pass an unnamed lake on your left, then ford its outlet stream. At a trail junction shortly after the stream, bear right. The trail to the left heads south and climbs 0.3 mile to Upper Velma Lake. After another 0.2 mile, the trail arrives at a junction with the Pacific Crest Trail. Again stay right and continue heading west. A turn south on the PCT would take you to Fontanillis Lake, 1 mile from the junction. Travel just 0.2 mile from the PCT junction, then descend cross-country to the shore of lovely Middle Velma Lake.

Middle Velma offers excellent swimming. Good swimmers play on its scenic rock islands. Anglers try for rainbow trout in its clear waters. Those with energy to spare can explore Upper Velma or Fontanillis Lakes. Most hikers simply relax and picnic at Middle Velma's lovely, shady shore.

Right: *Tamarack Lake*

CHAPTER 4

THE SOUTH LAKE TAHOE BASIN

The South Lake Tahoe Basin offers superb hiking and biking. The glacier-molded landscape includes lands rich in subalpine lakes and sculptured granite peaks. The south shore is also endowed with beautiful sandy beaches. This natural wealth, as well as the proximity of casinos and accommodations, brings crowds to the south basin. Hike early in the morning, midweek, or off-season for a measure of solitude.

The trips described cover the area south and east of Emerald Bay to the lands north of Highways 50 and 89 and south of Highway 207. A portion of Desolation Wilderness is included. For routes entering Desolation Wilderness (Trips 37, 39, 40, 47, 48, and 50), obtain self-issuing hiking permits at the trailheads. If you plan to camp in Desolation Wilderness, you must obtain a permit from the National Forest Service (see "Desolation Wilderness" in Chapter 1.).

Hikers with young children are encouraged to try the nature trails of the Lake Tahoe Visitor Center (Trip 34), the Angora Lakes Trail (Trip 38), the Mount Tallac Trail to Fallen Leaf Overlook (Trip 36), Benwood Meadow (Trip 46), Big Meadow (Trip 41), and Lower Horsetail Falls (Trip 50). Wheelchairs and strollers are manageable on the visitor center trails (Trip 34) and on the South Lake Tahoe Bike Path (Trip 35).

For those seeking a challenge (as well as a refreshing swim), try Grass, Gilmore, Round, Dardanelles, Tamarack, Ralston and Cagwin Lakes, and Lake of the Woods on Trips 39, 40, 42, 43, 48, and 49, respectively. For superb views and a real challenge, hike to the summit of Echo Peak or Mount Tallac (Trips 47 and 37). Excellent views also abound on the Tahoe Rim Trail (Trip 51).

Lastly, the South Lake Tahoe Bike Path (Trip 35) is perfect for biking with children. The bike path also offers easy access to the nature trails of Trip 34 and the sandy south-shore beaches.

34 LAKE TAHOE VISITOR CENTER NATURE TRAILS

Difficulty: easy, handicapped accessible with assistance
Distance: Smokey's Trail: 0.15-mile loop; Forest Tree Trail: 0.25-mile loop; Rainbow Trail: 0.5-mile loop; Trail of the Washo: 0.75-mile loop; Lake of the Sky Trail: 0.4 mile one way; Tallac Historic Site: 1 mile one way
Usage: high
Starting elevation: 6235 feet
Elevation gain: none
Season: spring, summer, fall
Map: USGS Emerald Bay

On the beautiful grounds of the Lake Tahoe Visitor Center on the shore of Lake Tahoe, the National Forest Service has built several very easy and informative trails that are perfect for children. Come to the center at the beginning of your visit for a fun and invaluable introduction to the history and natural history of the basin. As well as providing five self-guided trails, the visitor center hosts numerous guided walks and programs. From junior ranger programs to marsh walks to visits from Smokey Bear, there is something at the visitor center for every member of the family. These trails are also good choices for early- or late-season hiking, when snow covers trails at higher elevations.

The Lake Tahoe Visitor Center is located on Highway 89, 3.1 miles west of the intersection of Highways 89 and 50 in South Lake Tahoe. For information about naturalist-led activities and evening programs at the center, and hours of operation, call (530) 573-2674.

The trails described below can be combined to create longer hikes. Visitors may also include adjacent Kiva or Baldwin Beach in their plans. Cyclists should note that bikes are not permitted on the nature trails. The center provides bike racks for those visiting via the South Lake Tahoe Bike Path (Trip 35).

Smokey's Trail: 0.15-mile loop. This very brief trail demonstrates safe campfire building. The presentation is direct and effective. Children who complete this trail (and remember its lessons) receive a small award from visitor center rangers. Find this trail just south of the visitor center.

Forest Tree Trail: 0.25-mile loop. This short trail takes visitors through a fragrant Jeffrey pine forest. Signs describe the life cycle of the pine. The trail is an

Smokey Bear teaches children about fire safety at the Lake Tahoe Visitor Center.

enjoyable introduction to one of the most plentiful, and beautiful, of Lake Tahoe's trees. Children should take this trail, if only to learn of the marvelous vanilla scent of the Jeffrey pine. From the visitor center, walk a few yards north on the paved trail, then when the trail forks, head east (right) to find the Forest Tree Trail loop.

Rainbow Trail and Stream Profile Chamber: 0.5-mile loop. The paved trail passes from Jeffrey pine forest to a lovely grassy meadow. Signs describe natural features of the area. In 0.25 mile from the visitor center, hikers enter the Stream Profile Chamber, a partially submerged interpretive building on Taylor Creek. Through windows in the chamber, visitors watch numerous varieties of trout, kokanee salmon, and other aquatic life. Rangers feed the fish daily during a brief interpretive lecture. The unique Stream Profile Chamber is a must for families.

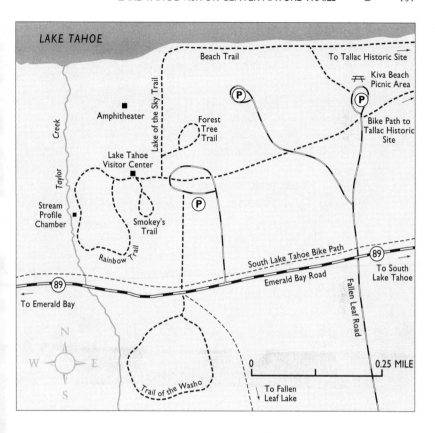

In the fall, check for special events at Taylor Creek and walk the Rainbow Trail to view colorful foliage.

Trail of the Washo: 0.75-mile loop. Learn about the Native Americans who lived in the Tahoe Basin for thousands of years before the arrival of white settlers. Signs along the trail describe the life of the Washo. Pick up the trail at the southwestern end of the visitor center parking lot. Walk south, cross Highway 89, and follow the loop trail southwest to Taylor Creek through a forest of fir and pine. Those interested in the ways of the Washo should also visit the Tallac Historical Site (see below) to view artifacts and enter replicas of Indian dwellings.

Lake of the Sky Trail: 0.4 mile one way. This smooth, mostly unpaved path courses past expansive meadows to the shore of Lake Tahoe. Along the way, read eloquent commentary about Lake Tahoe from Mark Twain and naturalist John Muir. The trail begins east of the visitor center and travels directly north to the lake. At Lake Tahoe's shore, visit the tranquil beach or continue to hike east toward the Kiva Picnic Area and the historic Tallac Site. Take a very interesting loop hike of approximately 2 miles via the Lake of the Sky Trail to the shore of Lake Tahoe, then head east on the Beach Trail to the Tallac Site, and return by the trail that travels southwest through open pine forest from the Kiva Beach Picnic Area back to the visitor center.

Tallac Historic Site Trail: 1 mile one way. From the visitor center, walk east on a level path 0.3 mile to the Kiva Beach Picnic Area, then continue strolling east to reach the historic remains of Lake Tahoe's turn-of-the-century estates. Visit Lucky Baldwin's Tallac House, gambling casino, and Tallac Hotel. Tour the grounds of lovely summer homes and take a scheduled indoor tour of the elegant Pope Estate. In addition, families shouldn't miss the Washo exhibit housed in the Baldwin-McGonagle House. The grounds of the historic site are beautiful and include a lovely arboretum as well as a gorgeous beach. Cultural events are frequently held here during the summer. Call (530) 541-5227 for information regarding events. To make reservations for a Pope House tour, call (530) 573-2674.

35 SOUTH LAKE TAHOE BIKE PATH

> **Difficulty:** easy, handicapped accessible with assistance
> **Distance:** 3.4 miles one way
> **Usage:** high
> **Starting elevation:** 6240 feet
> **Elevation gain:** none
> **Season:** spring, summer, fall
> **Map:** USGS Emerald Bay

The South Lake Tahoe Bike Path offers excellent riding for young families. Superb scenery, beautiful beaches, historic sites, and hiking trails can all be found on the effortless 3.4-mile trail. Ride through stands of aspen, beside green meadows, over wooden bridges, and on sandy paths beside the lake. Just be prepared to share these immensely popular trails.

The bike path parallels Highway 89 (Emerald Bay Road) along the south shore of Lake Tahoe. The western end of the trail is 0.8 mile west of Baldwin Beach Road and its eastern end is approximately 1.5 miles north of the intersection of Highways 89 and 50 in South Lake Tahoe. Those renting bikes can find convenient concessions along Highway 89 at the eastern end of the bike path or at Camp Richardson, approximately 1.8 miles west of the beginning of the trail. Free parking is available at the Lake Tahoe Visitor Center and the Tallac Historic Site. Since most cyclists ride east to west, the trail description is written accordingly. Note that there are many spur trails that cyclists may wish to explore. The best strategy is to meander leisurely through the area. It is nearly impossible to get lost since all trails intersect main roads that lead back to Highway 89.

From the trail's east end, ride northwest through a forest of pine and fir for approximately 1.5 miles to the trail's intersection with the road to Pope Beach. Pope Beach is a long sandy beach, superb for swimming and strolling.

Continuing west, pass Camp Richardson after another 0.3 mile. At the Camp Richardson Marina there is access to another sandy beach (usually very crowded). If you're ready to abandon your wheels for a while, rent a family-friendly kayak here. Across Highway 89, stables offer pony rides and guided tours. Also across the highway, a rental concession rents bicycles for the whole family. The flat, paved bike trail is perfect for cycling.

Continuing another 0.5 mile west from Camp Richardson, arrive at Kiva Beach

A surrey ride on the South Lake Tahoe Bike Path

Road. Kiva Beach is yet another long sandy beach, with many fine spots for swimming and picnicking. Due to the drought, the lake is very shallow for quite a distance from shore. At the Kiva Beach Picnic Area, eat at tables under magnificent 200-year-old pines. From the picnic area, cyclists can access trails to the fascinating and beautiful Tallac Historic Site (Trip 34) as well as ride along the lake behind the historic buildings.

The Lake Tahoe Visitor Center is only 0.1 mile east of the Kiva Beach Picnic Area. A wealth of gentle nature trails radiates from the center (Trip 34). Bicycles are prohibited on the nature trails, so please watch the signs. A bike rack is provided at the visitor center.

Continuing west on the bike path from Kiva Beach Road, riders reach Baldwin Beach Road after 0.7 mile. A short ride to the lake at Baldwin Beach brings cyclists to a quiet, exquisite beach with soft sand, clear water, and green-gold meadows. Dark, dramatic Mount Tallac lurks to the southwest, high above sunbathers. Baldwin

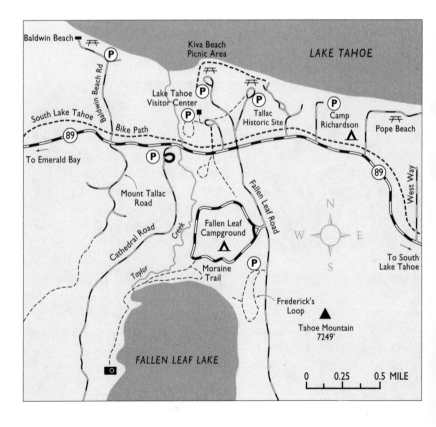

Beach offers perhaps the nicest stretch of beach on the south shore. After visiting the beach, cyclists can ride 0.7 mile farther west on a quiet and shady stretch of trail to its end.

All cyclists on the South Shore bike paths must exercise extra caution due to the congested trails. Many young and unsteady riders use these trails, so go slowly. In addition, the trails course through fragile meadows, so it is essential that riders stay on the trails. Meadows are easily damaged by tire tracks of careless cyclists; they filter the water flowing into Lake Tahoe and remove impurities, so their health is essential to the health of the lake.

36 MOUNT TALLAC TRAIL TO FALLEN LEAF LAKE OVERLOOK

Difficulty: easy
Distance: 1.2 miles one way
Usage: moderate
Starting elevation: 6440 feet
Elevation gain: 480 feet
Season: spring, summer, fall
Map: USGS Emerald Bay

Hikers need not climb all the way to the summit of Mount Tallac for breathtaking views. This trail climbs moderately to the crest of a forested moraine above Fallen Leaf Lake. Once atop the moraine, hikers have a splendid and effortless 0.5-mile crest walk with fabulous views of two beautiful lakes as well as prime vistas of the two most impressive mountains in the basin.

From the Lake Tahoe Visitor Center, drive 0.7 mile west on Highway 89 to an intersection where a road leads north to Baldwin Beach and a road heads south for the Mount Tallac Trail and Camp Concord. This intersection is approximately 4 miles south of Emerald Bay. Turn left (south) for Mount Tallac and drive about 0.3 mile to a junction and take a second left. Drive another 0.1 mile to another fork; this time keep right and drive 0.5 mile to a parking lot at the Mount Tallac Trailhead. Obtain a wilderness permit at the trailhead.

The trail begins on a gravel road heading south. After 100 yards, turn right at a junction and head briefly west, aiming straight for the impressive, dark hulk of Mount Tallac. Pass an old gravel pit, then follow the trail as it turns south again. The rocky path travels through Jeffrey pines with a fragrant understory of sagebrush.

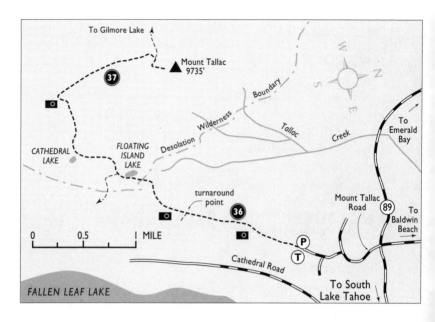

Commence a moderate ascent on a dusty trail to reach the ridge of the massive lateral moraine that borders Fallen Leaf Lake. The moraine was created by a glacier, perhaps more than 1500 feet thick, that moved north toward Lake Tahoe about 15,000 years ago. On its downward course, the glacier pushed stones and soil aside, creating huge piles of rubble on either side. The glacier never quite made it to Lake Tahoe, but the basin that it dug became Fallen Leaf Lake. In a similar fashion, another glacier to the north created Cascade Lake. In the case of Emerald Bay, an enormous glacier pushed its icy tongue all the way to Lake Tahoe. Its lateral moraines are now the steep forested slopes that flank the deep green bay.

As an alternative to geologic history, children might enjoy the Washo legend regarding the origin of Fallen Leaf Lake. According to the legend, the Evil One was in pursuit of an Indian brave. To protect the Indian, the Good One gave the Indian a magic branch. Leaves from the branch had the power to create lakes so that the Evil One would not catch the young Indian. But when the Evil One pursued the Indian across the eastern mountains, the Evil One closed in upon the poor brave. The Indian panicked and dropped the whole branch, except one leaf. From the branch, Lake Tahoe was formed and the Indian made a temporary escape. On Lake Tahoe's south shore, however, the Evil One again gained on the Indian. So the Indian dropped his last leaf, forming Fallen Leaf Lake. With this

Mount Tallac

obstacle in place, the Indian crossed safely into the Sacramento Valley.

Once upon the crest, the trail continues for an easy 0.5 mile until it leaves the moraine to head west, resuming its ascent of Mount Tallac (Trip 37). The 0.5 mile it spends on the moraine above Fallen Leaf Lake is one of the prettiest stretches of trail in the Tahoe Basin. Lovely, long-needled Jeffrey pines and white firs frame but don't obscure the views. To the east is Fallen Leaf Lake, with majestic Freel Peak (10,881 feet) prominent on the horizon above it. To the north is the great blue expanse of Lake Tahoe, and immediately to the west is, of course, the impressive southeast face of Mount Tallac.

Mount Tallac rises more than 2500 vertical feet from the crest of the moraine. Its summit was one of the few points of land that was not engulfed by the sea of glacial ice. Mount Tallac appears particularly sober and forbidding due to the dark composition of its steep rock face. Depressions on its northeast slope usually hold snow throughout the summer in the shape of a cross.

Walk to a rocky outcropping just south of where the trail leaves the moraine. Boulders there supply seats for a picnic. For solitude and maximum drama, try a sunrise breakfast atop the moraine.

37 MOUNT TALLAC SUMMIT

Difficulty: strenuous
Distance: 4.6 mile one way
Usage: moderate
Starting elevation: 6440 feet
Elevation gain: 3295 feet
Season: summer, fall
Map: USGS Emerald Bay
See Trip 36 for map.

The hike to the summit of Mount Tallac is infinitely rewarding but difficult. The very steep and rocky route can wear out the best young hikers. Nevertheless, the dark, dramatic summit with its unparalleled views certainly warrants an attempt. Two interesting lakes and plenty of great views along the way make any portion of this trail worth hiking. Bring plenty of water, warm clothes, and sunblock, for the majority of the hike is on exposed slopes.

From the Lake Tahoe Visitor Center, drive 0.7 mile west on Highway 89 to an intersection where a road leads north to Baldwin Beach and a road heads south for the Mount Tallac Trail and Camp Concord. Turn left (south) for Mount Tallac and drive 0.3 mile to a junction and turn left again. Drive another 0.1 mile to another fork; this time keep right and drive 0.5 mile to a parking lot at the Mount Tallac Trailhead. Obtain a wilderness permit at the trailhead.

Follow Trip 36 to the crest of the moraine. At approximately 1.3 miles, the trail leaves the crest to descend west to a gully. In the early morning, look for mule deer. From the gully, climb another moraine and enter a dark forest of red fir. Ascend south via switchbacks, cross the Desolation Wilderness boundary at 1.7 miles, and arrive at the north end of Floating Island Lake.

In 1890, the year it was named, this lake had a floating island of grass and low shrubs. In the intervening years, mats of grass have broken off from the lake's

Banner trees shaped by wind

shore. Sometimes more than one "island" floats in this small, pine-rimmed lake. Lucky hikers might see a newly formed island, although in recent years the lake has been islandless. Unfortunately, Floating Island Lake has a thriving mosquito population in midsummer, so most hikers are not likely to linger.

The trail skirts around the grassy eastern edge of the lake, follows its flower-lined inlet stream, then heads southwest on a gradual climb. Openings in the forest are occupied by sagebrush and a multitude of wildflowers, including Indian paint-brush and purple lupine. The headwall of Tallac provides a dramatically beautiful backdrop.

To the east, a rocky knoll at 2.3 miles offers excellent views to the east and north. Climb the knoll for the views, then descend to cross Cathedral Creek for more flowers. Soon arrive at a junction with a trail heading east to Fallen Leaf Lake. Stay right, travel south on the main trail, and arrive in 0.1 mile at the rocky basin that holds tiny Cathedral Lake.

The lake's shore is rimmed by barkless lodgepole pine snags. Note their spiral grain. Evolution has determined this spiral growth, for it gives trees more strength. It is especially pronounced in trees on windy sites, such as this one.

The trail becomes decidedly steeper after Cathedral Lake. Ascend beside manzanita, huckleberry oak, and a variety of flowers. Watch for loose rock. Fortunately, the views continue to improve, distracting hikers from the relentless climb.

At 3.3 miles, arrive at a rocky bowl. Hikers may stare in disbelief at the trail visible on the steep east face of the cirque. It travels nearly straight up the talus slope. To complicate matters, snow may remain in the bowl through August. (If snow persists, exercise extreme caution.) Follow the narrow trail up the bowl. At a fork near the rim, take the trail to the left, for it is the safer, more gradual route.

Arrive at the edge of the ridge at 3.5 miles and gain spectacular views to the east, south, and west. Hikers who have made it this far should feel well rewarded. The view of Desolation Wilderness is beautiful beyond words. Look for the Crystal Range's highest peaks, Pyramid (10,003 feet) and Ralston (9240 feet).

Tired hikers are given a short respite on top of the ridge as the trail leads gently northwest through brush-covered terrain. Stands of western white and whitebark pine dot the slopes. The trail soon resumes its steep ascent, and the expansive views improve. In midsummer, flowers are everywhere. Watch for red heather and yellow sulfur flowers.

Soon a spectacular view to the west of Gilmore, Susie, and Aloha Lakes emerges and you arrive at the intersection with the Gilmore Lake Trail (Trip 40) at 4.4 miles. Follow ducks (cairns) to the right and ascend on a rocky path. On mild, sunny days look for the indolent yellow-bellied marmots on the rocks. They look curiously at the exhausted hikers, surprised that any living thing would exert so much effort. The more industrious pikas can be glimpsed running to and fro across the boulders, gathering greenery for their winter stockpiles.

Shortly, reach an exposed ridge and gain views of nearly all of Lake Tahoe and Desolation Wilderness. Continue boulder hopping to the summit at 9735 feet. Lakes are everywhere. The deep blue of the sky and the dazzling blue expanse of Lake Tahoe sandwich the viewer in dizzying bliss. The heavenly 360-degree view defies description. Don't miss it.

38 ANGORA LAKES

Difficulty: easy
Distance: 0.7 mile one way
Usage: high
Starting elevation: 7200 feet
Elevation gain: 260 feet
Season: summer, fall
Map: USGS Echo Lake

The Angora Lakes are delightful. They are accessible, wonderfully scenic, and perfect for swimming and picnicking. Your youngest can walk or bike there. The bad news is they're terribly overused and beginning to show the stress. Busloads of children from local camps are dropped there almost every summer day. If you don't mind sharing a beautiful place and you're willing to treat this fragile area

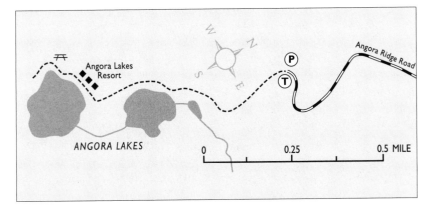

A joyful hiker and little friend

with the utmost care, spend a sunny afternoon at Upper Angora Lake. Your children will certainly be grateful.

From the intersection of Highways 89 and 50 in South Lake Tahoe, drive 3.1 miles west on Highway 89 to Fallen Leaf Road on the south side of the highway. Approaching from the west, find Fallen Leaf Road 0.9 mile after the turnoff for Baldwin Beach on Highway 89. Take Fallen Leaf Road 2 miles to Tahoe Mountain Road. Turn left and continue 0.4 mile to a fork and go right onto Angora Ridge Road. Drive 1.8 miles and pass the Angora fire lookout. Continue on this rugged road another 1.1 miles past the lookout to reach a large parking area at the end of the road. The trail begins on the closed road at the southeast end of the parking area. Remember to leave pets at home; they are prohibited at the upper lake.

Begin on the wide, sandy road. The walk, although initially steep, is sunny, open, and pleasant. Golden-mantled ground squirrels are abundant. These handsomely striped squirrels are often confused with chipmunks, their smaller relatives. They are, however, easily distinguishable by their stripes. A squirrel's stripes do not reach its face, while a chipmunk's stripes extend across its cheeks and through its eyes.

After only 0.4 mile (and an elevation gain of 190 feet), arrive at Lower Angora Lake. The attractive lake has shaded shores and boulders from which to fish for cutthroat trout. Private cabins line the far shore. Lower Angora Lake is the smaller and quieter of the two.

A short 0.2 mile brings you to the north side of Upper Angora Lake and the Angora Lakes Resort, comprising several cabins and a refreshment stand (serving fresh-squeezed lemonade in season). The resort rents small boats for fishing or paddling on the 14-acre lake. The main attraction, nevertheless, is the long sandy beach on the lake's western shore, where families spread out in the sun or picnic in the shade at tables facing the lake. The ridge that rises steeply west and south of the lake reaches 8200 feet, creating a dramatic backdrop. The striking cliffs on the lake's far shore unfortunately provide diving platforms for reckless youths. This author recommends vehemently against jumping from these cliffs. Many serious injuries have been caused by this activity.

Due to the Angora Lakes' intense popularity, take special care to tread gently there. Pack out what you bring, and do not short-cut on the trail. Short-cutting down the slopes will strip them of vegetation and speed erosion.

On your way back down Angora Ridge Road, stop at the Angora fire lookout for fabulous views of Lake Tahoe and Fallen Leaf Lake to the north, Mount Tallac (9735 feet) to the west, and Pyramid Peak (9983 feet) and the Crystal Range on the horizon to the southwest.

39 GRASS LAKE 🖊◀

Difficulty: moderate
Distance: 2.6 miles one way
Usage: high
Starting elevation: 6560 feet
Elevation gain: 680 feet
Season: summer, fall
Map: USGS Emerald Bay and Echo Lake

Grass Lake is a great destination. After the first somewhat disappointing 1.2 miles, hikers reach a sunny, rocky trail that is beautiful and fun to climb. Your goal is a delightful lake for swimming, picnicking, and fishing. The lake is classic Desolation Wilderness, surrounded by granite slopes, bright wildflowers, shiny green manzanita, and graceful conifers. Due to its proximity to the trailhead, however, Grass Lake can be terribly crowded on summer weekends.

To reach the Glen Alpine Trailhead, drive to Fallen Leaf Road, which is 3.1 miles northwest on Highway 89 from the intersection of Highways 89 and 50 in South Lake Tahoe. Approaching from the west, Fallen Leaf Road is 0.9 mile east of the Baldwin Beach turnoff. Turn south on Fallen Leaf Road (do not turn right into Fallen Leaf Campground) and drive 4.8 miles (do not turn left onto Tahoe Mountain Road) to a fork in the road at the south end of Fallen Leaf Lake. Take the left fork, signed for Desolation Wilderness Trails. Stay to the left again at a sign for Lily Lake. Proceed 0.4 mile to Lily Lake and cross a small bridge to reach a parking area, 5.6 miles from Highway 89. Obtain your wilderness permit at the trailhead.

Begin your hike on the rocky road heading west from the parking area. Willows and aspens border the road. The mosquitoes are voracious in these wet environs, so bring bug repellent. Reach a locked gate in 0.3 mile (it seems much longer due to the poor hiking surface). After the gate, the road surface becomes only slightly better. Modjeska Falls on Glen Alpine Creek at 0.5 mile is a welcome distraction. The falls acquired its unusual name when an actress of Polish origin admired them while visiting Glen Alpine Springs Resort.

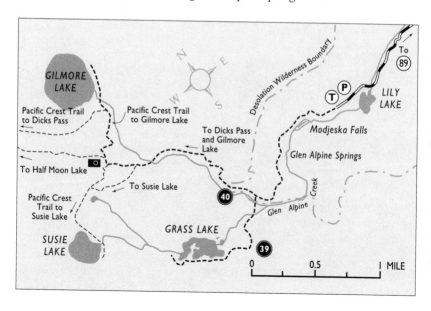

Grass Lake

The private road passes what seems like an endless stream of private homes. The last structure is a remnant of the renowned Glen Alpine Springs Resort, founded by conservationist Nathan Gilmore in the late 1800s. The once impressive stone building was designed by California architect Bernard Maybeck. Finally, at 1.2 miles, the road ends, and a trail, thankfully, begins at a sign for Susie and Gilmore Lakes.

Ascend gently through pine and fir. The trees soon give way to rocky, open hillsides. Pink mountain pride and manzanita line the trail, and Sierra juniper punctuates the landscape. Enter a shady grove of firs. Next pass a deep pool in a stream that is fed by a small waterfall. The spot is a shady and attractive rest stop.

Just after the falls, at 1.6 miles from the trailhead, arrive at a trail junction in a dense stand of trees. The junction is easy to miss; look for a wooden post to the left of the trail, signed for Grass Lake. (If you begin to climb an open staircase of boulders, you've missed the junction.) Take the trail to the left, heading west, for Grass Lake. The right fork climbs north to Gilmore Lake (Trip 40). Cross the boundary into Desolation Wilderness

Almost immediately, cross a creek on a log bridge. Ascend gently to a marshy pond, then cross Glen Alpine Creek. Look for a narrow V-shaped area below the pond for the easiest crossing. Regain the trail, then make a third creek crossing on rocks. Next head left (south) to skirt a granite outcropping. Rock hop on a steep section of trail. At 2.4 miles, the trail levels atop an open ridge.

Climb briefly again on rock stairs to reach a soft path in the shade of pines. A short distance northwest brings you to the south end of Grass Lake. After all the stark white rock, the blue lake, nestled among western white pines, mountain hemlock, and scattered boulders, is a pleasing site. Find good boulders for picnicking along the lake's west side. Swimming is excellent, for the lake's shallow water warms to a reasonable temperature by midsummer. Anglers should explore the northern end of the lake for secluded spots. Those seeking additional hiking could venture north to view the waterfall entering Grass Lake from Susie Lake.

40 GILMORE LAKE

Difficulty: strenuous
Distance: 3.9 miles one way
Usage: high
Starting elevation: 6560 feet
Elevation gain: 1760 feet
Season: summer, fall
Map: USGS Emerald Bay and Echo Lake
See Trip 39 for map.

The hike to Gilmore Lake is a moderately tough climb to a large, beautiful lake. After the first mediocre mile on a closed road, the trail offers splendid views and varied terrain. For backpacking families, Gilmore Lake makes an excellent base camp from which to explore the Velma Lakes (Trip 33) or climb Mount Tallac (Trip 37).

Drive to Fallen Leaf Road, 3.1 miles northwest on Highway 89 from the intersection of Highways 89 and 50 in South Lake Tahoe. Turn south on Fallen Leaf Road and go past Fallen Leaf Campground. Drive 4.8 miles, passing Tahoe Mountain Road, to a fork in the road at the south end of Fallen Leaf Lake. Take the left fork, signed for Desolation Wilderness Trails. Stay to the left again at a sign for Lily Lake. Proceed 0.4 mile to Lily Lake and cross a small bridge to reach a parking area, 5.6 miles from Highway 89.

Obtain your wilderness permit and begin at the Glen Alpine Trailhead, as described in Trip 39. At the fork at 1.6 miles, signed for Grass Lake and Dicks Pass, keep to the right for Dicks Pass and Gilmore Lake.

Switchback north up an open, rocky slope at a moderate grade. Occasional Sierra junipers and Jeffrey pines grow gnarled and stunted like beautiful sculptures on the rocky ledges. From the sunny trail enjoy expansive views and plenty of lupine, phlox, and Indian paintbrush. At the top of the ridge, head north on a shady path along a stream. At 1.8 miles from the trailhead (0.2 mile from the last fork), cross the stream and resume your climb. The path is wetter now, providing fertile soil for ferns and corn lilies.

Leave the shade and commence a steep and rocky ascent along the north wall of a narrow canyon. Below you to the left tumbles Lake Gilmore's outlet stream. At the head of the canyon, cross the stream. Immediately thereafter arrive at a trail junction. The trail to the left heads toward Lake Aloha and Susie Lake. Keep to the right for Dicks Pass and Gilmore Lake.

The trail leads gently northwest, rising above a picturesque tarn covered with lily pads. The grade soon steepens. Climb breathlessly to another trail junction at a splendid overlook to the south and west. Junipers frame the gorgeous views of red rock, white snow, and dramatic ridge lines. Continue straight; the trail to the left is for Susie and Heather Lakes.

In a few feet, arrive at another fork. The trail continuing straight takes you to Half Moon Lake. For Gilmore Lake, bear right at the junction and climb north for 0.5 mile on the Pacific Crest Trail. Climbing up switchbacks on the rocky trail affords fabulous views southwest to Susie Lake and majestic Pyramid Peak (9983 feet). Pass more Jeffrey pines, manzanita, lupine, and Indian paintbrush.

The trail levels and enters a lush meadow of delicate red heather and purple alpine aster, tall white corn lilies, and numerous other flowers. Arrive at a junction with the trail to Dicks Pass. Take the right fork, leaving the Pacific Crest Trail, and continue 0.2 mile to the south end of Gilmore Lake.

Gilmore Lake is lovely. It is almost perfectly round, with a rocky bottom shining through sparkling clear water. The lake is stocked with rainbow, brook, and lake trout. Campsites on its south shore have been overused, so be careful not to damage any stressed vegetation.

The lake is named for Nathan Gilmore (1830–98), an early environmental activist in the Tahoe Basin. In 1896, with help from the newly created Sierra Club, he organized prominent citizens of northern California to petition the federal government to protect the southwest shore of Lake Tahoe from private acquisition. In 1899, one year after Gilmore's death, President William McKinley signed a proclamation protecting more than 130,000 acres, including most of today's Desolation Wilderness. On the shore of the beautiful lake named for this generous and progressive settler, visitors should be abundantly grateful.

41   BIG MEADOW

Difficulty: easy
Distance: 0.5 mile one way
Usage: moderate
Starting elevation: 7200 feet
Elevation gain: 200 feet
Season: summer, fall
Map: USGS Echo Lake and Freel Peak
See Trip 42 for map.

A short, steep climb of only 0.5 mile brings hikers and mountain bikers to scenic Big Meadow. In late July and early August, the flowers are bountiful in this high, lovely, and expansive subalpine meadow, making it a wonderful site for a mid-summer picnic.

To reach the Big Meadow Trailhead from South Lake Tahoe, take U.S. Highway 50–State Highway 89 south to their split in 4.8 miles. Then take Highway 89 southeast 5.3 miles, watching on the right side of the road for a trail sign indicating the Big Meadow Trailhead. Opposite the trail sign is a parking area. From Echo Summit, take Highway 50 northeast for 4 miles to its junction with Highway 89, where you turn right. Since parking spaces are limited, come early on weekends. Additional parking is available in the Tahoe Rim Trailhead parking lot, 0.2 mile north on Highway 89.

The trail begins steeply, ascending a shady slope under red firs and pines. At 0.3 mile, slip through a cattle gate among aspen trees and colorful columbines. The trail then levels somewhat. Arrive at a fork where the trail on your left leads to Scotts Lake. Continue straight (south) on the main trail.

At 0.5 mile, the world brightens as the expanse of Big Meadow comes into view, filled with red-orange Indian paintbrush, white bistort, pastel phlox, purple-blue larkspur, yellow cinquefoil, and purple asters. Snow-covered peaks rise above the meadow at its south end. A wooden bridge takes you across clear, gurgling Big Meadow Creek and into the meadow.

The trail travels right through the center of Big Meadow. Across the lovely meadow, enter an open pine woods. Large downed trees at the edge of the meadow, bleached and smooth, provide perfect picnic benches. This is a wonderful place to contemplate early-morning bird songs, the changing light of dusk, or your children exploring, romping, and chasing butterflies in the wide, beautiful meadow.

Big Meadow is the stepping stone to two fine family hikes, Round Lake and Dardanelles Lake (Trips 42 and 43).

42 ROUND LAKE

Difficulty: moderate
Distance: 2.7 miles one way
Usage: moderate
Starting elevation: 7200 feet
Elevation gain: 870 feet
Season: summer, fall
Map: USGS Echo Lake and Freel Peak

A moderately challenging trail takes hikers to interesting and mysterious Round Lake. While not as classically scenic as other lakes in the basin, Round Lake is still worth a visit. The unusual volcanic formations surrounding the lake are

Round Lake

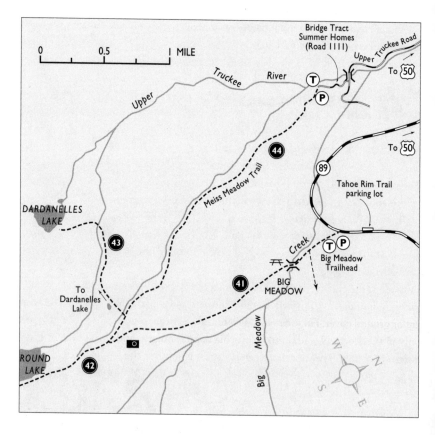

fodder for imaginative minds. Search out the natural gargoyles and weird mud-flow "moon" rocks as you discover firsthand the geological origins of the distinctive Round Lake environs.

From South Lake Tahoe, take U.S. Highway 50–State Highway 89 south to their split in 4.8 miles. Take Highway 89 southeast 5.3 miles to the Big Meadow Trailhead on the right. Since parking spaces are limited, come early on weekends. Additional parking is available in the Tahoe Rim Trail parking lot, 0.2 mile north on Highway 89.

Hike to Big Meadow (Trip 41). From the southern end of Big Meadow, go south on the well-defined trail. Enter a forest of lodgepole pine and red fir, then begin a moderate ascent.

The forest is interrupted by sunny patches where purple lupine and yellow mule's ears thrive. In midsummer, the trail is literally littered with them. As you rise, flowers and fragrant sagebrush increase, and forest thins. The loud clicking of flying grasshoppers and the calls of birds fill the air.

At approximately 1.5 miles, the trail becomes steeper but soon moderates again. The creek to your left is heard but not seen. Enter forest shade, which shelters delicate Jacob's ladder. This pretty plant sprouts delicate, bell-shaped blue flowers in early summer. The name of the plant derives from the arrangement of its narrow leaves opposite each other on the stem.

Ahead, the creek comes into view amid lush meadows of corn lilies. The trail then heads southwest and passes through another cattle gate. After climbing southwest for 0.25 mile to the crest of the saddle, the trail turns south once again and descends a west-facing slope graced with huge, sweet-smelling Jeffrey pines. Through the widely spaced pines, you have beautiful views to the green valley below and to the ridge to the west. Directly above the trail to the south is an ominous but majestic sphinxlike rock formation.

The path descends quickly to arrive at a fork 2.1 miles from the trailhead. Stay left and continue south for Round Lake. The right-hand fork takes you to Dardanelles Lake (Trip 43) and Christmas Valley.

Travel south along a stream, rising slightly. As the trail leaves the stream, the surroundings quickly change. The terrain becomes dusty and barren, lacking flowers or ground cover. Huge firs tower overhead and darken the path. Red firs grow only in the Sierra Nevada, the California coastal ranges, and the southern Cascades of Oregon. The mood of a red fir forest is somber, for few plants can grow within its heavily shaded stands. You can identify a red fir by its dark, chocolate red, deeply furrowed bark, which appears purplish when wet.

The trail climbs steeply up to a ridge, passes over it, then climbs again. Move through a strange landscape of oddly formed boulders and volcanic mudflows. The remains of this volcanic activity look curiously like the construction debris of a mad developer.

Travel through this odd setting, letting your imagination roam. Note the red firs that grow right out of these unusual rocks. Above you, the sphinx again comes into view, high to the left.

Arrive at Round Lake, an oval-shaped lake with a rocky beach at its northern end. Rock formations resembling gargoyles guard the lake's entrance and watch picnickers hungrily. Rising from the lake's east side, dark, steep volcanic cliffs, called the Dardanelles, loom ominously and challenge expert rock climbers. Be forewarned that the lake carries much sediment and is consequently brownish. Round Lake's water temperature is above average, however, so swimmers who don't mind the lack of water clarity have a great spot for a sunny Sierra afternoon.

For backpackers, good campsites are available near the lake's northern shore. The best one is found by hiking west from the northeast corner of the lake to a bench just west of the lake's dam. From the bench, the views are stupendous. For treatable drinking water, find the creek along the lake's eastern shore.

43 DARDANELLES LAKE

Difficulty: moderate
Distance: 3.6 miles one way
Usage: moderate
Starting elevation: 7270 feet
Elevation gain: 1460 feet
Season: summer, fall
Map: USGS Echo Lake and Freel Peak
See Trip 42 for map.

Dardanelles Lake is a lovely destination. The trail to the lake is long, but varied, with lots of flowers, streams, and terrain changes. The lake is an especially scenic spot for swimming, fishing, or picnicking.

Dardanelles Lake

From South Lake Tahoe, take U.S. Highway 50–State Highway 89 south to their split in 4.8 miles. Take Highway 89 southeast 5.3 miles to the Big Meadow Trailhead on the right. Since parking spaces are limited, come early on weekends. Additional parking is available in the Tahoe Rim Trail parking lot, 0.2 mile north on Highway 89.

Beginning at the Big Meadow Trailhead, hike to the fork for Round Lake (Trip 42). To reach Dardanelles Lake, take the trail to the right signed for Christmas Valley. Follow this trail north alongside a stream for 0.2 mile. At an unmarked but obvious trail junction, head left (west) over the small stream.

Continue traveling west through a sun-dappled landscape of quaking aspen. After a pretty 0.1 mile stretch of trail, cross another stream on a log. Continue to head west and enjoy the abundant flowers, which include red Indian paintbrush, purple larkspur, and yellow monkey flower.

Relish the level walking and pass a pond covered with lily pads on your left. In July and August, the pond lilies bloom in large, bright yellow blossoms. In the fall, the seeds of the lilies are an important food source for migrating waterfowl. Native Americans also utilized the rich seeds. Some tribes ground the seeds into flour, others roasted the seeds and ate them like popcorn. Indians also gathered, dried, and ate the lily's roots.

Past the pond, the trail angles northwest. Descend flower-covered slopes to follow a stream northwest for 0.5 mile. Like the last two streams, this stream originates at Round Lake. After passing through some willows, cross the stream on a downed log. Dardanelles Lake is only 0.4 mile from the crossing.

Next, the trail heads south and abruptly rises. Leave the gentle, green streamside for a boulder-filled landscape. Ascend the granite slabs, following ducks. Brilliant pink mountain pride accents the glacier-polished rock.

Briefly reenter a forest of lodgepole pine and fir, then arrive at campsites on the eastern shore of Dardanelles Lake. Trails to the right take you to the lake's edge.

The lake's setting is dramatic and beautiful. From its southern shore, cliffs rise 650 vertical feet, creating a haven for experienced rock climbers. For swimmers, Dardanelles Lake is a real treat. The large but shallow lake is one of the warmer lakes in the region. By mid-July, the lake's temperature usually exceeds 70 degrees. There is also a lot of room for anglers at this 16-acre lake. If you're planning to camp at the lake, look for good campsites on the east and northwest shores.

For an interesting side trip on the way back to the trailhead, hike an extra 0.6 mile (one way) to visit distinctive Round Lake (Trip 42).

44 MEISS MEADOW TRAIL 🐾🐾

Difficulty: moderate
Distance: 3.6 miles one way to Round Lake; 4 miles one way to Dardanelles Lake
Usage: low
Starting elevation: 6520 feet
Elevation gain: 1300 feet
Season: summer, fall
Map: USGS Echo Lake and Freel Peak
See Trip 42 for map.

This hike is an alternative route to Round and Dardanelles Lakes (Trips 42 and 43). On the downside, the route adds 0.9 and 0.4 mile, respectively, to the length of the hikes and misses scenic Big Meadow. Nevertheless, this route is recommended in the fall when the foliage along the trail is quite colorful. Hikers with two cars can make a scenic loop, entering via Big Meadow and returning via the Meiss Meadow Trail. If you're looking for solitude, consider this trail to explore a scenic tributary of the Upper Truckee River.

From the junction of Highways 50 and 89 in South Lake Tahoe, take Highway 50 south 5.2 miles to Upper Truckee Road. Turn left and drive 3.8 miles to a road marked "1111" with a sign announcing Bridge Tract summer homes. This road is the first right after a bridge over the Upper Truckee River and is 0.1 mile past another spur road, Road 12N13A, which leads to the Hawley Grade National Recreation Trail. Turn right on "1111" and drive 0.2 mile past summer homes to a trailhead sign and a parking turnout on the left.

The trail begins by ascending through a fir forest. Intermittent meadows host numerous wildflowers. Displays can be quite impressive in early summer. Lupine, mule's ears, and Indian paintbrush are just a few of the colorful participants. A lush green ground cover of bracken fern and thimbleberry surrounds the trail. Areas of aspen, alder, and willow grow thickly by the creek.

After a brief level stretch, climb steeply and pass through a cattle gate. Parallel the rushing river, which tumbles over rocks to the right of the trail, then descend through open forest almost to the level of the river.

Stroll along the river on an attractive and relaxing stretch of trail. Soon begin another ascent through a mixed forest of red fir, Sierra juniper, and Jeffrey, lodge-

Western toad

pole, and western white pine. At 2.7 miles from the trailhead, look for a trail junction on the right. The trail heading southwest over the creek leads to Dardanelles Lake and is described in Trip 43.

To reach Round Lake, continue 0.2 mile to another trail junction. From there, hike 0.6 mile to Round Lake, as described in Trip 42.

45 TAHOE RIM TRAIL: BIG MEADOW NORTH

Difficulty: moderate, strenuous to Hell Hole Viewpoint
Distance: 1.8 miles one way; 6.5 miles one way to Hell Hole Viewpoint
Usage: low
Starting elevation: 7300 feet
Elevation gain: 740 feet; elevation gain to Hell Hole Viewpoint, 2000 feet
Season: spring, summer, fall
Map: USGS Freel Peak

Hike this section of the Tahoe Rim Trail in midsummer when flowers are bounteous and in autumn when changing foliage is brilliant. Jump across creeklets, explore parklike forest, and hike through constantly changing terrain. This is an excellent trail on which to discover the different habitats of the upper montane zone. Those with higher ambitions can hike another 3 miles on the Tahoe Rim Trail to superb scenery at Hell Hole Viewpoint. In July, flowers are at their peak, but so are mosquito populations, so bring repellent.

To reach the Tahoe Rim Trailhead from South Lake Tahoe, take U.S. Highway 50–State Highway 89 south to their split in 4.8 miles. Then take Highway 89 southeast 5.5 miles, watching on the left side of the road for a trail sign indicating the Tahoe Rim Trail (TRT). Find the TRT Trailhead and parking lot on the north side of Highway 89, 0.2 mile beyond the Big Meadow Trailhead. Approaching from the east on Highway 89, the TRT Trailhead is 1.5 miles from Grass Lake. Park in the TRT parking lot.

Head north out of the parking lot following blue Tahoe Rim Trail markers. Bordering the trail are Jeffrey pines and white firs, with a glorious sprinkling of yellow daisylike mule's ears, purple lupine, pink and purple sky rocket gilias, yellow sulphur flowers, and tall pink Anderson thistles. In late summer, Anderson thistles can grow to a prickly 4 feet.

The trail climbs gently as it winds through the sun-dappled forest, broken by granite boulders. Meet a road and briefly follow it to the right (east). Then turn

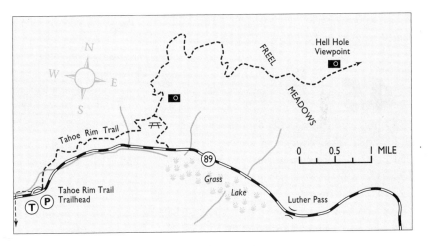

left (north) on a short stretch of paved road that leads to a creek bathed in willow, alder, quaking aspen, and colorful flowers.

After the creek, rise on a sunny, narrow path through more aspen with a carpet of purple asters. Over the length of this trail, hikers travel alternately through moist, open stands of aspen, drier hillside stands of Jeffrey pine, and dark, dense forests of fir. Even blindfolded, you could tell the forests apart. Lush undergrowth, warmth, and abundant bird, animal, and insect life characterize the aspen and pine habitats, while coolness, silence, and stillness dominate the fir stands.

Enter briefly one such stand of fir, then pass into another opening populated by aspen. In autumn, aspen leaves turn bright orange and yellow-gold. Trees in one stand will change color nearly in unison, independent of trees in a neighboring grove. This is because a stand of aspen is connected by a common root system and the trees are essentially clones. Aspen reproduce by sending out suckers from their roots that create genetically identical saplings.

This phenomenon also explains why aspen are often the first trees to come back after a disturbance, such as fire, avalanche, or logging. After the devastation, aspen roots remain alive below ground and send forth replacement suckers. The new suckers are nourished by an already established root system. Other trees must depend upon the much slower, and less dependable, germination of seeds. Because of the aspen's ability to "rise up from the ashes of destruction," it has been called the "phoenix tree."

The beautiful aspen are usually not long-term survivors in the forest. The presence of young firs in their midst indicates that forest succession is already underway. The firs eventually grow taller than the aspen and shade the sun-loving trees. The aspen, unable to thrive under the towering firs, ultimately die. The firs then take over until another cataclysmic event creates an opening for the aspen. Aspen, however, do not always yield to conifers. In areas bordering creeks, for instance, the soil is often too wet for needle-bearing trees.

Continue to climb gently on a smooth path, watched by the multiple "eyes" of the aspen. Pass by openings supporting huge colonies of yellow mule's ears and lupines. Cross over a stream, watching for red columbines and orange-speckled alpine lilies.

Next, enter an area of mature Jeffrey pines. Along this trail, there are occasional 5-foot-diameter pines and firs that may be more than 300 years old. Due to the intense logging of the basin in the late 1800s, such trees are scarce. Look also for tall pine snags, which provide homes for tree squirrels and smorgasbords of insects for woodpeckers and numerous other birds. Sweet treats for hikers are found in the lush growths of thimbleberry by the trail. Lift the bright red berry off the plant without crushing it, and it fits the end of your finger like a thimble!

Soon reenter the red fir forest. The forest floor is littered with broken branches. Loggers called red fir "the widow maker" for the proclivity of its crowns to break off and fall upon unsuspecting woodsmen. The forest, indeed, has the somber quality of a graveyard.

Arrive momentarily at a clearing, where again the change is dramatic. Flowers, sunshine, and lush ground cover return. Cross another small creek, where moisture-loving trees and flowers reappear. Alder trees shade the bouquets of red columbine and purple larkspur.

After the creek, the trail rises by switchbacks. Arrive at a rocky gorge where a creek flows beneath huge boulders. At the bank of the creek is a junction with a trail descending to Grass Lake. Explore the creek and picnic by the water, or keep left on the main trail and ascend north to a scenic viewpoint.

Hikers continuing northeast on the Tahoe Rim Trail rise moderately to the east side of a rock outcropping. From here, gain excellent views southeast across Luther Pass to Pickett Peak (9118 feet) and to the more dramatic Hawkins Peak (10,023 feet). Both are remnants of volcanoes that erupted approximately 10,000 years ago.

From this viewpoint, about 2 miles from the trailhead, the trail continues climbing northeast across gravely slopes, reaching Freel Meadows after approximately 3.6 additional miles. The trail then continues another 0.9 mile to a crest saddle above Hell Hole Canyon. From the saddle, there are dramatic views of the deep, steep-sided canyon, Lake Tahoe, and the majestic threesome of Freel Peak, Jobs Sister, and Jobs Peak. Completing the entire hike to the Hell Hole Viewpoint is strenuous; it covers 6.5 miles one way and gains approximately 2000 feet in altitude. Families with younger hikers will enjoy the first 2 miles of this diverse trail.

46 BENWOOD MEADOW

Difficulty: easy
Distance: 0.7 mile one way
Usage: low
Starting elevation: 7480 feet
Elevation Loss: 120 feet
Season: spring, summer, fall
Map: USGS Echo Lake

Benwood Meadow is a good destination for wildflower seekers. In late June and July, the lovely, quiet meadow is awash in color. The walk to the meadow is effortless and extremely pleasant, but be well prepared for the voracious mosquitoes.

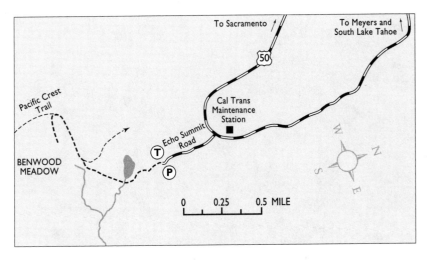

View from the Pacific Crest Trail above Benwood Meadow

Drive south 4.1 miles on Highway 50 from the Agricultural Checkpoint in Meyers to Echo Summit. Continue 0.2 mile past Echo Summit to Echo Summit Road on the left (south) side of the highway. Echo Summit Road is 0.1 mile southwest of the Cal Trans Maintenance Station. Turn left onto Echo Summit Road and drive 0.4 mile south past summer homes to a small parking turnout. A small sign on the right side of the road marks the Pacific Crest Trail (PCT) Trailhead.

Head south on a sandy path marked by blazes. The PCT weaves through granite boulders and patches of manzanita, huckleberry oak, and Sierra chinquapin. Descend gently to a lily-covered pond. From late June through August, large, bright yellow blossoms adorn the lily pads. Native Americans gathered the large seeds of the pond lilies in the fall and roasted them to make something that tasted remarkably like popcorn. Today the seeds are an important food for mallard ducks and Canada geese.

At the southeast end of the pond, bear right and cross the pond's outlet stream. The ground may be quite muddy in early summer and the trail indistinct. Head southwest around the pond. The trail becomes more defined once you reach the drier ground to the west. Descend a gentle slope through a forest of fir with a healthy manzanita understory and arrive at a trail junction, 0.5 mile from the trailhead.

Stay left, maintaining a westerly course. The trail to the right heads back to an alternate PCT trailhead off Highway 50. Shortly, Benwood Meadow appears to the left, bordered by lodgepole pines. A spur path takes you into the meadow.

Depending on the date of your arrival and the amount of rainfall received that year, Benwood Meadow can put on quite a show. Hikers may be greeted by giant red-orange Indian paintbrush, delicate white pennyroyal, and huge purple larkspur. In good years, dainty pink shooting stars burst forth from all directions through the meadow grass. This colorful flower is also known as "bird bill" because of the way its pink petals are bent back to expose a yellow conical "bill."

For more blossoms, walk east to a creek where more moisture-loving flowers thrive, including red columbines, bright yellow monkey flowers, and pink elephant's heads. Although the "monkeys" of the monkey flower usually elude all but the most imaginative of viewers, the delicate upraised trunks and floppy ears of elephant's head flowers please even the most serious observers. In late summer, tall white corn lilies and purple asters grace the meadow.

The advance of pines at the edge of Benwood Meadow may signal the start of "meadow invasion." Through meadow invasion, a meadow is slowly encroached on by a colony of trees. Eventually the trees take hold and a forest is born. Lodgepole pine is often the pioneering species because it can tolerate greater soil moisture than other Sierra conifers.

Wander through the meadow and enjoy uncovering colorful new discoveries. A bottle of insect repellent, waterproof footwear, a magnifying glass, a sketchbook, and a wildflower guide are handy items for this short but special hike.

Those interested in traveling farther on the Pacific Crest Trail can hike through beautiful coniferous forest for another mile or two on the moderately ascending trail. Mountain hemlocks, Sierra junipers, and western white pines frame fine views of Lake Tahoe and the Upper Truckee River Basin along the way.

47 ECHO PEAK

Difficulty: strenuous (moderate with water taxi)
Distance: 5.2 miles one way (2.5 miles each way with round-trip water taxi)
Usage: low
Starting elevation: 7420 feet
Elevation gain: 1475 feet
Season: summer, fall
Map: USGS Echo Lake

The climb to Echo Peak is steep and strenuous, but it amply rewards hikers with dramatic, breathtaking views. The trail travels through classic Desolation Wilderness, which is filled with the stark, desolate beauty of windswept ridges and dry rocky expanses. On the return, a short detour to Triangle Lake adds a tranquil and scenic rest stop to this difficult hike.

To reach Echo Lake from the intersection of Highways 50 and 89 in South Lake Tahoe, drive Highway 50 south for 9.7 miles to the sign on the west side of the road indicating Echo Lake. Approaching on Highway 50 from the south, the Echo Lake turnoff is 1.1 miles northwest of Echo Summit. Take Echo Lake Road east 0.6 mile to a junction. Turn left and proceed 0.9 mile to a parking lot above the Echo Lake Resort. Park in the upper lot, because the resort limits parking in the lower lot to two hours. Descend to the lake by a footpath located across the road to the right. Obtain a wilderness permit near the dock. The trail begins at the dam on Lower Echo Lake.

The trail to Echo Peak is one of the least crowded trails in the popular Echo Lake hiking area (see Trips 48 and 49). One reason for the area's popularity is the Echo Lake water taxi from Lower to Upper Echo Lake that cuts 2.7 miles off your hike each way. This is an attractive proposition, since you can quickly enter the heart of Desolation Wilderness from the west end of Upper Echo Lake. A phone at the taxi's western end allows you to call the resort for the ride back.

If you're taking the water taxi, go directly to the dock to purchase tickets. For die-hard hikers, cross over the dam on your right and pick up a trail that rises above the lake, heading northeast. The trail offers a fine view of Lake Tahoe, then turns west to parallel the shoreline for 2.7 miles. The rolling walk above the cabin-lined lakeshore is pleasant, offering fine views to the west of Ralston Peak (9235 feet) and of the more distant Pyramid Peak (9983 feet) slightly to the north.

At 1.3 miles, the trail switchbacks up to a forest of lodgepole pine, then descends to a rocky plateau at the lower (eastern) end of Upper Echo Lake. The trail then continues northwest on the forested slopes above Upper Echo Lake. At 2.7 miles, pass a junction on your left with the trail from the lake where the water taxi docks. Continue straight ahead. Those coming from the dock should hike up 90 steep feet to the trail and turn left.

View from Echo Peak

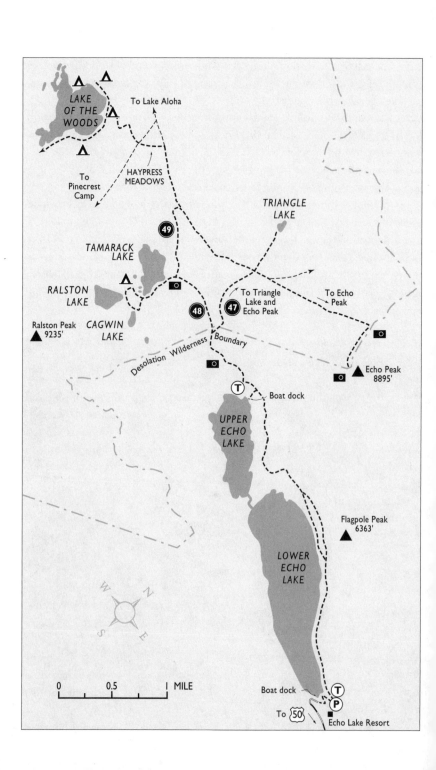

LAKE
OF THE
WOODS

To Lake Aloha

To Pinecrest Camp

HAYPRESS MEADOWS

TRIANGLE LAKE

49

TAMARACK LAKE

RALSTON LAKE

A Ralston Peak 9235'

CAGWIN LAKE

48

47 To Triangle Lake and Echo Peak

To Echo Peak

Desolation Wilderness Boundary

A Echo Peak 8895'

T Boat dock

UPPER ECHO LAKE

A Flagpole Peak 6363'

LOWER ECHO LAKE

W N S E

0   0.5   MILE

Boat dock **T** **P**

To 50

Echo Lake Resort

Lupine, mature Jeffrey pines, and a variety of flowering shrubs line the trail heading away from the lake. The trees frame, but do not obscure, the increasingly scenic views. Cross a stream, then continue to climb on the dry, rocky trail. Just before the trail heads northwest, look east to a grand view of Echo Lake dotted with picturesque islands. Prominent on the western horizon are Ralston and Pyramid Peaks.

Pass through a stand of lovely Sierra junipers with gray-green flattened foliage and shaggy cinnamon-colored bark. Junipers are commonly found in rocky, exposed areas where they are able to withstand harsh Sierra weather. The trees are often transformed by strong winds, ice, and snow to sculptural wonders. Under these conditions, their trunks are stunted, twisted, and stripped, their branches contoured by the wind, their heavy, gnarled roots exposed. The Sierra juniper's purplish berries are important spring and winter food for many Sierra birds. Crush one of the berries in your hand. Its scent will betray its use for flavoring gin.

Look on your right for a trail rising steeply to the east. The trail junction is just before the Desolation Wilderness boundary sign and before you enter a stand of lodgepole pine. Take a right on this narrow, rocky trail, which is marked Triangle Lake.

Climb steeply amid manzanita and purple asters. Enter a grove of pine and negotiate some downed trees. After a cluster of red fir, the trail climbs by a creek, the damp soil giving rise to tall corn lilies. After a tough 0.75 mile, arrive at a saddle and a four-way junction. Straight ahead is the trail descending 0.3 mile to Triangle Lake. The trail to the left leads to Lake Aloha. Take the trail to the right, which is signed for Lily Lake; it reaches Echo Peak in about 1.5 miles.

Shortly, come to a second fork. Take the right fork, which leads you northeast on an unimproved, often faint trail. Climb on the temporarily viewless trail through mature white firs, stepping over some fallen trees. On the ground are lots of gopher "garlands." These long, ropelike mounds of dirt are the remnants of winter tunnels excavated by the industrious pocket gopher. The pocket gopher is able to tunnel more than 100 feet in a single night through this rocky ground. The gophers are named for their external cheek pouches, in which they carry seeds and roots. Although the gophers themselves are rarely seen, evidence of their work is everywhere.

While your eyes are on the ground, note also the variety of tiny flowers by the trail. Observe the pussypaws, a low plant whose pinkish flowers bloom close to the ground in a circle around its stem. The soft, cottony, grayish pink clusters resemble the paws of kittens.

Continue to climb northeast through a grassy, flowered meadow. To your right (south), good views appear. When the top of the ridge is evident, hike cross-country to the ridge's edge. Since the trail is faint, you should take stock of its location so that you can locate it on your return. Once you arrive at the ridge, spectacular views of Lake Tahoe appear to the north. The two lakes immediately below you are the lovely Angora Lakes (Trip 38). To the northwest is the impressive bulk of Mount Tallac, elevation 9735 feet (Trip 37).

Walk southeast up along the ridge to Echo Peak (8895 feet) for more spectacular vistas. From the peak, look south and west to the Crystal Range. The view to the southeast, toward Carson Pass, is dominated by Round Top (10,381 feet).

Explore the ridgeline, or just pick a granite bench and picnic before the fabulous expanse.

If you want to visit Triangle Lake on the way back, retrace your steps and take a right turn at the second junction. The trail is signed for Triangle Lake, and the lake is visible as you begin your 0.3-mile descent. Head steeply down bedrock, following ducks. Near the lake, turn briefly east, then follow a creek bed to the lake's south shore. Hike to the lake's northwest shore for some fine picnicking boulders. To return to the trailhead, retrace your steps 0.3 mile to the four-way junction.

48 TAMARACK, RALSTON, AND CAGWIN LAKES

> **Difficulty:** moderate (easy with water taxi)
> **Distance:** 4.4 miles one way (1.7 miles each way with round-trip water taxi)
> **Usage:** high
> **Starting elevation:** 7420 feet
> **Elevation gain:** 460 feet
> **Season:** summer, fall
> **Map:** USGS Echo Lake
> *See Trip 47 for map.*

This is an easy and delightful hike through Desolation Wilderness to three beautiful and distinctive lakes. By taking the water taxi across Echo Lake, hikers can shave 2.7 miles each way off their hike. The boat ride allows you to make a quick and effortless entry into dramatically scenic Desolation Wilderness. This convenience makes the Echo Lake Trailhead immensely popular. Consequently, save this hike for midweek or fall, when the crowds won't detract from the inspiring scenery.

From the intersection of Highways 50 and 89 in South Lake Tahoe, go south on Highway 50 for 9.7 miles to the Echo Lake turnoff, as indicated by the sign on the west side of the road. From the south, the Echo Lake turnoff is 1.1 miles northwest of Echo Summit. Take Echo Lake Road east 0.6 mile to a junction. Turn left and drive 0.9 mile to the parking lot above the Echo Lake Resort. Park in the upper lot, because the resort limits parking in the lower lot to two hours. Descend to the lake by the footpath located across the road and to the right, and obtain a wilderness permit near the dock.

The trail begins at the Echo Lake Trailhead (see Trip 47). From the dam at Lower Echo Lake, hike 2.7 miles to the trail junction with the path from the dock at Upper Echo Lake. Alternatively, to save these 2.7 miles of hiking (each way) around Lower and Upper Echo lakes, take the water taxi from Lower Echo Lake.

Head to the first Triangle Lake Trail junction. To reach Tamarack Lake, continue straight ahead on the main trail past the junction. Pass through a stand of lodgepole pine, hike in and out of shade, and in approximately 0.5 mile, climb to another viewpoint where you can look back (east) at the Echo Lakes. Just after this scenic spot, at 3.9 miles from the Lower Echo Lake Trailhead (1.2 miles from the boat dock at Upper Echo Lake), arrive at the junction with the descending trail to Tamarack Lake. The main trail, which leads to Lake of the Woods and Lake Aloha (see Trip 49), continues to rise to the northwest.

Head left (southwest) for Tamarack Lake, descending on a very rocky trail. When the trail disappears over bedrock, watch for ducks. In July, bright pink mountain pride blooms amid the rocks beside the trail.

Tamarack Lake comes quickly into view and is reached at 4.1 miles from the trailhead. The large lake is scenically adorned with a tree-studded island. Tamarack Lake is rimmed by mountain hemlocks and pines, but its north side has numerous large rocks on which to sunbathe or picnic. Anglers may try for brook trout. There are good campsites at the lake's southern end.

To visit nearby Ralston Lake, continue on the faint trail that rounds the southeast end of the lake. Cross the outlet streams, then bear southwest following a faint trail up the west end of a low granite mound. Watch for ducks. From the top of the mound, gaze down on small Ralston Lake. The lake is half the size of Tamarack, but it delivers a scenic punch. From its south shore, Ralston Peak (9235 feet) rises abruptly. Streams of water from melting snow run off the mountain into the frigid lake throughout the summer. Walled-in Ralston Lake has a stark, forbidding quality. Winds sweeping down from the mountain add to its aura of isolation and desolation. Although Ralston Lake is only 1.7 miles from the busy Upper Echo Lake boat dock, a quiet picnic at its shore takes you worlds away.

To visit tiny Cagwin Lake, head east from the northern tip of Ralston Lake on a faint trail. Reach small Cagwin Lake after 0.1 mile. Cagwin Lake is shallower and not quite as scenic as the other two lakes, but it offers quiet spots for picnics. All the lakes provide fine shoreline for exploring, pleasant shade under pines, and fishing opportunities.

To return to Tamarack Lake from Cagwin Lake, follow an unimproved trail northeast from Cagwin Lake's northern tip. The trail soon turns northwest, crosses outlet streams, then brings you back to the southern, marshy tip of Tamarack Lake. Regain the main trail along the eastern shore of Tamarack Lake and then retrace your steps to the trailhead or boat dock.

49 LAKE OF THE WOODS

Difficulty: moderate
Distance: 5.1 miles one way (2.3 miles each way with round-trip water taxi)
Usage: high
Starting elevation: 7420 feet
Elevation gain: 1010 feet
Season: summer, fall
Map: USGS Echo Lake
See Trip 47 for map.

Lake of the Woods is a large, scenic lake, excellent for swimming in midsummer. It is very popular, but due to its size it is seldom overwhelmed by visitors. For families seeking a moderate hike, it is an excellent choice.

From the intersection of Highways 50 and 89 in South Lake Tahoe, go south on Highway 50 for 9.7 miles to the Echo Lake turnoff, as indicated by the sign on the west side of the road. From the south, the Echo Lake turnoff is 1.1 miles northwest of Echo Summit. Take Echo Lake Road east 0.6 mile to a junction. Turn left and drive 0.9 mile to the parking lot above the Echo Lake Resort. Park in the upper lot, because the resort limits parking in the lower lot to two hours. Descend to the lake by the footpath located across the road and to the

Mule deer

right, and obtain a wilderness permit near the dock.

The trail begins at the Echo Lake Trailhead (see Trip 47). From the dam at Lower Echo Lake, hike 2.7 miles to the trail junction with the path from the dock at Upper Echo Lake. Alternatively, to save these 2.7 miles of hiking (each way) around Lower and Upper Echo lakes, take the water taxi from Lower Echo Lake.

Follow Trip 48 until the Tamarack Lake Trail junction, 3.9 miles from the trailhead (1.2 miles from the boat dock at Upper Echo Lake). Head right and proceed on the main trail ascending northwest. A good view is gained looking down to Tamarack Lake, with impressive Ralston Peak (9235 feet) rising behind it.

Next climb a series of long switchbacks up dry hillsides covered with sagebrush and phlox, lupine and pussypaws. The trail levels and becomes less rocky as the hillsides turn green and grassy. Begin a stretch of easy walking on a wide trail of packed dirt. Pass through a shady forest of lodgepole pine and fir. This section can be very buggy in midsummer.

At 4.4 miles from the trailhead, arrive at another fork. Veer left for Lake of the Woods. Follow the edge of pretty Haypress Meadows with good views of peaks on the horizon. Haypress Meadows is named for the hay baling that occurred in this meadow in the late 1800s. Settlers cut the meadow grass, baled it, then transported it by ox cart to Virginia City and Placerville.

Head over a rise and arrive at a trail junction in 0.25 mile. Continue straight ahead to Lake of the Woods. To the left the trail heads south to Pinecrest Camp, and to the right the trail leads to Lake Aloha.

Descend moderately to the north shore of Lake of the Woods. Arrive at the lake in 0.4 mile. This large lake is popular with backpackers, anglers, and swimmers. For warmer and shallower water, head over to the lake's island-studded west side by taking the trail along the lake's north shore. The best campsites are also on the west shore. If you're camping at Lake of the Woods, be sure to set up camp at least 100 feet from the lake. Illegal campsites hasten the deterioration of the lake's water quality and fragile surrounding vegetation.

50　LOWER HORSETAIL FALLS

Difficulty: easy
Distance: 0.75 mile one way
Usage: moderate
Starting elevation: 6110 feet
Elevation gain: 200 feet
Season: summer, fall
Map: USGS Echo Lake

Hiking below Lower Horsetail Falls offers spectacular views and a wealth of splendid picnic sites. Explore a dramatic granite slope or find quiet streamside hideaways, all less than a mile from your car. Keep a close watch on youngsters on this hike, however, because there are treacherous drop-offs and slippery areas near streams along the way where a tumble could lead to serious injury. If you

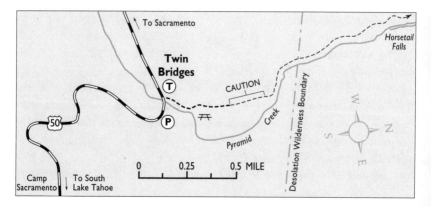

are accompanied by children who can't resist wandering, it's better to choose another, safer hike.

The trail begins at the Twin Bridges Trailhead on Highway 50. From the intersection of Highways 89 and 50 in South Lake Tahoe, drive 15.4 miles south on Highway 50 to the Twin Bridges Trailhead on the right (north) side of the highway. The trailhead is 1 mile beyond Camp Sacramento. Approaching from the south on Highway 50, the trailhead is 1.7 miles north of the town of Strawberry. There is parking at the trailhead, although it often fills up on summer weekends. Obtain a wilderness permit at the trailhead.

Walk carefully down Highway 50 to cross a bridge over Pyramid Creek. On the west side of the bridge, pick up a trail and head north, keeping the creek on your right. Climb to granite slabs where ducks point the way. Enter a shady forest of cedar and pine with a lush ground cover of bracken fern. The gurgling stream drowns out the traffic noise from Highway 50.

The trail ascends gently at first. Soon, it veers away from the creek, leaves the cool forest, and rises more steeply. Remarkable views of glacier-carved landscapes open up to the south. High moraines tower to the east and west. Round a bend and Horsetail Falls appears high above you to the north. This awesome torrent of falling water resembles a horse's tail in its impressive length and narrow breadth. The mist of the cascade mimics the fluidity of long hairs blowing in the wind.

In this expanse of granite, there are numerous hiking options. Following the trail takes hikers high up the open slope. The trail is easy to follow for approximately 0.5 mile. Hike among widely set Sierra junipers and Jeffrey pines to increasingly better views. Sure to accompany you are the golden-mantled ground squirrels and chipmunks who scurry over the rocks. Less common are the yellow-bellied marmots that also inhabit these rocky environs. Chubby marmots may be seen sunning themselves on the warmed granite. As the grade steepens, the trail becomes more obscure and more difficult, and consequently is not recommended for children.

Alternately, aim for Pyramid Creek and explore the bubbling cascades and cooling shade along the creek. Excellent picnic spots are abundant. Also abundant are western fence lizards. These small lizards have distinctive blue throats and bellies. Males can be seen puffing out their blue throats atop rock outcrops. The colorful western fence lizards are also known to do a type of push-up!

In either direction, huge glacial erratics punctuate the landscape. Thousand-foot tongues of ice broke off boulders high in the mountains and dragged the stones miles away. As the glaciers retreated 10,000 years ago, these boulders were left stranded.

Atop the granite boulders and slopes, note the many varieties of lichen. The crusty black, orange, brown, and green coatings on the rocks are actually plants. Exposed rock in the Sierra offers ideal habitat for these symbiotic unions of fungi and algae. Lichen play an important part in the production of soil in the Sierra. As the lichen grow, they secrete acids that gradually break down the rock.

These slopes provide fine areas to explore. There is little danger of getting lost, because following the creek brings you back to Highway 50. This is an especially convenient and flexible hike to take if Highway 50 is your route home.

51 TAHOE RIM TRAIL: KINGSBURY GRADE SOUTH

Difficulty: strenuous
Distance: 4 miles one way to Monument Pass
Usage: low
Starting elevation: 7520 feet
Elevation gain: 1330 feet
Elevation loss: 1000 feet
Season: summer, fall
Map: USGS South Lake Tahoe

This hike is rich with scenic views east over the Carson Valley and south to majestic Freel and Jobs Peaks. The trail's steep descent into Mott Canyon midway

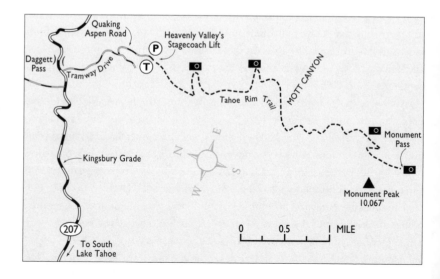

The Tahoe Rim Trail

through the hike is disappointing, but the views gained are ample reward. This hike will attract gung-ho hikers and won't let them down. Very ambitious trekkers can walk an additional 5 miles south on the Tahoe Rim Trail to quiet and lofty Star Lake, sitting at 9100 feet at the base of Freel Peak.

From the intersection of Highway 207 and Highway 50 in South Lake Tahoe, drive 3.1 miles east on Highway 207 to Tramway Drive. (The intersection of Highway 207 and Highway 50 is located 0.6 mile north of Stateline.) Turn right on Tramway Drive and travel another 0.6 mile south, then turn left onto Quaking Aspen Road. Drive 0.6 mile on Quaking Aspen Road to the parking lot at Heavenly Valley's Stagecoach Lift. The trail begins at the south end of the lot. Look for the blue Tahoe Rim Trail (TRT) sign.

Follow a narrow path through a field of grass and goldenrod, purple pentemon and white mountain pennyroyal. The trail soon leads to a road. Take the road up a steep hill to the ski area boundary. Following blue TRT signs, regain the trail and enter a shady forest.

The trail rises gently on switchbacks, providing views of Carson Valley to the east and Lake Tahoe to the west. The forest opens up, the ground cover of manzanita increases, and lichen-covered boulders are common. The hiking is pleasant and easy.

The trail turns south and begins a descending traverse of an east-facing slope. Cross a ski slope under a chair lift. The ski slope looks dramatically different than the undeveloped mountainside. The badly eroded ski slope is barren of soil-holding shrubs and vegetated only by sparse clumps of grass. The slope is an effective reminder of the environmental damage wrought by downhill skiing.

Next enter a dark forest of red fir on the other side of the ski slope. As is typical of red fir forests, the ground is littered with broken branches. Head east through the forest on a gentle ascent.

Soon cross another ski slope. Then turn south again and traverse a beautiful east-facing slope dotted with Jeffrey and western white pines. Switchback up the slope, gaining dramatic views of the Freel Peak massif to the southeast.

At approximately 1.5 miles from the trailhead, meet a ski-lift maintenance road descending very steeply to Mott Canyon. Follow this road as it leads down the canyon. After the road curves to the east and you've descended a discouragingly large distance, look to the right (south) for the blue Tahoe Rim Trail sign. Leave the road to pick up a trail heading south.

From this point on, mule deer tracks are common in the trail's sandy soil. Early morning and dusk are good times to spot mule deer. Most mule deer in the Sierra are migratory. They winter at lower elevations, such as the Carson Valley, then move up the mountains in spring. Deer are browsers and eat the leaves and stems of shrubs and trees. Watch for them at the edges of forest openings.

Watch also for ancient western white pines by the trail. One trailside pine measures 6 feet in diameter and is probably 300 years old. Identify western white pine by its checkerboard-patterned bark and its needles in bundles of five.

Pass under another chair lift, then rise on a path cut dramatically into a steep slope. Watch your footing, for the trail is very narrow. Rocks increase as you ascend. Round a bend, and a panoramic view to the east explodes.

Spectacular views continue as the trail traverses the rocky, open slope heading south. Switchbacks lead you up to Monument Pass at 8850 feet. Climb a rock outcropping south of the pass for excellent views of Freel Peak (10,881 feet) and Jobs Sister (10,823 feet). These two peaks are the highest in the Lake Tahoe Basin. (The next highest is Mount Rose at 10,776 feet; see Trip 1.) The steep north face of Freel Peak makes the mountain look particularly imposing, and its ascent is indeed extremely strenuous. South of Monument Pass, the Tahoe Rim Trail continues to traverse these scenic western slopes, rising gently 300 feet to reach Star Lake.

Right: *A beach on Lake Tahoe's east shore*

CHAPTER 5

THE EAST LAKE TAHOE BASIN

The East Lake Tahoe Basin offers unique hiking and biking opportunities. Like the north shore, it is often less crowded than the west and south shores. The topography of the east basin is somewhat gentler and more forested than its neighbors', for the eastern crest of the Sierra did not form glaciers and undergo the intensive sculpting that occurred in the south and west. The eastern basin also receives less precipitation. Therefore, eastern routes may be clear of snow in the spring when western routes are still snowbound.

The trips described in this chapter are located south of Sand Harbor State Park and north of Kingsbury Grade. The chapter includes several trails in Lake Tahoe–Nevada State Park. Fall hiking and biking is especially recommended in the park because of its many deciduous trees. Look also to beautiful Sand Harbor State Park for fine beach walking in the fall, when the hordes of sunbathers leave the sand to lovers of nature and solitude. Wildlife enthusiasts will also enjoy the east basin, for large mammals such as mule deer, black bears, and pine martens can be found in Lake Tahoe–Nevada State Park. The park also provides homes for a large variety of birds.

For hiking families, an easy trail to a lovely, sandy beach is described in Trip 52. A great hike for children around fishable Spooner Lake is found in Trip 56. For a more challenging hike, the Tahoe Rim Trail offers two magnificent scenic routes, one to Snow Valley Peak (Trip 57) and the second south to South Camp Peak (Trip 58).

Family mountain biking trips are described in Trips 52, 53, and 54. All are intermediate level. Trip 53 is the gentlest of the three, offering a well-graded single-track trail through forest to a large meadow. Trip 54 is longer and steeper, but riders are well rewarded when they arrive at pretty Marlette Lake. Skunk Harbor (Trip 52) is a breeze to ride down, but a killer to ride up. Nevertheless, the lovely beach and the trip's end are well worth the effort. Finally, the classic and difficult Great Flume Mountain Bike Trail (Trip 55) is a must for skilled mountain bikers comfortable with narrow singletrack and steep drop-offs.

52 SKUNK HARBOR

Difficulty: easy (moderate for mountain bikers)
Distance: 1.4 miles one way
Usage: low
Starting elevation: 6807 feet
Elevation loss: 567 feet
Season: spring, summer, fall
Map: USGS Marlette Lake

The "trail" to Skunk Harbor is a long, curving dirt road that descends to a small sandy cove on the east shore of Lake Tahoe. This easy hike is a pleasant way to arrive at a quiet and pretty beach. For a special treat, bring a late snack and flashlights for a beautiful sunset picnic. For mountain bikers, the descent is steep and sandy, and the climb back is extremely demanding.

To reach the trailhead, find the turnout on the west side of Highway 28, 5.4 miles south of Sand Harbor State Park and 1.8 miles north of the entrance to Lake Tahoe–Nevada State Park (Spooner Lake Picnic Area). Look for the locked gate on the unpaved logging road (Road 15N07). There are only a few parking spaces in the turnout.

Begin on the logging road beyond the locked gate. Descend moderately on the smooth dirt road. Beautiful and towering Jeffrey pines line the way. Ask your children to smell the bark of these magnificent three-needled pines. The bark's vanilla scent has inspired my children to name this pine the "cookie tree."

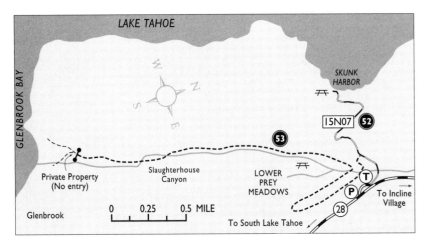

Watch and listen for red-capped woodpeckers and numerous other species of tree-dwelling birds inhabiting this forest.

As you descend, look below to the south for a glimpse of beautiful Lower Prey Meadows (Trip 53). These meadows may be reached by a 1-mile (one way) diversion from the main road. This is a pleasant and much-recommended side trip.

The shrub prominently lining the trail is gray-green rabbitbrush. Jackrabbits are known to favor its long, thin, silvery leaves. In midsummer, its bright yellow flowers bloom profusely.

After only 0.25 mile, arrive at a junction with a trail heading east to Lower Prey Meadows. Stay on the road and continue to descend in a westerly direction. Large boulders line the trail along with white fir. Firs can be distinguished from pines because their needles are short, flat, and soft to the touch. The white fir is so named because its needles have two white lines on their underside, creating a silvery or whitish cast.

The road winds gracefully down to a lovely sand beach at intimate Skunk Harbor. Mountain bikers should show consideration for hikers, control their speed, and exercise caution on the sandy turns. Above the beach, the remains of a stone foundation reveal part of a summer lodge built in this bay in the 1930s. Remaining also is the skeleton of a boat pier.

A few leisurely hours could easily be spent here, enjoying the beach, taking in the exquisite westerly views, and observing a variety of waterfowl.

53　LOWER PREY MEADOWS

Difficulty: easy
Distance: 1.5 miles one way to meadows
Usage: low
Starting elevation: 6807 feet
Elevation loss: 367 feet
Season: spring, summer, fall
Map: USGS Marlette Lake and Glenbrook
See Trip 52 for map.

Mountain bikers especially enjoy the trail to Lower Prey Meadows. Although the trail is narrow, its grade is never steep. Cyclists can descend effortlessly through deep forest to reach the spacious flower-filled meadows just east of Lake Tahoe. Unfortunately, private property at the trail's end bars access to the lake. To reach

Lake Tahoe, one must climb back up and descend via the far steeper and sandier Skunk Harbor road (see Trip 52).

To reach the trailhead, find the turnout on the west side of Highway 28, 5.4 miles south of Sand Harbor State Park and 1.8 miles north of the entrance to Lake Tahoe–Nevada State Park (Spooner Lake Picnic Area). Look for the locked gate on the unpaved logging road (Road 15NO7). There are only a few parking spaces in the turnout.

Begin on the logging road beyond the locked gate. Descend steeply 0.25 mile on the sandy dirt road to the junction with the trail to Prey Meadows, which enters on the left. Turn sharply left at this junction and proceed east on the narrow trail.

The trail to Lower Prey Meadows travels the route of a narrow-gauge railroad built in the 1870s. The Lake Tahoe Railway was built to haul lumber from the mills at Glenbrook, on the shore of Lake Tahoe, to Spooner Summit, 1000 feet above the lake. From Spooner Summit, the lumber was floated via a wooden flume or chute to Carson City, then transported by rail to the Virginia City mines. In the 1880s, four lumber mills operated at Glenbrook, producing more than thirty million board feet annually. The surrounding slopes, from Glenbrook to Incline, were entirely denuded. By the 1890s, the mines were in decline and the demand for lumber radically decreased. In 1900, the Lake Tahoe Railway was dismantled.

Cyclist on Lower Prey Meadows Trail

Descend among beautiful Jeffrey pines framing views of Lake Tahoe. Bikers should be careful of downed trees and the plentiful pine cones along the trail that can cause skids. On this dry slope, look for blue lupine, orange Indian paintbrush, and the very abundant yellow mule's ears. These yellow composites are easily recognized by their distinctive leaves, which are large and fuzzy like the ears of a mule.

A fanciful legend recounts the origin of the mule's ear. It is said that a miner carrying sacks of gold from nearby hills was anxious to sell his ore and started down the mountains in early spring by mule train. In his haste to sell his gold, however, the miner left too early. Melting snows made the roads impassable. The roads were so wet that his wagon became hopelessly stuck in the mud, and the miner could escape with neither his gold nor his mules. The lost riches and animals have turned up every summer in mining country ever since, as golden-petaled, furry-leafed mule's ears.

Different flowers appear as the trail crosses a wet area. Where alders replace the pines and white firs, look for yellow monkey flowers, orange-spotted alpine lilies, and red and yellow columbines. In spring and early summer, this area may be very muddy.

Continue south, leaving the wet area. Negotiate a hairpin turn, then follow the gently descending switchbacks. Bikers should control their speed at all times due to the presence of hikers, a few steep drop-offs, and occasional low overhangs.

Cross over another wet and rocky area, then descend on an improving trail to the meadow. When the meadow is in view to your left (north), the trail becomes wider and more level. To reach the meadow, leave your bike and hike cross-country a few hundred yards through pine forest. It is best to visit the meadow in early summer. If you've timed it right, the meadow is alive with vibrant flowers and chirping birds. In June, purple penstemon is abundant.

At the meadow, watch for hawks circling the sky, looking for prey. Among the brush at the edge of the meadow, there may also be coyotes. Both predators are indications of the abundance of rodents rustling beneath the meadow grass.

The trail continues to descend through Slaughterhouse Canyon for about a mile to Glenbrook, where a gate finally blocks the trail. Even if the lake is not accessible, it is a pretty ride or walk down to the Glenbrook boundary. From overhanging branches, nimble chickarees drop pine cone grenades on the path. Discordant squawks from the gray-headed, black-winged Clark's nutcracker assail you. This handsome bird breaks pine cones to pieces with its sharp, pointed beak to dislodge the seeds. Find them high on pine branches or hanging acrobatically from pine cones.

Thanks to the gradual grade of the narrow-gauge railroad, the return trip is not too strenuous. For those with energy remaining, try the road to Skunk Harbor's charming beach. To reach Skunk Harbor, turn left where the trail meets the main road and descend to the beach. To return to the trailhead, turn right on the main road and ascend 0.25 mile.

54   MARLETTE LAKE

Difficulty: strenuous
Distance: 5 miles one way
Usage: moderate
Starting elevation: 6950 feet
Elevation gain: 1200 feet
Season: summer, fall
Map: USGS Glenbrook and Marlette Lake

The trail to Marlette Lake offers meadows, flowers, a scenic canyon, and a superlative lake for swimming or picnicking. The long, steep trail is challenging but rewarding. Although this demanding trip is a superb bike route, hikers enjoy it also. Take it in autumn, for it offers some of the finest fall color in the Tahoe Basin.

Drive to the Spooner Lake Picnic Area of Lake Tahoe–Nevada State Park. Approaching from the north on Highway 28, the park entrance is 12.25 miles south of the junction of Highways 28 and 431 near Incline Village. From South Lake Tahoe, drive north on Highway 50 to its junction with Highway 28. From the east, take Highway 50 to its junction with Highway 28. Take Highway 28 north just 0.7 mile to the park entrance on the east side of the highway. After entering the park, bear to the left and park in the northernmost parking circle.

From the parking lot, enter the picnic area on a paved path. Proceed about 25 yards, looking northeast and down the slope (to the left) for an unpaved trail. Turn left on this trail, which becomes more defined as you head north. Follow this trail to a closed road marked North Canyon Road.

Continue north on the unpaved road. The trail follows an 1880s logging road for the entire 5-mile route. Had you traveled this road a hundred years ago, you would have seen the surrounding hillsides entirely denuded. Loggers clear-cut this area to supply lumber for the silver mines of Virginia City. Today second-growth forest covers the slopes.

Pass through lodgepole and Jeffrey pines, then through groves of quaking

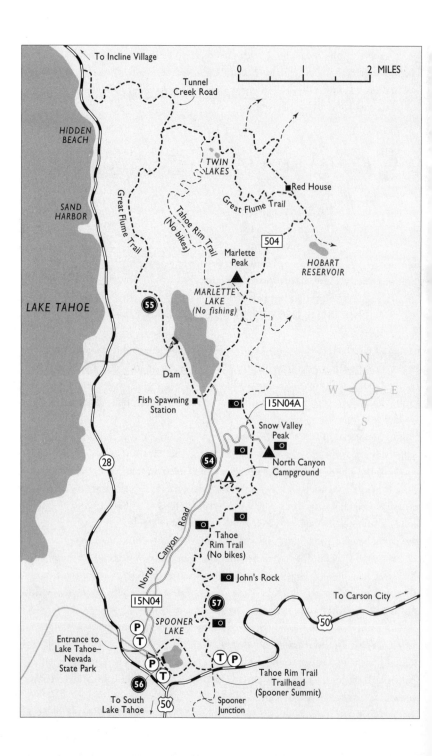

View from the south end of Marlette Lake

aspen. The tree's name comes from the fluttering of its delicate leaves, which move in the lightest breeze. The lovely leaves turn shades of orange and yellow in fall, providing a striking contrast with the dark green of the conifers. Unfortunately, vandals have carved the bark of many aspens along the trail. This is an ugly and destructive practice that can kill the tree if the carvings girdle the trunk. Please instruct your youngsters to respect the trees.

Next cross North Canyon Creek. As you enter the canyon, bird songs replace highway noise. The road rises gently but steadily as white fir is replaced by red fir. Savor the open views and wealth of fragrant green-gray sagebrush. Treeless Snow Valley Peak rises to the east.

Flowers line the trail and fill the intermittent meadows. In early summer, yellow woolly mule's ears, deep purple larkspur, and blue lupine predominate. The mule's ears (or wild sunflowers) are a favorite of youngsters. They are easy to recognize and fun to touch. The leaves are large and resemble the shape of a mule's ear. On their surface are small white hairs that make the leaves feel silky and fur-covered.

In July, watch for the flowers of the lovely pink bog mallow and creamy yarrow. In August, deep pink fireweed is plentiful. Throughout the summer, look along the willow-lined creek for red Indian paintbrush. Paintbrush is easy for children to recognize because the flowers look like scruffy green paintbrushes whose tips have been dipped in red-orange paint.

In the sandy soil, tracks of deer and other small mammals are usually visible. If you're lucky, you may even see the prints of a black bear. Early in the morning or at dusk, there is a good chance of seeing mule deer. The deer, once abundant in the meadows of the Tahoe Basin, are distinguished by their oversized mulelike ears. At any time of the day, chipmunks and ground squirrels abound.

After 2.5 miles on the rising road, arrive at a trail junction. To the right find North Canyon Campground and access to the Tahoe Rim Trail, 1.3 miles uphill to the east (see Trip 57).

Pass a large meadow after this junction. At the north end of the meadow, the trail becomes considerably steeper and shadier. In 0.3 mile from the meadow, arrive at a junction with Road 15N04A, which rises very steeply to the east. The road meets the Tahoe Rim Trail after 0.9 mile of steep switchbacks, and Snow Valley Peak (9214 feet) after 1.2 miles. Even if you don't plan to hike all the way to the peak, shed your packs (or drop your bikes) and hike a few minutes up this road. In a short time you'll be rewarded with a fabulous view of Lake Tahoe. The views continue to improve as you gain altitude. (If this whets your appetite for the ascent, see Trip 57 to hike the gorgeous Tahoe Rim Trail.)

To go directly to Marlette Lake, continue on Road 15N04 (North Canyon Road) heading north. The road continues to rise steeply. At the top of the ridge, large Marlette Lake comes into view and cool breezes welcome you. Descend to the lake on a moderately steep trail that drops several hundred feet. After the 0.75-mile descent, reach a trail junction above the lake's eastern shore.

Head left at the junction to reach Marlette Lake's more scenic western shore. The level trail takes you south, then north along the shore. The trail is exquisite. Pines frame but don't obscure the lake views, which are set off nicely by white granite and the shiny green leaves of the abundant manzanita. Enormous trout swim languidly in the clear water, protected from hungry anglers by the park's strict fishing prohibition. Travel 1.3 miles north on this lovely trail to the lake's dam.

The dam at Marlette Lake was built in 1873. Marlette's water was used to supply the mining towns of Virginia City and Gold Hill. Water from the lake was also used to feed the flume that carried lumber from the slopes south to Spooner

Summit and then east to Carson City. Although lumbering has ceased, Marlette Lake still supplies water to Carson City and Virginia City. Before this lake was rendered so productive, the Washo Indians regularly camped on its shores in a flat area west of the dam near Washoe Creek. The Washo name for the lake was "Phagathsami."

Today Marlette Lake is also used as a stock pond for cutthroat trout, a native species of trout that has been pushed out of its original habitat by more competitive species introduced by commercial fishermen. At the lake's south end, you passed the fish spawning station. Be sure to observe the year-round fishing prohibition and thereby aid the resurgence of the distinctive cutthroat trout.

At the dam, the infamous Great Flume Trail begins. This advanced bike route follows the trail of the nineteenth-century flume 6 miles north to Tunnel Creek Station. It is recommended only for experienced riders, as the single-track trail is narrow, drops off steeply in sections, and can be slippery if damp.

55 THE GREAT FLUME MOUNTAIN BIKE TRAIL

Difficulty: Strenuous, only for experienced mountain bikers
Distance: 13.75 miles one way (use two cars or shuttle service) or 23-mile loop
Usage: moderate
Starting elevation: 6990 feet
Elevation gain: 1885 feet, after dropping to 6295 feet
Season: spring, summer, fall
Map: USGS Glenbrook and Marlette Lake
See Trip 54 for map.

Some consider the difficult, and occasionally harrowing, Great Flume Trail a rite of passage for mountain bikers. The trail is physically very demanding, requiring solid skills, including confidence on narrow singletrack trails. Riders follow an abandoned flume line, perched on a ridge more than 1500 vertical feet above Lake Tahoe. Four and a half miles of trail involve steep drop-offs and truly magnificent lake views. Comfort with heights and excellent vehicle control are prerequisites. For the intrepid and careful rider, the rewards are unequaled. This is easily the most beautiful and exciting mountain ride in the entire Tahoe Basin. Try it in the fall for spectacular foliage. Watch the weather, however, because wet surfaces can make the singletrack slick, and avoid the exposed ridge ride if lightning threatens.

On Highway 28, drive 12.25 miles south of the junction of Highways 28 and 431 near Incline Village to get to the Spooner Lake Picnic Area of Lake Tahoe–Nevada State Park. From South Lake Tahoe, drive north on Highway 50 to its junction with Highway 28, then take Highway 28 north 0.7 mile to the park entrance. Park in the northernmost parking area.

Begin this trip by riding 5 miles to Marlette Lake, as described in Trip 54. Before reaching the lake, riders reach a road diverging to Snow Valley Peak at 3.9 miles from the Spooner Lake parking lot (Forest Road 15NO4A). A tough but rewarding 1.5 mile struggle up this extremely rough and rocky road takes you to the top of the peak (elevation 9214 feet). This exhausting diversion is only for the most hardy and committed, but the views are fabulous (see Trips 54 and 57).

Most will want to ride straight to Marlette Lake. At the south tip of the lake, bear left to ride along the lake's west shore to reach the dam at 6.2 miles. To the left, there is a sign for the Great Flume Trail. Descend (some may want to walk bikes down) a steep and rocky trail which turns right as it levels out. Cross Marlette Creek to begin the Great Flume Trail.

Marlette Lake

The singletrack Great Flume Trail follows the path of a flume built along the west-facing ridge in the 1870s. The flume carried water and logs from Marlette Lake to Virginia City during the heyday of silver mining. Although the original flume was wooden, pipes replaced the original and can still be found along the trail, so use caution when riding in wet weather. The 4.5-mile flume is perched 7700 feet high along the ridge. Consequently, the views are tremendous. The trail offers classic Tahoe beauty. Coasting atop sparkling white granite, sandwiched between deep blue sky and deep blue lake, the ride is heavenly and dazzling. If, nevertheless, the narrowness or exposed nature of the trail bothers you, retrace your steps to Marlette Lake.

At 10.6 miles from Spooner Lake, after 4.5 miles of ridge riding, the Great Flume Trail arrives at Tunnel Creek Road. Those who have cars waiting at Hidden Beach or Sand Harbor, or who plan to take the shuttle back to Spooner Lake, should turn left and descend 3 miles to Highway 28. Tunnel Creek Road is named for a tunnel that was blasted 4000 feet through the mountain to carry water to the dry eastern side. Exercise caution on this steep run. Portions of the switchbacking road are sandy or washboarded. Once at Highway 28, wait for your shuttle ride or turn left for Hidden Beach, Sand Harbor, and Lake Tahoe–Nevada State Park, or right to Incline Village.

Advanced riders can turn right at Tunnel Creek Road to circle back to Marlette Lake, via another portion of the Great Flume Trail and Forest Road 504. This is an extremely strenuous and rugged ride. To circle back to Marlette Lake, turn right and climb to the top of the ridge, about 0.5 mile from the junction. At the top of the ridge, note, but do not take, a signed road to the right headed to Twin Lakes, about 0.5 mile south. Continue straight ahead (east). Just 0.7 mile past the Twin Lakes junction, reach another portion of the Great Flume Trail. (Watch carefully; it is easy to miss this junction.) Experienced riders can turn right and follow the narrow, tightly curving trail for 2.4 miles. Watch for downed trees. Those who miss this junction can continue straight to the junction with the next main road and turn right. This road passes the "Red House," a 1910 flume tender's house, and meets up again with the Great Flume Trail after about 1.75 miles.

The Great Flume Trail ends at a small dam. Carefully walk across or around the dam and meet the main road and turn right (south). After 0.5 mile, turn right onto another main road, Forest Road 504, which crosses Franktown Creek. After the creek, riders must climb 1 mile to the top of a ridge. Ride along the ridge briefly until the road forks. Continue straight ahead (do not descend). After a bit more ridge riding, the road begins to drop to Marlette Lake, where you can retrace your path via the steep and sandy North Canyon Road to Spooner Lake and your car.

Options: The Spooner Lake Outdoor Company offers guided Great Flume Trail trips, including experienced guides, shuttle services, and bike rental. They also offer shuttle service from Highway 28 to Spooner Lake Day Lodge. The shuttle runs hourly on weekends, 12:00–6:00 P.M. during the summer. In spring and fall, the shuttle runs less frequently. Tickets may be purchased at Spooner Lake Day Lodge or from the driver. For more information, call (775) 749-5349 or 1-888-858-8844.

56 SPOONER LAKE

Difficulty: easy
Distance: 1.6-mile loop
Usage: moderate
Starting elevation: 6950 feet
Elevation gain: none
Season: spring, summer, fall
Map: USGS Glenbrook
See Trip 54 for map.

Spooner Lake is rich in history, wildlife, and flowers. The easy trail that circles the lake is fun and interesting for the youngest hikers. On its shoreline, fish for cutthroat trout while you watch for a variety of birds and mammals. The hike also provides an opportunity to learn about the Native Americans that inhabited the area, because Spooner Lake occupies the site of a former Washo settlement. Lastly, return to the lake in the fall for a spectacular show of foliage.

On Highway 28, drive 12.25 miles south of the junction of Highways 28 and 431 near Incline Village to get to the Spooner Lake Picnic Area of Lake Tahoe–Nevada State Park. From South Lake Tahoe, drive north on Highway 50 to its junction with Highway 28, then take highway 28 north 0.7 mile to the park entrance. Park in the upper lot.

Pick up the paved path at the southeast end of the parking lot and follow it through mule's ears, lupine, and sagebrush to a sunken granite display that describes the history, flora, and fauna of the lake. After this informative introduction, backtrack approximately 50 feet to an unpaved trail leading south. Follow this trail to its intersection with a dirt road, then head left. Shortly, look to the right and leave the road to take a narrow path that crosses a wet meadow. This is

Indian grinding stone at Spooner Lake

the start of the trail that circles Spooner Lake, roughly paralleling the shore. Begin here and move counterclockwise around the lake.

Walk through the wet meadow, which is rich with flowers in the spring and summer. Early in the season, look for marsh marigold, an enchanting flower with shiny green leaves, white petals, and bright yellow centers. In summer, watch for deep purple larkspur and waxy yellow buttercups.

As you pass along the south end of Spooner Lake, look closely in the grass for the nests of killdeer. The killdeer is a brown-backed, robin-size shorebird, distinctive for two black bands marking its white throat. It builds its nest in open areas among the sparse grasses of the gravely shore. The small nests are easily overlooked, for they are merely shallow holes in the dirt, thinly lined with grass. The killdeer's blotchy buff-colored pear-shaped eggs are also difficult to see. With luck, you may see some of the mottled chicks. If you do find a nest, do not disturb it or linger too long. The mother is probably not far away and will return only if you leave.

Western terrestrial garter snake

Next follow the trail into a delightful forest of quaking aspen. Some of the largest aspen in the Tahoe Basin grow around Spooner Lake. Aspen are easily identified by their small, fluttering leaves and whitish gray bark. The smallest puff of wind causes their leaves to tremble. The quaking aspen's scientific name, *Populus tremuloides,* reflects this trembling motion. The quaking is caused by the way the leaf is attached to its long slender stem. An early missionary to the north country recorded that superstitious woodsmen believed that Jesus was crucified on a cross made out of aspen and that the tree has been trembling ever since. In autumn its leaves turn bright shades of yellow and orange.

Within the aspen forest, look for moisture-loving flowers of many colors and varieties. One of the more interesting to young hikers is the purple shooting star. True to its name, it is recognized by its purple petals that flare backward, revealing a bright yellow center with prominent protruding stamens.

Trails to the lake beckon small explorers. Spooner Lake is warm and shallow, but waders must be careful of leeches. Distract would-be swimmers with a frog hunt. Look near the shore for black-spotted western toads. These large toads are common throughout the Sierra in meadows and woods near water. During the day they may be found under the shelter of rocks, logs, or in rodent burrows. If you're lucky, you might see a yellow-legged frog. These smallish frogs are dark green or black with yellow hind legs. Gently pick one up; it smells of garlic! Watch also for small, nonpoisonous snakes.

In the early morning or at dusk, mule deer often browse at the lake. The deer are reddish tan in summer, with a small white rump patch and black-tipped white tail. Their large, mulelike ears are extremely sensitive and can move independently, endowing the deer with a superior sense of hearing. During the summer, does are seen with their twin spotted fawns, provoking squeals of delights from children familiar with Bambi.

At the south end of the lake, ignore a trail to the right. That trail leads to Highway 50 and takes you to the trailhead for the Tahoe Rim Trail (see Trip 57). Stay left, and travel north up the east shore of Spooner Lake in the shade of aspens and western white and lodgepole pines. Canada geese, with their long black necks and white chin straps, are likely visitors at the shoreline. Look for downy gray goslings under close supervision.

At the north end of the lake, the trail heads west through superb bird habitat. Look on alder and aspen trees for the small holes made by the colorful red-breasted sapsucker. With their pointed beaks, sapsuckers poke small holes in the trees' bark. Sap collects in the tiny wells, and the bird returns to lap it up with its hairy tongue. The sapsucker's method of capturing sap is similar to the way we tap maple syrup. Sapsuckers seem to know that girdling the trees with holes would kill or injure the tree, so rows of holes are usually found on one side only. Other small birds and mammals such as tree squirrels, warblers, and humming-birds also take advantage of the sweet wells of sap.

In late summer, yellowing willow thickets adorn the shoreline. The earliest recorded inhabitants of this area were the Washo people, who built summer settlements in this vicinity. The Washo used willow stems to weave brush into domed houses whose entrances always faced east. Stripped and split willow branches were also used to weave baskets used for gathering, cooking, and transporting their belongings. The Washo were so skilled at basket weaving that their baskets were even used to hold water. Many baskets, adorned with intricate geometric patterns, survive today as works of art.

As the trail heads south on the lake's west shore, before the lake's dam, look for large granite boulders at the water's edge. Find the rocks with several round, shallow depressions marking the surface. Hundreds of years ago, Washo women prepared meals on these boulders. The Indian women placed nuts, seeds, or acorns in the circular holes of the rock, then used another stone to grind. Flour made from pine nuts or acorns was made into gruel or baked into biscuits. Children who wish to try grinding can visit the Lake Tahoe Museum in South Lake Tahoe, where an Indian grinding stone is displayed and its use encouraged.

Continue south to the lake's dam, a popular place to fish for cutthroat trout. This native trout got its name because of the blood-red stripe running across its lower jaw. Remember that those over age sixteen must possess a Nevada fishing license. The trail returns to the picnic area after 1.6 miles.

Lake Tahoe–Nevada State Park rangers occasionally lead interpretive hikes around Spooner Lake and host special children's programs there. For information on activities at Lake Tahoe–Nevada State Park, call (775) 831-0494.

57 TAHOE RIM TRAIL: SPOONER SUMMIT NORTH TO SNOW VALLEY PEAK

Difficulty: strenuous
Distance: 5.25 miles to Snow Valley Peak
Usage: low
Starting elevation: 7150 feet
Elevation gain: 1670 feet to Tahoe Rim Trail viewpoint; 2064 feet to Snow Valley Peak
Season: summer, fall
Map: USGS Glenbrook and Marlette Lake
See Trip 54 for map.

This uncrowded trail offers superlative views of the Lake Tahoe Basin and Carson Valley. The trail is long, but never excessively steep. A spur trail to treeless Snow Valley Peak provides additional spectacular views. Along the Tahoe Rim Trail, view awesome 400-year-old firs, a variety of flowers, and constantly changing terrain. The trail also offers opportunities for loop hikes with North Canyon Road (see Trip 54). For the loveliest views, hike in the morning so the view to the west is not obscured by the sun.

From the junction of Highways 28 and 50 on Lake Tahoe's east shore, drive 0.7 mile east on Highway 50 to an unpaved pullout on the left (north) side of the highway, designated by a Tahoe Rim Trail sign. Alternatively, pull into a paved parking lot on the south side of the highway. If you use the south parking lot, exercise caution crossing busy Highway 50. The trail begins just north of the trailhead sign.

Begin a gentle ascent on a very sandy trail. The walking is pleasant, but the roar of Highway 50 snaps at your heels. Travel quickly through the semi-open forest of Jeffrey pine, bitterbrush, and sagebrush. Within the open stands of pine, watch for mule deer, which favor bitterbrush foliage.

After approximately ten minutes, a view of Spooner Lake opens to the west. Next, enjoy filtered views of Lake Tahoe. At a fork, stay right (east) and feel the grade steepen. Cross a road and head into a forest of red fir. Here the sounds of wind and birds finally overcome the drone of the freeway.

A series of marked vista points awaits you in the next few miles of trail. Approximately 1.75 miles from the trailhead, look to the right of the trail for a vista signpost. Take the indicated spur trail to see Lake Tahoe, Genoa Peak to the south, and Carson Valley to the southeast.

Next, return to the trail and travel north 0.25 mile to the "John's Rock" vista at the next signpost, an excellent place for a snack break. Climb atop a rocky knoll for fine views of Lake Tahoe and the Carson Valley. Refreshed, return to the trail and hike west and then north for 0.5 mile to a third vista reached by a spur trail to the left. Again, climb a rocky outcropping, this time for truly lovely views of Lake Tahoe and Spooner Meadows. The rugged peaks of Desolation Wilderness and Granite Chief Wilderness tower above the blue expanse of water.

Back on the trail heading north, the views change once again, revealing the Pine Nut Mountains to the east. In the early morning, their layered, purple silhouettes extend to the horizon. The Pine Nut Mountains are named for the trees that provided the Washo Indians with their winter food supply. Until the late nineteenth century, the Washo migrated each fall to these mountains from their summer homes at Lake Tahoe. There they harvested pinyon nuts, built winter homes, and remained until spring. The spring thaw brought the Washo back to Lake Tahoe to take advantage of the spawning fish.

This trail provides an opportunity to experience the forest of times long past, before the devastation wreaked by white settlers. Enter a stand of 300- to 400-year-old red firs. Old-growth stands like this one are highly unusual in the Tahoe Basin, for nearly the entire basin was clear-cut in the late 1800s to supply lumber to the mines of the Comstock Lode and to the Union Pacific Railroad. Miraculously, this stand escaped the decimation.

The ancient trees stand massive and majestic, their thick branches hanging heavily downward like powerful arms. A sculptor could not recreate the imposing sense of majesty and age that the trees darkly convey. Time is measured here in centuries. Before leaving, have your children measure the trees' monumental girth with their arms. This tactile memory can be vividly relived when they return to an ordinary sampling of trees. It is tragic that the basin has so few areas of old-growth forest remaining.

Continue north to good eastern views. Soon, barren Snow Valley Peak appears. Approximately 4 miles from the trailhead, arrive at an intersection with a trail to the left. That trail descends to North Canyon Road and eventually heads back to the trailhead, forming an 8-mile loop. For backpackers, the connector trail accesses North Canyon Campground.

Keep to the right to continue on the Tahoe Rim Trail, which jogs east for more views, then continues its northerly route on the west flank of Snow Valley Peak. Traversing this sunny slope affords fabulous open views of the canyon below, Marlette Lake to the north, and Lake Tahoe to the west. A variety of sun-tolerant flowers grace the slope, including lavender lupine, purple penstemon, scarlet gilia, white mountain pennyroyal, and delicate mousetail. The tiny white blossoms and delicate stems of the mousetail resemble baby's breath. This flower was named for the dense, silky hairs that cover the long, thin, tail-like leaflets gathered at the flower's base.

At approximately 5.5 miles, meet an unpaved road entering on the left. To hike an 11-mile loop, descend left (west) on this road to meet North Canyon Road. The Tahoe Rim Trail continues north. To climb Snow Valley Peak, follow the road climbing steeply to the southeast.

Prepare for very high winds as you ascend 400 feet to reach the peak. The powerful west wind shaped the peak's few trees, contorting their trunks and branches until they all leaned east. In 0.3 mile, the road reaches the summit, which unfortunately holds a radio relay station. Nevertheless, there are spectacular views in all directions from the broad summit. Hikers can easily pick out Emerald Bay and the snowy peaks of Desolation Wilderness to the southwest, the craggy summits of Granite Chief Wilderness including Squaw Peak to the west, the volcanic mass of Mount Rose to the north, Reno and Carson City to the east, and majestic Freel Peak to the southeast.

If the day is too windy or you're looking for a less demanding goal, hike 0.25 mile farther north on the Tahoe Rim Trail from the intersection with the unpaved road. A truly spectacular view of Marlette Lake unfolds. This is a fine alternative to the steep, windy climb up Snow Valley Peak. The Tahoe Rim Trail continues north for another 7.5 awe-inspiring miles, offering additional fabulous views. When the Tahoe Rim Trail is completed in the fall of 2001, hikers will be able to hike 23 scenic miles north from this trailhead to the Mount Rose Highway.

58 TAHOE RIM TRAIL: SPOONER SUMMIT SOUTH

Difficulty: strenuous
Distance: 3.25 miles one way to viewpoint; 5.25 miles one way to South Camp Peak
Usage: low
Starting elevation: 7120 feet
Elevation gain: 1000 feet to 3.25-mile viewpoint; 1680 feet to South Camp Peak
Season: summer, fall
Map: USGS Glenbrook

Hike this uncrowded stretch of the Tahoe Rim Trail for miles of quiet forest walking and rewarding vistas of the Washoe Valley and Lake Tahoe. For a short excursion, turn back after the 3.25-mile viewpoint. For a longer walk, continue to climb gently to a panoramic viewpoint at 5.25 miles. Be flexible rather than goal-oriented; the peaceful solitude of the forest walk is reward in itself.

From the intersection of Highways 50 and 28 on the east shore of Lake Tahoe, drive 0.7 mile east on Highway 50 to the Tahoe Rim Trail parking lot on the

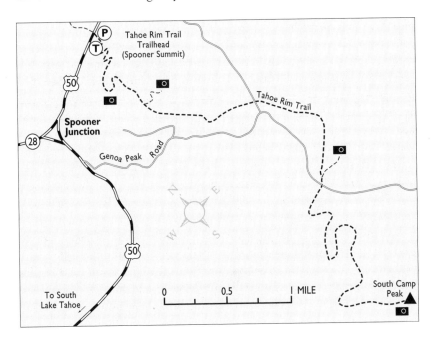

right (south) side of the highway. The trail begins to the left of the prominent trailhead sign.

The trail switchbacks up a north-facing slope through a dark forest of fir and lodgepole pine. At first there is little understory to break the monotony. Look for pinedrops, an unusual reddish brown plant with yellow bell-shaped flowers on the upper portion of its single stalk. Although totally lacking green leaves, this strange plant resembles a model of Jack's giant beanstalk.

Occasional breaks in the forest are filled with impenetrable tobacco brush and manzanita. Climb rather steeply to a nice view northwest to Spooner Lake and Lake Tahoe after about 0.75 mile.

Next head east and continue the ascent. Leave the dreary lodgepole and fir forest to enter a parklike stand of Jeffrey pine. Bitterbrush brightens the walk, particularly in early summer when the shrubs are in bloom. Bitterbrush is a popular browse plant for mule deer. Watch for them, especially in the early morning.

After approximately 45 minutes of pleasant hiking (gaining another 0.75 mile of trail), a spur trail to the left leads you to the top of a rock outcropping. From this sunny spot, there are fine views east to the purple, layered hills of the Washoe Valley and dramatic vistas west across Lake Tahoe to the peaks of Desolation Wilderness. This is an excellent place to spread a picnic.

To continue, return to the trail and hike to the south, climbing gently. Lake Tahoe remains visible to the west. Travel in and out of forest, losing then regaining views. Reach a sagebrush-covered ridge top, dotted with yellow mule's ears and offering fine views, then descend to the east into a forest of fir.

Cross an old logging road and again enter an area of open forest. Waist-high angelica, its white flowers clustered atop towering stems, is conspicuous along the trail. In late summer, tall prickly pink Anderson thistles sway dangerously and white pennyroyal begs for you to kneel to catch its scent. Mountain pennyroyal is a member of the mint family. Its flowers can be dunked in hot water in place of a tea bag for mint-flavored tea.

Look on the left for a rock outcropping and travel almost past it until you pick up a trail that heads northeast to the top. Gain good views on a pleasant rocky perch amid purple lupine and red Indian paintbrush. The outcropping is approximately 3.25 miles from the trailhead.

To continue on the Tahoe Rim Trail, descend, regain the trail, and head west to cross a logging road (Genoa Peak Road). Continue to travel west through a dense forest of fir and western white pine. From the logging road, the trail gains 700 feet in 2 miles to reach the northwest edge of South Camp Peak. The peak is a worthwhile goal reached via a well-graded switchbacking trail through firs and whitebark pines. The panoramic views reveal much of the Tahoe Basin, including Desolation Wilderness to the west and southwest, Squaw Valley Peak and Granite Chief Wilderness to the northwest, and Rifle Peak and Mount Rose to the north in the Mount Rose Wilderness.

APPENDIX A. Trip Finder

<small>KEY TO SYMBOLS:</small>

(H) = Handicap access with assistance

Difficulty: E = Easy; M = Moderate; S = Strenuous

Distance = miles one-way, unless noted otherwise

Usage: L = Low; M = Moderate; H = High

Biking: beg = beginning; int = intermediate; adv = advanced; No = prohibited;
   NR = not recommended

Point of Interest: R = Rock climbing or boulder hopping; H = Historical interest;
   I = Interpretive signs, P = Peak; W = Wildlife; S = Swimming

	DIFFICULTY	DISTANCE	USAGE	BIKING	BACKPACKING	FISHING	SCENIC VIEWS	FALL FOLIAGE	POINT OF INTEREST
North Lake Tahoe Basin									
1. Mount Rose	S	5.9	M	adv (2.5)	X		X		P,W
2. Mount Rose Relay Station	S	4.0	L	adv					P
3. Tahoe Rim Trail: Tahoe Meadows Interpretive Trail (H)	E	1.25 loop	L	No					I,W
4. Tahoe Meadows	E	0.25–0.75	L	No					W
5. Ophir Creek	E	2.0	L	beg					W
6. Tahoe Rim Trail: Watson Lake to Lava Cliffs	E	1.5	L	int			X		
7. Pacific Crest Trail to Mount Judah, Mount Lincoln, and Anderson Peak	M/S	2.3/6.2	M	No	X		X	X	H,P
8. Loch Leven Lakes	M	2.0/3.5	M	NR	X	X			R,S
9. Stateline Fire Lookout Trail (H)	E	0.4	M	NR			X		I
10. Incline Village Bike Trail (H)	E	2.5	H	beg				X	S
West Lake Tahoe Basin									
11. Northstar-at-Tahoe Mountain Biking	E-M	3.0/9.0 round-trip	H	beg-int					
12. Squaw Creek Trails	E	0.5–1.5	M	NR				X	S
13. Squaw Creek Meadow	E	1.0	M	NR				X	
14. Granite Chief Peak	S	5.6	L	No	X		X	X	R,W,P
15. Squaw Valley Mountain Biking at High Camp	E-M	1.0–3.0	H	beg-int (1–3)			X	X	P

Left: Building a sand castle at Sand Harbor State Park, Nevada

West Lake Tahoe Basin, con't

West Lake Tahoe Basin, con't	DIFFICULTY	DISTANCE	USAGE	BIKING	BACKPACKING	FISHING	SCENIC VIEWS	FALL FOLIAGE	POINT OF INTEREST
16. Five Lakes Trail	M	2.1	H	NR		X	X		S
17. Truckee River Bike Trail (H)	E	5.0–7.3	H	beg-int		X		X	H,S
18. West Shore Bike Path (H)	E	11.5	H	beg		X			H,S
19. General Creek Loop Trail (H)	M	6.0 loop	M	beg-int		X		X	
20. Ward Creek Bike Trail	E	4.0	L	beg		X		X	
21. Ward Creek Mountain Bike Loop (Paige Meadows)	S	13.0 loop	M	adv			X	X	S
22. Blackwood Canyon Bike Route	S	7.0	M	int-adv			X		
23. Sugar Pine Point State Park Nature Trails (H)	E	0.25/1.25 loop	H	No		X			I,H,S
24. Lake Genevieve and Crag Lake (H)	S	4.6/4.9	M	beg (1.3)	X	X			S
25. Rubicon Trail to Rock Pinnacles	E	0.5	M	NR			X		R
26. Rubicon Trail to Emerald Bay	M	3.1/4.5	M	NR			X		R,S
27. Balancing Rock Nature Trail	E	0.5 loop	M	No					I
28. Emerald Bay, Vikingsholm, and Eagle Falls Trail (H)	E	0.9/1.1	H	NR			X	X	H,S
29. Upper Eagle Falls	E	0.5	H	No			X	X	
30. Eagle Lake	E	1.0	H	No	X	X	X	X	S
31. Cascade Falls	E	0.7	H	NR			X		
32. Granite Lake	M	1.1	H	No	X	X	X		S
33. Velma Lakes	S	4.5	M	No	X	X	X		S
South Lake Tahoe Basin									
34. Lake Tahoe Visitor Center Nature Trails (H)	E	0.15 loop/ 1.0	H	No			X		I,H,S
35. South Lake Tahoe Bike Path (H)	E	3.4	H	beg				X	H,S
36. Mount Tallac Trail to Fallen Leaf Lake Overlook	E	1.2	M	NR			X		
37. Mount Tallac Summit	S	4.6	M	No	X	X	X		P,W,R
38. Angora Lakes	E	0.7	H	beg		X			S
39. Grass Lake	M	2.6	H	No	X	X		X	S
40. Gilmore Lake	S	3.9	H	No	X	X	X	X	S

South Lake Tahoe Basin, con't

	DIFFICULTY	DISTANCE	USAGE	BIKING	BACKPACKING	FISHING	SCENIC VIEWS	FALL FOLIAGE	POINT OF INTEREST
41. Big Meadow	E	0.5	M	int				X	R
42. Round Lake	M	2.7	M	NR	X	X	X	X	S
43. Dardanelles Lake	M	3.6	M	NR	X	X		X	S
44. Meiss Meadow Trail	M	3.6/4.0	L	NR	X	X		X	S
45. Tahoe Rim Trail: Big Meadow North	M/S	1.8–6.5	L	adv			X	X	
46. Benwood Meadow	E	0.7	L	No					
47. Echo Peak	M/S	2.5/5.2	L	No	X	X	X		P,S
48. Tamarack, Ralston, and Cagwin Lakes	E/M	1.7/4.4	H	No	X	X	X		S
49. Lake of the Woods	M	2.3/5.1	H	No	X	X	X		S
50. Lower Horsetail Falls	E	0.75	M	No			X		R
51. Tahoe Rim Trail: Kingsbury Grade South	S	4.0	L	adv	X		X		W
East Lake Tahoe Basin									
52. Skunk Harbor	E	1.4	L	int		X			S
53. Lower Prey Meadows	E	1.5	L	int			X	X	H
54. Marlette Lake	S	5.0	M	int-adv	X			X	S,W
55. The Great Flume Mountain Bike Trail	S	13.75	M	adv		X	X		H
56. Spooner Lake	E	1.6 loop	M	No		X		X	W
57. Tahoe Rim Trail: Spooner Summit North to Snow Valley Peak	S	5.25	L	No	X		X	X	P
58. Tahoe Rim Trail: Spooner Summit South	S	3.25/5.25	L	adv	X		X		P

APPENDIX B. Lake Tahoe's Beaches

South Shore	SANDY BEACH	PICNIC AREA	BARBEQUE PITS	PLAY-GROUND
Baldwin Beach	X	X	X	
Camp Richardson	X	X	X	X
Eldorado Beach	X	X	X	X
Kiva Beach	X		X	
Pope Beach	X	X	X	
Reagan Beach	X	X		X
Tallac Historic Site	X			
East Shore				
Nevada Beach	X	X	X	
Round Hill Beach	X	X		X
Zephyr Cove	X	X	X	
Skunk Harbor	X			
Hidden Beach	X			
Sand Harbor	X	X	X	
Chimney Beach	X			
West Shore				
D. L. Bliss S. P.	X	X	X	
Emerald Bay S. P.	X	X		
Kaspian Beach		X	X	
Meeks Bay	X	X		X
Sugar Pine Point S. P.		X	X	
William Kent		X	X	
Tahoe Commons Beach		X	X	X
North Shore				
Lake Forest Beach		X	X	X
Patton Beach		X	X	
Agatam Beach	X	X	X	
Moon Dunes Beach	X	X		
Secline Beach		X	X	
Kings Beach	X	X	X	X
Coons Beach	X	X	X	
Speedboat Beach	X			

APPENDIX C. Recommended Reading

The books and periodicals listed below promote understanding, appreciation, and respect for the environment. Through reading, children can build upon their outdoor experiences and prepare for their next adventure.

The Lake Tahoe Visitor Center is an excellent place to find books about the Tahoe Basin. Proceeds from sales benefit park educational programs. The visitor center is located on Highway 89 in South Lake Tahoe. On the west shore of Lake Tahoe, visitors can find a small selection of books in Sugar Pine Point State Park at the nature center. The League to Save Lake Tahoe offers books and maps at their two locations, 955 Emerald Bay Road, South Lake Tahoe, or 600 North Lake Boulevard (Lakehouse Mall), Tahoe City. Visitors to North Lake Tahoe should check out the Incline Village Public Library for their excellent regional collection.

The following organizations also offer excellent nature books by mail:

The League to Save Lake Tahoe, 955 Emerald Bay Road, South Lake Tahoe, Califonia 96150, (530) 541-5388, *www.keeptahoeblue.com*

The National Wildlife Federation, 1400 16th Street NW, Washington, D.C. 20036, 1-800-432-6564, *www.nwf.org*

The National Geographic Society, Educational Services, Washington, D.C. 20036, 1-800-368-2728, *www.nationalgeographic.com*

The Sierra Club, 730 Polk Street, San Francisco, California 94109, (415) 923-5500, *www.sierraclub.org*

Field Guides For Children

Alden, Peter. *Mammals—A Simplified Field Guide to the Common Mammals of North America*. Boston: Houghton Mifflin Co., 1987.

Biesot, Elizabeth. *Natural Treasures Field Guide for Kids*. Boulder, Colorado: Roberts Rinehart, Inc., 1996.

Peterson, Roger Tory. *Peterson First Guide to Birds of North America*. Boston: Houghton Mifflin Co., 1998.

————. *Peterson First Guide to Mammals of North America*. Boston: Houghton Mifflin Co., 1998.

Peterson, Roger Tory, and Peter Alden. *A Field Guide to Birds Coloring Book*. Boston: Houghton Mifflin Co., 1982.

————. *Wildflowers—A Simplified Guide to Common Wildflowers*. Boston: Houghton Mifflin Co., 1986.

Game and Activity Books

Peterson, Roger Tory, and Peter Arden. *A Field Guide to Mammals Coloring Book*. Boston: Houghton Mifflin Co., 1987.

Peterson, Roger Tory, and Francis Tenenbaum. *A Field Guide to Wildflowers Coloring Book*. Boston: Houghton Mifflin Co., 1982.

General Nonfiction for Children

Arnosky, Jim. *Crinkleroot's Guide to Knowing Animal Habitats*. New York: Aladdin Paperbacks, 2000.

The Earthworks Group. *50 Simple Things Kids Can Do to Save the Earth*. New York: Universal Press Syndicate, 1990.

Evans, Lisa Gollin. *An Elephant Never Forgets Its Snorkel*. New York: Crown Books for Children, 1992.

Parker, Steve. *Pond and River*. New York: DK Publishing, 2000.

Picture Books

Cooper, Ann. *Above the Treeline*. Boulder, Colorado: Roberts Rinehart, Inc., 1996.

————. *Around the Pond.* Boulder, Colorado: Roberts Rinehart, Inc., 1998.

Donahue, Mike. *The Grandpa Tree*. Illustrated by Susan Dorsey. Boulder, Colorado: Roberts Rinehart, Inc., 1991.

George, Jean Craighead. *One Day in the Woods*. New York: Harper Trophy 1995.

Mazer, Anne. *The Salamander Room*. New York: Alfred A. Knopf, 1994.

Siebert, Diane. *Sierra*. New York: Harper Collins Publisher, 1996.

Steptoe, John. *The Story of Jumping Mouse*. New York: Mulberry Books, 1989.

Yolen, Jane. *Owl Moon*. New York: Philomel Books, 1987.

Fiction for Young Readers

Connolly, James E., et al. *Why the Possum's Tail Is Bare and Other North American Nature Tales*. Owings Mills, Maryland: Stemmer House, 1992.

George, Jean Craighead. *Julie of the Wolves*. New York: Harper Trophy, 1974.

————. *My Side of the Mountain*. New York: E. P. Dutton, 2000.

Laurgaard, Rachel K. *Patty Reed's Doll: The Story of the Donner Party*. Fairfield, California: Tomato Enterprises, 1989.

Mowatt, Farley. *Never Cry Wolf*. Boston: Skylark, 1983.

Rawlings, Marjorie Kinnan. *The Yearling*. New York: Collier Macmillan Publishers, 1938.

Rylant, Cynthia. *When I Was Young in the Mountains*. New York: E. P. Dutton, 1992.

Savage, Deborah. *A Rumour of Otters*. Boston: Houghton Mifflin Company, 1986.

Seuss, Dr. *The Lorax*. New York: Random House, 1971.

Periodicals for Children

National Geographic World, National Geographic Society, Washington, D.C. 20036. Ages 8–13.

Ranger Rick, National Wildlife Federation, 1400 16th Street NW, Washington, D.C. 20036. Ages 7–12.

Your Big Backyard, National Wildlife Federation, 1400 16th Street NW, Washington, D.C. 20036. Ages 3–5.

Books for Parents

Brown, Tom, Jr., with Judy Brown. *Tom Brown's Field Guide to Nature and Survival for Children*. New York: Berkley Publishing Group, 1989.

Caduto, Michael J., and Joseph Bruchac. *Keepers of the Earth: Native American Stories and Environmental Activities for Children*. Golden, Colorado: Fulcrum, Inc., 1999.

————. *Native American Stories and Wildlife Activities for Children*. Golden, Colorado: Fulcrum, Inc., 1997.

Carson, Rachel. *The Sense of Wonder*. New York: Harper & Row, 1984.

Cornell, Joseph Bharat. *Sharing Nature with Children*. Nevada City, California: Dawn Publications, 1998.

Forgey, William. *Campfire Stories, Volume 1: Things That Go Bump in the Night*. Merrillville, Indiana: ICS Books, 1985.

Hampton, Bruce, and David Cole. *Soft Paths*. Harrisburg, Pennsylvania: Stackpole Books, 1995.

Lingelbach, Jenepher. *Hands on Nature: Information and Activities for Exploring the Environment with Children*. Hanover, New Hampshire: University Press of New England, 2000.

McGivney, Annette. *Leave No Trace*. Seattle: The Mountaineers Books, 1998.

First-Aid Books

Gill, Paul G., Jr. *The Ragged Mountain Press Pocket Guide to Wilderness Medicine*. New York: McGraw-Hill, 1997.

Lentz, Martha J., Steven C. Macdonald, and Jan D. Carline. *Mountaineering First Aid*. Seattle: The Mountaineers, 1996.

Natural History

Balls, Edward. *Early Uses of California Plants*. Berkeley: University of California Press, 1989.

Carville, Julie Stauffer. *Hiking Tahoe's Wildflower Trails*. Chicago Park, California: Mountain Gypsy Press, 1997.

Horn, Elizabeth L. *Sierra Nevada Wildflowers*. Missoula, Montana: Mountain Press Publishing Co., 1998.

Inter-Tribal Council of Nevada. *WA SHE SHU: A Washo Tribal History*. Salt Lake City: University of Utah Printing Service, 1976.

Schaffer, Jeffrey P. *The Tahoe Sierra: A Natural History Guide to 106 Hikes in the Northern Sierra*. Berkeley: Wilderness Press, 1998.

Stall, Chris. *Animal Tracks of Northern California*. Seattle: The Mountaineers Books, 1990.

Stollery, David J., Jr. *Tales of Tahoe*. Reseda, California: Mojave Books, 1969.

Storer, Tracy I., and Robert L. Usinger. *Sierra Nevada Natural History*. Berkeley: University of California Press, 1989.

Strong, Douglas H. *Tahoe: From Timber Barons to Ecologists*. Lincoln, Nebraska: Bison Books Corp., 1999.

Van Der Ven, William. *Up the Lake with a Paddle—Lake Tahoe and Sierra Lakes*. Anacortes, Washington: Mountain Biking Press, 2000.

Whitehill, Karen, and Terry Whitehill. *Best Short Hikes in California's Northern Sierra*. Seattle: The Mountaineers, 1990.

Whitney, Stephen. *A Sierra Club Naturalist's Guide to the Sierra Nevada*. San Francisco: Sierra Club Books, 1982.

APPENDIX D. Making a Difference: Protecting the Lake Tahoe Basin

Those interested in the preservation and restoration of the Lake Tahoe Basin can look to two excellent organizations dedicated to the defense of the lake and its environs.

The League to Save Lake Tahoe

Since 1957, the nonprofit League to Save Lake Tahoe has established a solid record of accomplishments. It stopped the construction of a proposed freeway over Emerald Bay in 1966 and won a federal ban on new casinos at the lake. The league promotes environmentally sound regional planning and was instrumental in the creation in 1960 of the Tahoe Regional Planning Compact. The league has also launched legal challenges to land-use plans incompatible with the environmental health of the basin. Through effective lobbying, the league secured $200 million in state and federal funds to buy sensitive lands and to fund erosion-control projects around the lake.

Members of the league receive quarterly newsletters containing information on timely environmental issues. Membership dues support the league's invaluable watchdog and legal efforts. To "Keep Tahoe Blue," contact the League to Save Lake Tahoe, 989 Tahoe Keys Boulevard, Suite 6, South Lake Tahoe, California 96150, (530) 541-5388, *www.keeptahoeblue.com*.

The Tahoe Rim Trail

Since its inception in 1984, The Tahoe Rim Trail Association (TRTA) has constructed and linked 150 miles of spectacular trail following the ridges and mountain tops that surround Lake Tahoe. The Tahoe Rim Trail (TRT) circles the entire lake, crossing national forest, wilderness and state park lands, thick conifer forests, wildflower-filled meadows, and aspen-bordered creeks. Built to accommodate hikers, mountain bikers, and equestrians, the TRT provides unparalleled access to beautiful Lake Tahoe, the majestic peaks of the Sierra Nevada, and the dramatic expanse of western Nevada's Great Basin. In recognition of the TRT's role in preserving open space, interpreting natural history, and encouraging recreation, the TRT was named as one of the fifty Millenium Legacy Trails in 1999.

The nonprofit Tahoe Rim Trail Association depends on donations and volunteers to preserve and protect the TRT. The association works year-round to maintain this spectacular trail and to address issues that threaten its integrity. You can help support the TRTA and preserve this important resource by becoming a TRTA member, by participating in the association's Adopt-a-Mile Program, by volunteering to attend a trail maintenance day, by becoming a Charter Trail Guardian, or by purchasing maps, books, and other merchandise from the TRTA website.

To find out more about the Tahoe Rim Trail Association, visit their website at *www.tahoerimtrail.org* or contact them at P.O. Box 4647, 297 Kingsbury Grade Suite C, Stateline, NV 89449, (775) 588-0686.

INDEX

ABOUT THE AUTHOR

Lisa Gollin Evans extends her professional focus from environmental law to environmental advocacy by helping families appreciate nature. She is the author of *Rocky Mountain National Park: An Outdoor Family Guide, Outdoor Family Guide to Yellowstone and Grand Teton National Parks, Outdoor Family Guide to Acadia National Park, Sea Kayaking the Massachusetts Coast,* and the award-winning children's book *An Elephant Never Forgets Its Snorkel.* She is continuously inspired by her husband and her three daughters who live with her in Marblehead, Massachusetts. She is currently working for the Clean Air Task Force, a national environmental organization based in Boston.

THE MOUNTAINEERS, founded in 1906, is a nonprofit outdoor activity and conservation club, whose mission is "to explore, study, preserve, and enjoy the natural beauty of the outdoors. . . . " Based in Seattle, Washington, the club is now the third-largest such organization in the United States, with 15,000 members and five branches throughout Washington State.

The Mountaineers sponsors both classes and year-round outdoor activities in the Pacific Northwest, which include hiking, mountain climbing, ski-touring, snowshoeing, bicycling, camping, kayaking and canoeing, nature study, sailing, and adventure travel. The club's conservation division supports environmental causes through educational activities, sponsoring legislation, and presenting informational programs. All club activities are led by skilled, experienced volunteers, who are dedicated to promoting safe and responsible enjoyment and preservation of the outdoors.

If you would like to participate in these organized outdoor activities or the club's programs, consider a membership in The Mountaineers. For information and an application, write or call The Mountaineers, Club Headquarters, 300 Third Avenue West, Seattle, WA 98119; 206-284-6310.

The Mountaineers Books, an active, nonprofit publishing program of the club, produces guidebooks, instructional texts, historical works, natural history guides, and works on environmental conservation. All books produced by The Mountaineers Books fulfill the club's mission.

Send or call for our catalog of more than 500 outdoor titles:

The Mountaineers Books
1001 SW Klickitat Way, Suite 201
Seattle, WA 98134
800-553-4453
mbooks@mountaineers.org
www.mountaineersbooks.org

The Mountaineers Books is proud to be a corporate sponsor of Leave No Trace, whose mission is to promote and inspire responsible outdoor recreation through education, research, and partnerships. The Leave No Trace program is focused specifically on human-powered (nonmotorized) recreation.

Leave No Trace strives to educate visitors about the nature of their recreational impacts, as well as offer techniques to prevent and minimize such impacts. Leave No Trace is best understood as an educational and ethical program, not as a set of rules and regulations.

For more information, visit *www.LNT.org*, or call 800-332-4100.

Other titles you might enjoy from The Mountaineers Books:

BEST HIKES WITH CHILDREN® Series
Fully detailed "where-to" and "how-to" guides to day hikes and over-nighters for families. Includes tips on hiking with kids, safety, and fostering a wilderness ethic. Titles in the series include:
BEST HIKES WITH CHILDREN®: SAN FRANCISCO'S NORTH BAY
BEST HIKES WITH CHILDREN®: SAN FRANCISCO'S SOUTH BAY

CALIFORNIA STATE PARKS: A Complete Recreation Guide, *George & Rhonda Ostertag*
Features complete details on more than 230 parks and state-managed outdoor areas, ranging from the ocean to the mountains to the desert.

100 CLASSIC HIKES IN™ NORTHERN CALIFORNIA, Second Edition, *John R. Soares & Marc J. Soares*
A full-color hiking guide written by experts who have personally researched every trail. Includes a mix of day hikes and overnight backpacking trips

BICYCLING THE PACIFIC COAST: A Complete Route Guide, Canada to Mexico, Third Edition, *Tom Kirkendall & Vicki Spring*
The most detailed and professional guidebook for the 1,816.5-mile route— broken up into 35 day trips averaging 53 miles per day, with options to shorten or lengthen individual trips.

MAC'S FIELD GUIDE SERIES, *Craig MacGowan*
Two-sided plastic laminated cards with color drawings, common and scientific names, and information on size and habitat. Cards in the series include:
CALIFORNIA COASTAL BIRDS
CALIFORNIA COASTAL FISH
CALIFORNIA COASTAL INVERTEBRATES
CALIFORNIA GARDEN BUGS
YOSEMITE/BIRDS & MAMMALS
YOSEMITE/TREES & WILDFLOWERS

KIDS IN THE WILD: A Family Guide to Outdoor Recreation, *Cindy Ross & Todd Gladfelter*
Practical advice on hiking and camping with children. Includes suggestions on the best outdoor activities for families, from backpacking and camping to boating, biking, and skiing.

GPS MADE EASY: Using Global Positioning Systems in the Outdoors, Third Edition, *Lawrence Letham*
Updated for today's more precise GPS receivers ("Selective Availability" removed), this popular guide covers how GPS works, features of common receivers, and practical examples of GPS use in the outdoors.

WILDERNESS 911: A Step-by-Step Guide for Medical Emergencies and Improvised Care in the Backcountry, *Eric A. Weiss, M.D.*
Covering the injuries and accidents most likely to occur in the backcountry, this quick access guide provides tips and techniques from *Backpacker* magazine experts.